# Exposed

# Exposed

Inexcusable Me. . . Irreplaceable Him

## Shannon M. Deitz

Pleasant Word
A Division of WinePress Group

Pleasant Word (a division of WinePress Publishing, PO Box 428, Enumclaw, WA 98022) functions only as book publisher. As such, the ultimate design, content, editorial accuracy, and views expressed or implied in this work are those of the author.

Unless otherwise noted, Scripture is taken from the *New American Bible*®, Copyright © 1960, 1962, 1963, 1968, 1971, 1972, 1973, 1975, 1977, 1995 by The Lockman Foundation. Used by permission.

Free Bird lyrics w & m Ron VanZant & Allan Collins. Copyright Judy VanZant Jenness (W), Tammy VanZant, Melody VanZant © RE0000852176/2001-12-28 and renewal registration: EU0000450840/ 1973 –12-05

ISBN 13: 978-1-4141-1582-5
ISBN 10: 1-4141-1582-2
Library of Congress Catalog Card Number: 2009908022

"My job is just to give you the message; it is up to you whether you believe it or not."

—St. Bernadette of Lourdes

For Sweetgraw

Your faith transcended this world and continues
to inspire beyond the gates of heaven.

# Content

# Acknowledgments

THERE IS NOT one family member, either immediate or distant, or high school friend, college friend, sorority sister, co-worker, neighbor, fellow parishioner from old or recent parishes, past or present critique group, youth group student, student who has heard me speak and sent me encouraging emails, fellow youth minister, speaker, priest, nun, counselor, or partner in crime that I would want to leave out of this feeble attempt of praise and thanksgiving.

Whether I have known you for an instant or a lifetime, you have affected me, and therefore you have affected what lies beneath this story of my life's journey. Thank you for your memories, patience, guidance, support, hope, confidence, and, most of all, your love.

And to God: thank you for never letting me go.

# Author's Notes

MOST NAMES AND descriptions of characters in this book have been changed or altered in order to maintain the dignity and privacy of others.

The tone of this book depicts the viewpoint of myself as a child and later as a teenage girl. These memories are mine and in the perception of the age in which they were experienced. In some segments of the book the reaction to a situation (or lack there of) is told with an honest remembrance of the logic and reasoning I embraced in the moment.

# Preface

**W**HY ME?
I have asked this question many times in my life. Growing up, I wondered why I felt so ugly and wanted so much attention, why my older sister told me secrets I never wanted to hear, why it felt like our family was falling apart and I couldn't do anything to stop it, and why it felt like bad things kept happening to me and I never could catch a break.

The most common response would be that "it all happens for a reason." Looking back, however, it is obvious to me that is not necessarily true. I cannot ignore the decisions that were made on my part, or my sister's, friends', family's, or acquaintances', and not recognize the course life took because of our decisions.

Some would argue that God is the reason. God is in the illnesses or forces of nature that strike hard and uproot your core existence, forcing your hand in strength and causing your tomorrows to change. Everything else? Well, that is due to an abuse of God's gift of free will. I cannot look back at my life and ignore the fact that free will, on my part or the part of others in my life, led to life-altering circumstances.

What it comes down to is the reaction.

How do I respond? How do I move forward? What do I internalize? To whom do I turn?

When a stranger among the 1.2 million Catholic Young Adults that had gathered for the 2005 World Youth Day festivities in Köln, Germany called me by name, I didn't have time to respond, react, or internalize. I only knew that I needed to go and listen.

Once I heard the message, I could no longer feel sorry for myself or throw out blame. I was called by name, and it was about time I reacted.

Why me? Why not?

# The 'Nothing' Child

Amen, I say to you, whoever does not accept the kingdom of God
like a child will not enter it.

—Mark 10:15

IN THE BEGINNING, under the watchful eye of an enormous
thunderbird, wings outstretched, in the barren, blistering city of El
Paso, outlined with white rock alongside Coronado Mountain, our
family of six struggled against the clashing waves of good and evil.
At the age of seven, far too young to comprehend the very real but
incomprehensible battle, I was sucked into the undertow.

Perched like a vulture on the arm of the couch, with her bronze
legs folded up to her chest, my thirteen year old sister Carrie smirked
and said, "I'm not your sister." My older brother, Kyle, who was only
seventeen months younger than Carrie, sat beside her and laughed,
"Yeah! We're not your brother and sister!"

"Yes. You. Are!" I protested each word sharply and with great
calculation. Carrie and Kyle were inclined to gang up on me, when all
I longed for was to be accepted and involved in everything my siblings
did and invited to every place they went.

1

"Nope," Carrie said. "Daddy is not my daddy."

My undeveloped mind could not grasp what she was trying to say. Of course Daddy was her daddy! We had the same sandy hair. My face was a little more round than theirs, but they were all I knew as family. No one was supposed to look alike anyway. In a flash of a moment, the world I knew to be predictable and safe was shaken and unrecognizable.

I ran to Mom, who was busy in the utility room sewing a dress for one of us girls, flung my arms around her waist, and wailed, "Carrie says she's not my sister!" Carrie and Kyle, who had been running close behind me, stopped short and nearly toppled on top of us when they reached the door. My sobs were muffled in Mom's lap, but I could still hear the disappointment in her voice.

"She is your sister, and that is not nice to say."

My head shot up in a flash. "See! You're lying!"

"No we're not!" Kyle insisted. "Dad is not *our* dad, Mom."

Mom sighed a long, slow, "the weight of the world had just been dumped on her shoulders" sigh. I looked into her green eyes, and for the first time I really saw her. She had jet black hair that was cropped and straight—completely the opposite of my waist-length, wavy mop– and a beautiful, small oval face with a smile that radiated warmth and love. We looked nothing alike.

Fear came alive within me. "Am I adopted?"

"No, Shannon," she sighed again, "but your daddy did adopt Carrie and Kyle."

"See," Kyle said as he tapped my shoulder. "I told you so." He and Carrie started to laugh, and I wailed louder.

Mom called for my father. "Tom!"

"What?" he shouted from the living room.

Mom pulled me up with her as she stood. "Let's all go into the TV room. We need to have a family talk."

Within the sanctity of my home, amidst those closest and dearest to me, who I knew to be my family, I was prematurely stripped of the honor young children have to be naïve and carefree.

Tears began to build at the corner of Mom's serene eyes as she explained the details of her first marriage in a way that my young mind could comprehend. It wasn't until I was in college, struggling through my own personal trials, that I finally understood the story and became privy to the rest of her secrets.

Mom's first marriage was sad, abusive, and short-lived. It began soon after high school and ended when her husband returned home from Vietnam. The demise of her innocence, however, began much earlier.

Mom's earliest memory goes back to when she was still in her crib, and it is the first of ten years of memories of a stolen childhood and loss of innocence. The eldest of five, she was the only one to claim the pink bow in her testosterone filled home. "Thank God," she'd say. If her brothers had been girls, they, too, would have suffered at the perverted hands of her father.

Like many girls who suffer in silence, to the outside world my mother seemed to have it all. She was captain of the cheerleading squad, bubbly, bright, and envied by her friends. At home, she was envied by her mother. But my mother did not ask for the kind of attention she got from her father. Instead, she spent her teen years pushing every memory of him into a tiny black box in the corner of her mind, and began seeking after the love her young soul craved.

Pregnant too young and married too young, Mom entered into a new world of abuse, orchestrating a spiraling descent that eventually led her into recovery. The box was opened, and she wanted to heal, help, and forgive.

As a seven-year-old, I couldn't help but wonder where this past marriage left me. Where did I fit in? Was this why Carrie and Kyle were always giving me a hard time, when all I wanted was to be with them?

My mind reeled as I realized the obvious gap that had formed between us as children. Carrie and Kyle were so close in age, and they were five and six years ahead of me. Morgan and I were three years apart. Morgan was the baby. She was cute and entertaining, and I felt

3

like an annoyance. The divide between us created a festering knot of insecurity.

"I'm nothing!" I wailed, perched on Dad's lap with my head tilted back dramatically.

Giggling, Dad mustered a serious tone. "You are too something. You're my little girl."

"No!" With great zeal, I shook my head and added, "Carrie's the oldest, Kyle's the only boy, and Morgan's the youngest! What am I? Nothing!" For my young mind, this was the truth.

One afternoon, Carrie changed course with a simple gesture of kindness. Desperate for her acceptance, I jumped at the opportunity.

"Hey, Shannon, come here for a sec," Carrie called as she walked past my room and into her own.

"Is this a trick?" I thought. Fueled by excitement and honor, I jumped up from the floor. She never asked me into her room, but, after hesitating, I stepped in.

"Hey, come here," she said. "I want to show you something." She was on her stomach with her legs fanned out on the bed.

Without hesitation, I hopped up onto her bed and sat Indian style beside her. Her profile was magnetic, and in that moment I couldn't help but stare. As far as I knew, my time in her room and presence was limited. But the more I stared, the sadder I felt. Carrie was a classic beauty. Her eyes were a petite almond shape and tortoise green. Mine were round as quarters and mint blue. The slope of her nose finished into a defined and delicate tip, and mine formed a small but not so delicate round ball. Everything about Carrie was distinct and defined yet feminine at the same time, and, even though I was still a young girl, everything about me was unusual. I had big round eyes, full lips, and a widow's peak that came to a dramatic point in the middle of my forehead.

She held a shiny piece of paper that looked like a small poster. I looked over her shoulder to see what held her attention. It was a list including photographs of pills in all shapes, sizes, and colors, with their names below them.

"I've done this one, and this one…and this one," she said, smiling with a strange satisfaction as she pointed out the various medications she had taken. That was what I thought, at least—that they were just pills. Medicine. I never understood why she was pointing out pills, and giggled as she did so, but then again, I was in her room and she was paying attention to me. That was all that mattered.

Of course, I knew nothing about recreational drugs. I knew there was a big scare about not accepting stickers from strangers because there was some kind of poison called LSD on the backs of them. I knew not to talk to strangers or take anything from them. Carrie was not a stranger.

That wasn't the last of the invites into her room. No longer was I nothing. Instead, I felt like something, because Carrie, the most beautiful, funny, and perfect girl was finally taking notice of me, her bratty half-sister.

For months I trailed behind Carrie and her new boyfriend, Jose. I sat in on their conversations and make-out sessions, being sure not to be seen but staying close enough to be there if she needed me for anything. It was fascinating to witness the same girl who would sometimes rant and practically spit bile at my parents become giddy when this boy was around, often to the point of being taken over by hysterical laughter. The medications she had pointed out in her room were never seen. I was unsure if she was taking anything. If anything, this boy was a cure for whatever had made her sad and angry.

I noticed that the more Jose was around, the more Mom and Dad would yell at night when I was supposed to be sleeping. I would hear the door to Carrie's room slam, and I would press my ear up to the wall that separated us and listen to her muffled cries and curses. Sitting on the corner of my bed, I would pray to God, asking him to make my parents leave her alone. All I knew of God was that he was our protector and I needed him to protect her.

One night, I gathered up the courage to leave the safety of my room and enter Carrie's without her permission. She was sitting in the corner, scratching on her desk with the tip of a ballpoint pen. "What do you want?" she grumbled.

"Are you OK?" I whispered, afraid that if my parents heard me in her room she would get in more trouble.

She shrugged her shoulders with little effort. "They don't get it. They are so stupid."

"Yeah," I said in bogus agreement. I didn't think my parents were stupid, but I was desperate for Carrie's approval.

Her face softened when she turned to look at me, and she stopped tormenting her desk. I smiled because I knew I had said the right thing. I am not sure what she saw in me at that moment, or if she ever truly considered me a friend, but I was the only one around who was eager to listen. A sense of trust began to develop between us.

Weeks and months passed, and I became more knowledgeable about what Carrie was doing as I listened in on various conversations of her sexual prowess, hearing words that made no sense, and feeling the air around me thicken with sounds and moans that sounded as if she were being wounded. And during her last years in our home, I unintentionally witnessed these acts that were beyond my years and understanding.

When it came to Carrie, nothing ever felt right. She was like an injured animal that had lost trust in the ones who wanted to help her most. When I was sucked into this vortex, spinning uncontrollably as Carrie whirled around in the air above, battling the unfair tactics of parents and social propriety, I hadn't even reached puberty. She was beyond reach, and although I had become so immersed in her teenage world, I was still a helpless child, looking up and desperately trying to save her.

None of us were aware. My mother's demons had entered into my sister's world, wreaking this havoc in our family. Carrie was only six when her innocence was stolen. Mom thought she could protect us by keeping a watchful eye and she took a chance by taking us with her to attend a family reunion. Unfortunately, my grandfather's disease was never cured. Tainted by someone she loved and trusted, my sister did not know how to create that tiny black box in the corner of her mind to block the sickness of what he did to her. Instead, she retaliated against the pain she held inside, never sharing her dark secret. Like my mother, she, too, sought after love and healing, but never through healthy means or relationships.

In many ways, he hurt me, too—not physically, but through Carrie's retaliation and through her search for the love that his disease created. All I did was love my sister. All I wanted was to see her happy and be able to witness God's protection. I wanted to finally rest inside, because I knew she would be OK. Instead, my hope faded with each passing day.

# Devil's Eyes

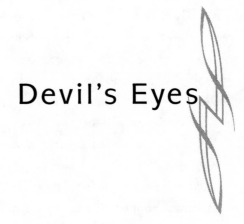

Then the dragon became angry with the woman, and went off to
wage war against the rest of her offspring, those who keep God's
commandments and bear witness to Jesus.

—Revelation 12:17

LIVING IN CARRIE'S shadow allowed me to soak up a plethora
of information like a sponge, leading to the beginnings of my taste
for the dramatic. We had lived in El Paso for a year when I turned eight,
and even though I performed a great act of playing the pesky little sister,
inside I felt the oldest child in the family.

Often I would obscure myself in a corner and listen to various
conversations, trying to keep myself abreast of everything going on.
Not only was my sister fertilizing my awareness of the sinister world of
drugs, as well as a young woman's clumsy entrance into sexuality, but
also the adults were frantically whispering about the continued epidemic
of laced stickers—and also about satanic cult activity near the border
in Juarez, Mexico. I wasn't too concerned with any of this talk; I never
really understood the effect of the laced stickers, and I didn't know what
the word "cult" meant. Living in that environment, our young minds

were saturated with that sort of talk—talk of drugs, cults, and the Devil. It was all around, and my parents could not have shielded me from it even if they had tried. A neighbor boy who lived at the end of our street even jumped off his roof to see if he could fly. According to rumor, he was found in a tangled mass at the foot of his front door with a Daffy Duck sticker on each hand. He survived, but he broke two legs and was in a body cast for months.

During an afternoon recess, spurred by the various rumors and terrifying stories we had heard concerning this cult, my friends and I decided to form a new club. We gathered together inside a giant tractor tire that was about four feet high, five feet wide and could fit six of us when we squeezed in tight. These tires were located at the far end of the school playground, close to a chain link fence that separated the school property from a vast amount of barren land that had been scorched by the desert sun. On that land was a hill and no tree in sight. At the very top of the hill sat an ominous white church that resembled the kind in storybooks, with a single steeple and long, narrow stained-glass windows on the sides. The windows had been boarded up, and the cross that should have been on the tip of the steeple was no longer there.

Vince, the tallest in our group (and also the oldest, because he had been held back in the first grade), spoke up first. "We are the Mighty Rivera's. And whatever we do and say stays here." He looked pointedly around the tire, pausing at each face to make sure we understood the gravity of his words. Besides Vince, there were three girls and two other boys. We all nodded in agreement but didn't say a word. I anxiously waited for Vince to continue, as the French braid my mom had woven tightly into my hair that morning was beginning to make my scalp itch. I absently reached up to my head to rub it.

"What do you want to say?" Vince asked.

As quick as a puppy sneaking forbidden food from his master's plate, my hand flew back to my lap. I was not shy, but I had never been part of an elite group before. I didn't want to mess anything up. "Nothing," I whispered.

"So what are we gonna do, Vince?" demanded Danny, the freckle-faced smart-mouth.

"As you all know," answered Vince, in a low, conspiring voice, "the Devil lives in that church." A ripple of bone-chilling air coursed over my body, raising the hair on my arms. The only thing I knew about the Devil was that he was the epitome of every scary monster, boogieman, fear, and phobia, intertwined into one creature.

"Yeah, Cooper told me that the other day when we passed it going home," said Jennifer, her black hair and deep brown eyes veiled by the dense light in the tire. Despite her small size, she was often the loudest and most talkative, which kept her from being overlooked.

Olivia, John, and I said nothing. The inside of the tire had become stuffy and cramped with our legs hanging over the lip of the wheel. Despite the cold chill I felt, the heat from the rubber tire began to irritate my bare skin.

Danny broke the silence. "So what?"

"I say we scare him away," answered Vince without hesitation. He sat forward and clasped his hands together. "My Sunday school teacher told me any time we thought the Devil was bothering us to say 'In the name of Jesus, go away!' and the Devil would have to leave because Jesus' name is that powerful."

"Well," Vince prodded. "Is everyone in?"

I looked over at Olivia, and she shrugged her shoulders. If she could do it, then I guess I would to. I nodded my head.

"Yeah!" Danny yelled as he thrust out a fist.

Vince stood up before the others could say anything. "OK, let's go before the bell rings!" He hoisted himself up over the edge of the tire, and the rest of us followed.

At my CCE class (Continuing Catholic Education), I had never heard about invoking the name of Jesus against evil, but, then again, we never spoke much about the Devil. I knew Jesus, and I knew he was God, which made him all-powerful, but actually dealing with the Devil himself was new to me. I was reminded of a song from a Bible school

I had attended with a friend: "Shut the door, keep out the Devil. Shut the door, keep the Devil in the night. Shut the door, keep out the Devil, light a candle, everything is all right."

I repeated those words again and again in my mind, until they chased away the chill and filled me with courage. That made me smile, but I wasn't brave enough to suggest that we get candles for fear that they would not allow me to stay in their group.

Forming an unbreakable line by holding hands, we walked over to the hurricane fence and stared up at the church.

Before, the church was just an old, white, unkempt wooden building, but now it loomed before us, very daunting. My skin bristled again from the chill of anticipation.

Vince cleared his throat. "OK, on the count of three, we all yell at the church. Ready? One…two…three!"

"In the name of Jesus, go away!" we yelled in unison.

"No!" replied a deep, bone-chilling voice that sounded as though it came from every crevice of the earth around us. In the same instant, a flicker of green pierced through the farthest window of the old church. For a breath of a second, we stared at the decrepit building, and then, screaming, we broke our bond to run toward the safety of the school.

One on top of another, we collided into a heap on the entrance steps. No one spoke. The only sound that could be heard was fast and heavy breathing. The playground had already been cleared, and we were the only ones left outside. None of us were able to look at each other, and we never spoke of that day again.

In fact, it was as if it had never taken place. I don't recall praying about it, asking God for protection, and I don't remember being concerned that the Devil would really try and come get me. In fact, I continued to walk to and from school without a hint of anguish.

A few months later, while walking home from a friend's house after school, the nightmarish incident was reinforced by another and tested my childlike faith.

I was sitting in my friend Katy's room, listening to records, eating Ding-Dongs®, and playing with Barbies®. Katy lived a few blocks away from me on the other side of a highway.

"Is your mom home yet?" I asked as I hopped off her bed to look out the window. It was getting late, close to dinnertime, and I knew my mom was going to get worried if I didn't get home soon.

Katy, who was busy looking through her album collection, shrugged her shoulders. "I don't know."

I saw her mom's car in the driveway and turned away from the window. "I think she is. Will you go ask her to take me home now? My mom's going to get mad if I don't go home soon."

Katy sighed, agitated, and leaned back on her heels. "Why can't you just walk home? It's only a few blocks away."

"Yeah," I said frantically, "but I have to cross the highway to get to my street! My mom would never let me do that!" We had a carpool take us home from school that day, and that was the only reason my mom let me play at her house.

"Then why don't you call your mom and ask her to come get you?" Katy turned back to her collection and picked out the new Olivia Newton John album. I knew that if I called Mom after promising her that Katy's mother would bring me home, I'd never be able to go over to her house to play again.

"Katy, you said your mom would take me home. Why don't you just go ask her?"

"Fine!" Katy huffed, and she stood up and left the room. She came back a few minutes later and told me her mom had a headache and couldn't take me home.

"Why don't you walk? I'll walk with you up to the end of my street, and then I'll watch you on our monitors."

"Monitors?"

"Yeah, we have these monitors on our TV that can follow you all the way home to make sure you got there OK."

I knew Katy liked to twist the truth at times, but I didn't think she'd do it about something so serious. Earlier, she had told me she was Olivia Newton John's cousin and was going to visit her in Australia that summer. I looked up at the clock again and saw that it was getting closer to six. I was running out of time.

"Fine," I said. I was forced to give in. "Then walk me to the end of the street."

I grabbed my red Tupperware® lunch box and rainbow backpack and walked out Katy's front door without trying to find her mother to make sure she was telling the truth. I did not ask for a demonstration of the monitors. Blindly, I trusted.

Katy grudgingly walked me up to the end of her street that met the four-lane highway. I hesitated. "Are you sure your mom can watch me on that monitor?"

Katy tried to reassure me with a smile and a nod. "Uh-huh," she said. She watches me walk to school all the time." She quickly gave me a hug. "Thanks for coming over," she said. "I'll see you at school tomorrow!" Then she walked away, leaving me standing alone at the stop sign.

I watched her leave, and as she got smaller and smaller in my vision, the knot in my stomach tightened. I knew that if my mom found out I had walked home alone she would be angry, but I wanted to be able to go to Katy's house after school again. So, with a deep breath in and an exhale out, I gathered my courage and looked to the highway. Traffic was light, and most of the evening rush hour was gone. Looking both ways before making the decision to brave the daunting asphalt, I held my breath and dashed across to the other side of the street.

When I had made it safely to the other side, relief flooded through me. I had only one more block to walk before I came to my street. A vision of Katy and her mom watching me on the monitor came to mind, and I thought about doing something funny to see if Katy would laugh about it the next day. I set my lunch box down to wave when a boy turned the corner from the direction of the elementary school. I didn't want to embarrass myself so I picked up my lunch box and continued walking.

The boy got closer, and I wondered whether I should say "Hi" to him when he passed or keep staring straight ahead. He was a stranger, and although I knew not to talk to strangers, I would have hated to be rude if he were to smile or say "Hello" to me.

He had short black hair and dark, deep set eyes covered with bushy eyebrows that were not threatening. He was coming from the junior high or high school, carrying a violin case, and he looked to be about fourteen or fifteen years old. He seemed nice enough, and I decided that if he said "Hi" to me then I would say "Hi" back.

When he was about two feet away from me, he stopped walking. The sour smell of cigarette smoke and oranges burned my nostrils. He stood ominously before me, dressed in black jeans and a black T-shirt, and even though his hair looked black I could now see that it was just real dirty. I had slowed my pace and moved to the edge of the sidewalk to pass him. As he got a little closer, I started walking to the curb so he could pass. I kept my head down, feeling too awkward to look at the stranger passing me, and before I knew it I was staring down at his black tennis shoes and jeans. He had blocked my path. The only way around him was to step off the curb into oncoming traffic or scoot to the other side onto the lava rock yard. I looked up, far up, for he was taller than me, and softly said, "Excuse me." Then I tried to pass him on the right. He moved in front of me again and set his violin case down on the sidewalk.

This time I scooted to the left and tried to walk off the sidewalk into the rock yard to go around him. My heartbeat increased with raw fear. What was he doing?

He moved again to prevent me from going around him, and then he reached out with both hands, grabbed me by the elbows, and my lunch box fell to the curb. "Hi, Shannon," he said in a very clear and distinct voice.

Instead of feeling relieved that somehow he knew me, the adrenaline in my veins began to flow, causing the acid in my stomach to churn. "How do you know my name?"

15

His grip tightened. "I was told to get you. You are what we want."

"Who told you to get me?" I pleaded. A shard of hope caught in my throat. I thought maybe my Mom had sent some neighbor boy to look for me.

"He's not too happy with you, Shannon. You've been a bad girl."

Suddenly, he pulled me to his chest, violently turned me around, and wrapped one arm firmly around my chest, pinning my arms to my sides. My back was flat against his chest. In a panic, I tried to wiggle free, but he reached up with his free hand, and I felt something cool and sharp against my neck.

"Don't move, you little twit or I'll slice your throat!"

The warmth of urine running down my leg went unnoticed.

"Get away from her!" a strange male voice from behind us yelled. The boy let go of my neck and took off running towards the yard.

Weak with fear, I slumped to the ground. I saw a man run past me, chasing the boy through the yard, and as I lay there sobbing into my hands, trying to grasp what had just happened, I heard a car door slam.

"Oh, my dear God!"

Hope surged through me because I recognized that voice. It was my mom!

I stood up, willing my legs to move, and ran towards her. She shoved the car keys into my hand. "Get in the car and lock yourself inside! Don't move till I get back!"

She shoved me toward our white Oldsmobile and ran after the stranger and the boy. I did not think to question where she was going. I went straight to the car. It took three tries to get a grip on the car door handle, but once I was inside I locked the doors and looked through the passenger window. I quickly scanned through the other houses and yards, but I couldn't see my mom, the unknown man, or the boy.

It felt like an eternity had passed when my Mom appeared from behind the house. She was panting like a rabid animal, her skirt was stuck between her legs, and her blouse was plastered to her chest with perspiration. She smiled when she saw me through the window. The tension in my limbs eased as the tears streamed down my face, and I unlocked the door to let her in.

"That man got the little twerp," she said.

She turned on the ignition and drove us home, all the while saying something about how she didn't want me to have to look at him again. The rest is a blur.

In fact, the only thing I can recall after walking home that day is finding out what the boy was talking about when he said *they* were looking for me. That next morning, I heard my parents discussing the incident. The young man who had accosted me was only fifteen years old and could not be arrested because he had not afflicted any physical harm. The police, however, were able to get some information out of him before they let him go. According to the young man, he was a member of a satanic cult, or gang, as it would be called today. I don't know why he chose me or how he knew my name. Sacrifices are said to be complete wives' tales, but I had fit the description of the perfect victim—a young virgin girl with blonde hair and bright blue eyes.

At that moment, I became aware of the presence and power of the Holy Spirit. I knew He was with me and wanted to use me. He presented himself in the gift of wisdom, but it would take me nearly twenty years to embrace the complete understanding and meaning of having a purpose. A very gentle, slight whisper let me know that God wanted me to work for him, and the Devil was the opposition.

# Saved

For whoever wishes to save his life will lose it, but whoever loses his life for my sake and that of the gospel will save it.

—Mark 8:35

MY FATHER WAS desperate to save his children from a corrupt world, so in 1982, a few months after that incident, he took a demotion and moved our family hundreds of miles away to his hometown.

The summer before my tenth birthday, approximately a year after the incident in El Paso, I went to stay with my aunt Denise, uncle Jack, and their two children, Nikki, eight, and Nate, six. "Be good for your aunt and uncle," Mom whispered into my ear as she kissed my forehead. I nodded with great enthusiasm, crawled back into the "camp" we had constructed in the bed of the truck with sleeping bags and pillows, and nestled between Nate and Nikki. I was happy that for one brief moment that summer I would be the oldest. I no longer would be the annoying little sister, waiting for a sign of recognition or acceptance. I would be the one that others would look up to—the one that my cousins would come to and want to be around.

The trip was planned quickly. One day, we were at my grandparents' home for a family reunion, and a few days later, with nothing but the few clothes I had brought with me, I was off by myself, with cousins I only saw on once-a-year occasions. This was an adventure. We bumped and thumped with the groove of the road and giggled till we nearly peed ourselves. The distance was of no importance. It could have been endless for all I cared. But before long, the vibrations of the tires beneath our backs lulled us to sleep.

A few hours later, we stopped at a rest area for a break and a bite to eat. The vibrations of the tires coursed through my body. Still groggy from sleep, Nikki, Nate, and I obediently sat at the picnic table for lunch. "Let us pray before we begin," Aunt Denise said.

I made the sign of the cross, but halfway through it I realized that my hand was the only one moving. Everyone else's hands were folded in front of them. Their heads were bowed and their eyes were closed. Although I was prepared to hold hands and recite the blessing I had known practically since birth, I lowered my hand and did the same. I sat silent through the prayer that Uncle Jack led, realizing for the first time that I had family who were not Catholic. In my naïveté, I had assumed that everyone related to me would have been.

This realization came quickly and soon was forgotten as we tore into the lunch that had been blessed. Not until the next morning, when I awoke in a guest room that was devoid of any items and knickknacks other than a lone picture on the wall and a dresser and chair in the corner, did I realize that for the next three weeks I would be experiencing an entirely new family dynamic. I would not have Morgan to take up half the room or mess with my things, Kyle would not chase me around the house, snapping the back of my knees with wet dish towels as I cried out in pain, and I would not have Carrie to shadow and protect.

I sprawled out in the full-sized bed, reaching wide with my fingertips and long with my toes, covering as much of the surface as I could.

"Nice!" I giggled to myself.

But beyond my closed door were the faint sounds of someone else's giggles. As I jumped out of bed and ran into the hall, the giggles grew louder, and the high-pitched voice of Mickey Mouse tickled my ears. Nate and Nikki were on the couch in the living room with their eyes transfixed to the Disney Channel. What a treat! We didn't have the Disney Channel at home, and even if we had, there would have been no chance that I'd get to have control over what we watched. With great pleasure, I hopped onto the couch and wiggled in between them. There were no protests, shoves, or kicks to throw me off. There was only acceptance.

That afternoon, Aunt Denise was on a mission to find some dresses for me to wear to church—a mission I was not too thrilled about because dresses were not my style. My lack of agility and athleticism and my fear of getting hurt kept me from being a tomboy, and I only tolerated playing dress-up. I was misplaced.

Any feeble protests on my part were unheard by Aunt Denise, because there was a Wednesday evening service at the church they attended. When we stumbled upon a great sale of one-piece miniskirt dresses, Aunt Denise exclaimed, "Oh, look, Shannon! The Good Lord guided us here!"

"What does the Lord have to do with me wearing a dress?" I wondered.

She picked a purple one off of the rack and held it up to my neck. "You'll have to try it on," she said. "We don't want you shocking the young men with those tan legs of yours."

I rolled my eyes and obediently went to the dressing room. The dress was comfortable, not too girly, and was a definite change from the big puffy dresses my mom made me wear as a little girl that caused me to constantly fidget in discomfort. At the same time, this dress mustered enough feminism to be appropriate for church. I studied my reflection in the changing room mirror, and for the first time I looked at my legs and wondered about what Aunt Denise had said. Would a boy look at my legs?

After spending a day on my aunt and uncle's turf, I realized that church was not just something they went to on Wednesday nights and Sunday mornings. It was their life. Nearly every sentence out of Aunt Denise's mouth was about the Lord. It was intriguing and different.

In my family's Catholic household, we diligently attended Mass every Sunday and on holy days of obligation. Of course, I wasn't sure why those days were obligations, but my parents made sure I went. I received the Sacraments of Baptism and First Communion, attended CCE, and we said the blessing before every meal. In many ways, we were just as consumed with church as my aunt and uncle's family . We believed in Jesus Christ, and we were Christians, but without stepping foot into my aunt's church building, I could see that my family's Christianity was not lived in the way I experienced with Aunt Denise and Uncle Jack.

"Oh, Shannon, I can't wait for everyone to meet you tonight!" said Aunt Denise over a snack of delicious mint and chocolate Keebler® Grasshopper® cookies.

"Who will I meet?" I asked wearily. I was not a shy girl, but Aunt Denise's eyes twinkled with expectation, and I didn't want to fail her.

"Everyone," she giggled. "You're my niece, and I know everyone is going to love you!" Her enthusiasm was infectious, and I couldn't help but get excited. Excited about church! It was an odd feeling, but a welcoming one, too.

As we drove into the parking lot, I saw a group of kids who were a year or two older than me going up the back stairs to the church. Aunt Denise turned in her seat to look at me, motioning to the kids outside. "Do you see the girl in the blue shirt? She sings in the choir."

I caught a glimpse of a girl in blue just before the door closed behind her. I nodded politely, unsure if I was supposed to be impressed or if this was simply one of the many random facts Aunt Denise divulged.

"One year ago, she couldn't sing if she had to save her own precious life!" She laughed, mouth wide open, as she hit Uncle Jack on his arm.

We parked, filed out of the car, and Aunt Denise kept talking. "The poor thing wanted to sing so badly, she'd go up to the front and pray for a voice to glorify God. We prayed over her and prayed for her, till one day she got up in front of the entire church and sang the most beautiful hymn." As Aunt Denise told me this story, her gaze seemed to be looking into the past.

She had caught my attention. Someone who couldn't sing, who was so bad that even Aunt Denise would laugh about it, prayed for a voice, and then, suddenly, could sing? If I prayed hard enough, could Carrie be happy? If my prayers were as heartfelt as that girl's, would I see a true smile from Carrie and have the peace that she would be all right? I was anxious to enter this church of miracles, but I was equally nervous.

Unsure if fairies or wizards who would snap their wands to grant wishes would greet me, we entered the church, and, much to my relief, it was simply a church. No bells and whistles—just pews, a stage, some band equipment, and a bare cross hanging front and center, directly above what looked to be a small swimming pool. It definitely wasn't ornate like the Catholic altar. At that age I didn't understand the difference between a crucifix and cross, so I stared at the bare cross, wondering why Jesus wasn't on it. Later, I came to realize that was a source of contention between Protestants and Catholics. Most Protestant denominations believed that Catholics were glorifying Christ's crucifixion and not focusing on his resurrection. Of course, I would later learn that this was a misconception and not true, but at that moment, all I realized was that Christ was missing. To me, the bare cross was odd.

We were separated into age groups on Wednesday nights for classes. But thankfully there were no surprises. We learned about Jesus, his love, and the Bible—many topics I had been introduced to in my own parish and in other vacation Bible schools I had attended along the way.

But the second Wednesday night, toward the end of the evening, when all ages gathered for a closing service, my simple world was rocked. Somehow, I found myself sitting by an older man to my left, and I was on the edge of the pew by the aisle. At the time, the band was playing. The drums were making a hypnotic rhythm, and the tambourine added just the right amount of zing to the entire ensemble. That girl, the one who could never carry a tune, was belting out praise that raised the hair on my arms. As things began to quiet down, the man next to me spoke out deeply and with great strength—but in a language I could not understand. As he continued talking, his words came out faster and more fervently. His hand rose in the air, and my heart nearly stopped beating.

Across the aisle, a woman cried out just as fervently and strong, but this time I could understand her, because she cried out in English. The man next to me ceased speaking but he kept his hand raised and his eyes closed. The congregation began "Amening" the woman's outcries of necessary obedience and servitude to our Lord Jesus Christ.

I wanted to run.

I loved Jesus. I loved Bible school, going to church, and my aunt, uncle, and cousins, but I wanted to get out of there. Even so, my feet remained planted to the floor, as I stood helpless, desperately looking for Aunt Denise. And then, except for a few calm mutterings of Jesus' name and the stream of voiced prayer, it was quiet.

It seemed to have been a dream, and as quickly as it all began, it dissipated, as people suddenly snapped back into reality and began filing out of the pews, making conversation with their neighbors about the daily grind and obligations of their lives. I seemed to be the only person with her cheeks wet, eyes wide, and hands still shaking.

Nikki found me first but never commented about what I had experienced. Instead, as she guided me in the direction of the parking lot, she chatted excitedly about our plans for the next day.

In the car I found my voice. "Aunt Denise?" It came out in a jagged whisper.

She turned in her seat to look at me.

"What was that man next to me doing?" I could feel the tears well up again, and I bit the inside of my cheek to keep them from surfacing.

She smiled, and in her eyes I could see only compassion and love, which calmed me down. "He was speaking in tongues," she answered. "It's a gift of the Holy Spirit. It doesn't happen often, but when it does it's amazing." Her smile widened, and she turned back in her seat, content that she had given me what I needed to know.

Unfortunately I was still clueless. But soon enough, Nate said something funny that made me giggle, and my young mind let it go.

Nothing more was spoken of the happenings of that Wednesday evening, of the gifts of the Holy Spirit, or of any other mind-bending things. Instead, we spent the next three days playing around the house, watching Disney movies, eating Grasshopper® cookies, being extremely silly, and getting the most out of each other with what little time I had left to be submerged in their world of comfort. Time seemed to go by too quickly, and we were set to pack up Aunt Denise's car that Monday morning to make the ten hour drive to take me home.

Sunday would be my last service with their church. I had grown to enjoy the liveliness and simplicity, but in many ways I missed the comfort of the Mass I had always known. There was a feeling I got when I walked into our church that I didn't get in theirs. At first, I thought it was the absence of seeing Christ on the cross, but it was more than that. I missed the familiar prayers, the jolt of excitement that ran through me when I received the Eucharist, and the warmth I felt as I sat with my family—a warmth I didn't know was there until I wasn't around them.

This last service, however, felt different. It was tainted with an edge of anxiety. Something in the air pricked my skin and took me back to the oddness of the previous service when I witnessed the speaking of tongues. I could feel that energy in the air, and once the music began to play, all of the anxiety seeped out of my pores, and I relaxed once again, listening to the message that was being delivered.

Toward the end of his sermon, the preacher began talking about living our lives in the comfort of Jesus' arms, accepting him as our Lord and Savior, and saying, "Yes!" to Jesus so we could be protected from the evil in the world around us.

I understood wanting to be protected. I had escaped evil in a way that most people around me had never experienced, and I certainly didn't want to experience it again. But it was the concept of being saved that was new to me. On the last day of my visit, it wasn't the service or the congregation that shocked me. It was *me!*

Filled with the energy coursing through my veins, I left my seat and went up front, just before the preacher's feet, and then collapsed in a heap on the steps. My face was mashed into the carpet, and all I could see were odd visions of family, friends, and even faces I didn't recognize, all of whom were in sadness, pain, and torment. The energy within me became a heavy, suffocating weight. It was like watching a slide show in ultrafast speed, while feeling each of the various emotions represented on the faces as the slides flashed by. Vaguely, I was aware of my aunt kneeling over me, her arms and upper torso wrapped protectively over mine.

The preacher was at my head, saying something I couldn't hear, because the pain I felt inside strangled my senses of hearing and sight. I wept—not for myself or my own salvation, but for the many people that seemed to encompass me at that moment. And then finally my voice broke free, and I cried to Jesus, saying his name over and over again. "Jesus...Jesus...Jesus. Please always be with me."

And then it stopped. My aunt's body behind me was suddenly overpowering, and the preacher's voice was loud in my ear. I could hear sobs and low groans, and as I lifted my head I realized they were coming from me, and that no one else was up front. Embarrassed, I went to stand, but I could barely lift my shaking arms.

With Aunt Denise's support, I stood on my feet, and then the preacher put a hand on my forehead. "Do you, my child, accept Jesus as your personal Savior?"

"Of course!" I thought to myself. Since I had started talking, I had been taught that Jesus had died on the cross for me and everyone else in the world. But I couldn't say this. My voice was gone. I nodded. Claps arose from the congregation behind me. Gone was the pain, torment, and suffering, and in their place I felt elation, joy, and love. "I guess this is what 'being saved' is," I thought as I smiled.

If anything could upset the Devil, it is the open acknowledgment of Jesus Christ in your life. That night, he came to visit me once again, this time in my dreams. I struggled, kicked, and writhed about in the vast bed that I had claimed for myself but had now claimed me, as he held me in my nightmarish sleep. He hated me. He wanted me. It was a clear, horrific feeling that burned into my consciousness.

Green eyes and fear. The eyes are a vivid memory, casting their eerie glow on the vague recollection that remains in the recesses of my mind. It is the fear that remained like a dormant disease, flaring up in moments of insecurity.

The sunlight splashed the walls, uncovering every dark corner and crevice of the room. My eyes were wide open, already squinting from the brightness of the day, and staring at Aunt Denise, who was sitting in the chair in front of me. The fear had subsided, and was shrinking away from the light. I was awake and safe.

Slowly, I sat up. "Aunt Denise?"

She was slouched over with her head in an awkward angle on the armrest. When she heard me speak, she mumbled something and sat up straighter, eyes still closed.

"Aunt Denise," I said with more force, but not loudly enough to wake everyone else.

She opened her eyes, and as they caught mine, for a split millisecond of a moment, there was uncertainty on her face. But then it was gone, and concern contorted her every feature and movement.

She was on the bed, cradling me in her arms. "Shannon, honey, are you OK?"

"Yes," I said, very curious as to when she had come into my room.

She hugged me tightly to her chest. "You gave me such a scare last night. I had no idea what was going on with you."

"What are you talking about?" I asked, afraid that if she knew about my dream she would call me crazy.

She withdrew and gave us enough distance to look me in the face. "You were kicking and moving all about this bed as if you were fighting the Devil himself. And you kept saying something about eyes."

When she said the word "eyes," the sight and physical repugnance of the ones in my dream rushed through my senses.

"Honey, you're trembling. Are you OK?"

At that moment, at the age of nine, I made the conscious decision to cover up what I knew in the depth of my soul to be real—the insane reality of a spiritual struggle. "I'm fine, Aunt Denise. It was just a bad dream."

"Well, you scared me to death. The way you were crying out and going on about those eyes, I knew I needed to stay in here with you and pray over you while you slept."

It was a genuine smile that I gave her, because I finally understood that it was prayer and Christ that saved me.

# Rejected

Therefore, you are without excuse, every one of you who passes judgment. For by the standard by which you judge another you condemn yourself, since you, the judge, do the very same things.

—Romans 2:1

GREEN EYES, PRAYERS in tongues, displaced pain and suffering, and nightmarish struggles with the unreachable depths of the spiritual world may scare most sane or even insane adults into a spiral of anxious uncertainty. As my aunt and uncle piled us into the backseat of my aunt's car for the ten-hour ride home, however, those experiences dissolved into the pores of my consciousness, and the landscape smoothed out into the vast plains of North Texas.

These events didn't fit the life of a typical nine year old. I knew my parents wouldn't understand their daughter seeing evil as reality, so as time passed the incidents became more and more detached, and soon I stored them away as memories.

For the next few years, I followed my parents' lead and settled back into our way of life. Sundays were always for church, but the morning never began with excitement and anticipation of the message. Instead, with our family of four, chaos ensued from the moment Mom tried to get us up, dressed, and in the car to make it to Mass on time.

My parents had good and holy intentions in giving us a Catholic based foundation. Morgan and I were enrolled in Catholic grade school, and we all attended CCE and were not allowed to skip Mass on Sunday. Still, we never discussed our relationships with Christ or made it a part of our home life as my aunt and uncle's family did.

The Catholic Church did not have a youth group, and by the time I had turned 12 and was in the seventh grade, I had tucked away the strangeness of that summer. Other than in the occasional nightmare, the green eyes were behind me.

I wanted to live a normal life. I wanted the relationship with God, but I didn't want everything else that seemed to accompany my faith.

The lesson I learned in my aunt's church continued as I learned that the walls of separation between denominations had been built long before I would even begin to dream of tearing them down.

"Are you sure your parents are OK with you going to Camp Fall Creek?" my best friend Stacy's mother asked.

"Yeah, why wouldn't they be?" I snapped, as I grabbed a registration form from the table at her church's family life center. I was twelve and full of sassiness. I didn't care one way or the other what my parents thought about me going to Fall Creek.

"Well, because it *is* a Protestant camp," Stacy's mother said.

I shrugged my shoulders and rolled my eyes. "They let me come here every Wednesday and Sunday night. I'm probably more Protestant than Catholic at this point anyway!"

How naïve I was to take religion so lightly. Not long into our first day at Camp Fall Creek, the differences hung around my neck like a noose.

"Where's your Bible?" a fellow cabin mate asked me as we headed to the evening service.

"I don't have one," I said, putting my empty hands behind my back.

"You don't have a Bible?" Her voice rose up through the tips of the trees and spread like fire all around us.

Stacy, who was walking ahead of me, stopped and waited for us to catch up. "She's Catholic," she said, simply. She offered it up as a tell-all explanation, but it only fueled the fire.

"Catholic?" the girl asked with wide eyes. "Don't you worship Mary and statues?"

Frantically, I turned to Stacy for support, but instead she returned my silent plea with curiosity. "No," I answered petulantly, afraid to say more. I didn't know how to explain why we said Hail Mary's and prayed to saints for intercession.

"Thou shall not have other gods before Me," she sang out before leaving us to find a pew with worthier company.

"We don't worship Mary," I grumbled under my breath to Stacy, who continued to stand beside me, looking at me with pity.

By the time the week had drawn to a close, I had managed to make it through with a little less taunting and come out with a few new friends. I thought I was home free—that is, until the final church service.

The minister gave us his final sermon, and we had our heads bent in the final prayer. "If you have not accepted Christ in your life and you want to say yes to Jesus, please come and join us here at the front." I felt Stacy move beside me, and I picked my head up enough to see her edge out of the pew and go forward.

My ears began to burn. Flashes of my aunt and her preacher covering me on the stairs, and the pain and anguish I felt for others seeped back into my awareness, knocking the air out of me. Bent forward, I held onto the pew.

"It's OK," I heard from a gentle voice above me, as a hand stroked my hair. "Let it all out."

I wanted to shake my head "no"—not because I didn't want Jesus, but because I didn't need to go up there again! I was torn between the memories of the summer, years before, and the humiliation of everyone around me, who thought I was a heathen because I wouldn't go up front. There was so much pressure. In the end, I remained in my seat with my head down, ignoring the many gentle touches and words to nudge me forward. "God will understand," I told myself. He still loved me, right?

Back home, in the rotating cycle of Catholic Mass and Protestant church services, the pressure continued to build up from the youth group I had considered a part of my life for the past three years. My senses were heightened to the underlying accusations towards the Catholic church. Most of the time, I didn't blame them for asking questions or assuming things that I knew were untrue, but I was not bold enough to give them answers. I didn't really know the answers. When given the chance, however, I remained loyal enough to my initial upbringing to defend it as best I could.

This new atmosphere changed the dynamic of the group. Before, I was one of them—accepted, loved, and taken in without preconceptions or expectations. Now, the barrier was broken—enough for the expectations to suffocate.

"The Bible is God's Word," the youth minister proclaimed as he held up his KJV. The look in his eyes pierced my soul. "You do not need anything but his Word! Remember! God is a jealous God! You do not need to turn to saints or Mary for answers to prayer! You must live your life in his truth, which is right here." He brought the Bible down and slapped the palm of his hand on the cover. "And his truth shall set you free."

It was eerie how he seemed to fix his gaze in my direction. I turned slightly to see who was behind me, only to find the row empty. For the first time, I felt attacked, and I couldn't understand why. I had never proclaimed my devotion to Mary or to any saint. I was in Confirmation class that year so I was learning quite a bit about them. I understood why each saint had been canonized, considering the miraculous events that had surrounded their lives. I did not personally own a Bible, but that didn't mean I had never read one or that we Catholics didn't read out of the Bible. The whole Mass was taken from the Bible, Gospel readings and all!

When the youth minister was done, I slipped away and phoned home. My mother answered on the third ring.

"Hello?"

"Mom?" Hearing her voice made me cry.

"Shannon? What's wrong?"

"Will you come get me? It ended early tonight, and Stacy wants to stay."

"Are you OK?"

I sniffed and tried to wipe the tears away with the back of my hand before anyone could turn the corner and witness my breakdown. "Yeah, I just want to go home."

"OK, I'll be there in five minutes."

I hung up and decided to wait outside on the steps. Before I could reach the front door, the youth minister was at my side.

"Everything OK?" he asked.

Afraid my voice would betray me, I nodded in reply.

"Listen," he said. "I've wanted to talk to you about something since this summer." He moved in front of me and looked directly into my eyes.

"You've been a part of our group for almost three years. I know the rest of your family is Catholic, and I think now that you are about to go into high school you should be able to make a decision as to what you want to be."

What I want to be? The phrase ricocheted in my head. What was wrong with who I was?

"I think, Shannon, that it's time you choose your faith. Do you want to stay with us or remain Catholic?"

I paused, dumbfounded, in the position he had forced me into, for what seemed to be a lifetime.

It was long enough to allow the betrayal to fester. I was surprised by my self-control. "I will always be Catholic," I said firmly, and I walked past him and out the door.

I sat on the steps waiting for my mother, and as my tears dried up, all I could think about was how I felt judged for being Catholic. For the past three years, that youth minister had taught God's love and compassion, but in one breath, the picture had changed. His words, which, in hindsight, could have been quite innocent, tore apart the protective layer that kept me secure—the reassurance that God would love me, no matter what. Here was a man I looked up to, held in high regard, and often believed had a direct line to the Lord Almighty, telling me he did not approve of my faith.

The differences between our denominations were obvious, but in that moment they were as segregated before my eyes as black and white. Which was the right way to go? Confusion set in. Had God rejected me because I was Catholic? But how could I not be Catholic? It was who I was! I was firm and stoic on the outside, but inside my soul was shattered. I felt that God had stared me down and given me an ultimatum.

The loving, forgiving, merciful Lord who had been preached to me by all the churches I had visited no longer made sense. What I saw and experienced now, not only because of that man but also through my failed prayer requests and sadness, was that God was to be feared.

# The Quick Fix

We often think of sin as breaking God's law. But at its core, sin is really breaking our relationship with God and distancing ourselves from God (*Live It! The Catholic Youth Bible*, NAB commentary in reference to Romans 3:21–31)

ANGER AND RESENTMENT settled deep into the marrow of my bones. At the impressionable age of thirteen, the message was loud and clear: *"You are not worthy!"*

Instead of a loving God, I now knew a fearful God. Could I have listened to the message given at Mass that God loved me? That he was merciful and forgiving? Sure, I could have, but I wasn't listening.

For four years, I refused to write in my journal. I was a petulant, stubborn teenager, and I was upset that the personal bond, the touch of his favor, seemed to be out of reach for no good reason. I don't need a journal, however, to remind me of those four years. I recall those tumultuous days, weeks, months, and years with great clarity, as a long trip into what I like to refer to as the "Valley of Shadow and Death."

In the midst of the valley, the Devil spun his web of artificial joy and happiness. He knew what I wanted and offered it to me in a variety of ways. I had the time of my life—*fun!* Sin was fun! Sin was easy! Sin was also addicting.

The summer after eighth grade, my family had a party at our home. I had a girlfriend over, and for the first time we tried beer. We mixed it with Sprite. We were desperate to feel the intoxicating joy of drunkenness, but after tasting the bitter fizzle of one beer, we couldn't stomach another.

In a country town such as ours, however, it didn't take long to meet up with older, more mature kids who were willing to supply us with alcohol. Normally this was because my girlfriends' older siblings let us tag along. I enjoyed the feeling of being included with older girls rather than treated like a pest by my sister at home.

The first time I got drunk, nothing seemed to matter. After a while, all of the drunken nights seemed the same. I would stay the night with friends, go out with siblings or older friends to parties, and then try to get back home safely so I could pass out.

It was cool. I was lighter than air. I was almost fourteen. My braces had come off, my hair had grown out, and my body was filling out. Cute, older boys took notice of me, and I didn't even have to pray to God to get them to. Flirting was fun. This was what I had been waiting for—to be noticed, feel liked, and be wanted.

I didn't realize the impression I was giving.

"Oh! I love those jeans! They are so awesome!" squealed my friend Lauren with envy.

Spurred on by her excitement, I scuttled over to the full-length mirror that hung on the back of her bedroom door. My jeans were a second skin, stonewashed with manufactured tears and rips strategically placed, and the inside of the rips revealed a patch declaring the brand name: Used. Twisting to see my backside, I smiled at my reflection. After all the years of crying on my father's lap about my hideous unworthiness in this world, I finally felt confident that I looked good.

That evening, we tagged along with Lauren's sister, Natalie, who was four years ahead of us in high school. We were entering our freshman year, and she was a senior. That summer, we found ourselves at countless parties at college students' apartments, playing drinking games and flirting well beyond what my fourteen years could handle.

At one of these parties, an extremely good-looking college freshman named Taylor Brinkman sat at the table next to me. We were playing "quarters" and somehow, he managed to bump the table every time I tried to bounce the quarter into the cup, faulting me into drinking. Not until I got up to use the restroom did it dawn on me that he may have been playing with an ulterior motive.

"'Used?'" Taylor said as he grabbed the belt loops on the back of my jeans and pulled me closer to him. "Are *you* used?" He dragged the word out and kept his hands on my hips.

Rather than push me to leave, the attention invigorated me. This older and very cute guy was paying attention to me. If he thought I knew what I was doing, then so be it. I shrugged my shoulders and smiled.

Before I could get deeper into his web, Natalie caught on to our exchange. She stood up from the table and called into the other room where Lauren had been messing with the stereo. "Lauren! It's time to go." She grabbed my elbow and pulled me out of Taylor's grasp. "Nice try, Taylor."

Taylor winked and I crumbled inside. "Nah," he said. "She's too young. We're just talking."

"Um-hum," Natalie grunted, as she escorted Lauren and me out the door.

"He's so cute!" I exclaimed once I was settled in the back seat of Natalie's car. Although my vision was blurry and my hands and feet felt like someone else's appendages, the majority of my alcohol-induced buzz had been consumed in the adrenaline of the attraction.

"Watch yourself, Shannon," Natalie warned, looking at me wearily in the rearview mirror. "Taylor's a good guy, but you never know. Both of you are so naïve right now," she said as she sighed.

Lauren looked at me over the back seat, and we both answered with giggles.

Those summer months were a rocky journey of leaving behind the good young girl I had always been and morphing into the young lady that intrigued yet frightened me, all the while keeping me on edge. At the end of the summer, the two parts of my personality collided.

"Surprise!"

A loud chorus of whoops and hollers from all of my friends surrounded me as I entered my best friend Jenny's backyard. I thought I was going to an end-of-summer swim party, but instead she had thrown me a surprise fourteenth birthday party.

I was humbled and overwhelmed by the effort it took for Jenny to pull this off, and by the group of friends that were there to celebrate. I was the youngest of them all. Normally my birthday would have been forgotten—lost in Labor Day festivities and the first day of school.

It was nice to settle back into the evening and enjoy it with a clear mind, free from alcohol. The pressure to impress was off, but I still had to keep my head above the inner circle of the "cool" waters.

The party wasn't the only gift Jenny gave me.

"OK," she said. "I have my gift for you, but I don't know if you'll want to open it in front of everyone." I followed her into the house to her room. When we entered, she grabbed a small wrapped package off the nightstand. "You've been coming to the church for so many years, I thought you might like to have this."

My heart tinged with pain when she mentioned church. I didn't tell what her youth minister had said to me, or how it had made me feel. She didn't even know all the horrible things I had been doing all summer! Jenny was one of my best friends, but I felt that we were slipping apart, solely because I could not live up to the standard she had set for herself.

Ever since we'd met in the sixth grade, our relationship was more of a sisterly bond. She was the mature one, the bold one, the one that knew where we should go, what we should do, and, when I was with her, it was always as if the path would fall into place. I loved her for her stamina and charged, positive attitude. As we grew older, however, I felt more and more incompatible to her intellect, gifts, and talents.

Carefully, I unwrapped the package and held the gift gingerly in my hands: The Holy Bible.

Jenny reached over and flipped open the cover. "Look, I wrote in it and dated it. I would've had it embossed with your name, but I didn't have time." Her face glowed with excitement. The tears came in a rush. It was the best gift I could have received.

I didn't deserve it, but, somehow, I managed to thank her.

She began to cry, reached over, and hugged me. I wrapped one arm around her neck, cradling the Bible against my chest. I didn't deserve it, and I didn't deserve her as a friend. What kind of best friend was I to hide the things I had done that summer from her?

For a brief moment, I thought about coming clean and telling her everything—how I wanted to get away from what I knew would only get worse. I wanted to keep going to church events and being everything that "good" entailed. But I couldn't.

I couldn't go back.

Before I knew it, my freshman year in high school had ended, and sophomore year began. It didn't take long to realize that a lot of my friends were finding ways to party—except for the select few, including Jenny, who remained true to the principles by which we had all been raised.

Life revolved around guys and parties. Who did I like? Where was the party after the Friday night game? Whose house could we stay at and find a way to go to the party without getting caught? Who would buy us the Keystone®, or Boone's Farm®, or should we go the cheaper route, get MD 20/20®, a faster buzz, and risk the possibility of blacking out?

"Your parents are out of town?" My friend Brittany asked, her voice filled with hope. There was a party that weekend, but she was grounded to an earlier curfew. "If I can get my mom to say I can spend the night with you, we can go and not have to worry about getting home so early!"

"Yeah, I wish," I mumbled, still pissed that my parents didn't trust me enough to stay in the house with Morgan by myself. I was fifteen and couldn't drive, but that didn't matter. We could bum rides off of friends. Instead, they asked my great aunt Debbie to come stay with us. She was a wonderful older woman, close to my grandmother's age, with a tremendous amount of history behind her, and she was a stickler for order. "Aunt Debbie is staying with us."

"So?" Brittany rambled on, "She's great and she never bothers you. She'll go to bed and not even realize when we're home!"

She had a point. Aunt Debbie did go to bed early. "OK, whatever. But I think we have to stick with my midnight curfew."

That evening, we dressed to impress in our best jeans. This was one of the biggest parties of the year, and it was at a senior's house, so all of the senior guys would be there.

One foot in the door, with a half-empty bottle of Strawberry Hill® in my hand, I was handed a glass of MD 20/20® for a game of "quarters." One shade shy of wasted, I was so bad at the game that I had already drunk a full bottle of MD 20/20® and polished off my wine by the time someone handed me a large plastic glass filled with vodka and orange juice. The Screwdriver. Boy, did that ever put me over the edge.

Brittany managed to drive us home, down the dark, winding country road to my parents' house. Sitting next to her in the passenger seat, I rolled down the window and rested my head on the door, just enough to allow the cool breeze to kiss my forehead.

A ferocious pain in my stomach jolted me out of the sticky black pool of drunken sleep. My eyes shot open, but the room was dark, and nothing seemed familiar.

"Where am I? What's going on?" I thought I was saying these things out loud, but when I tried to swallow I realized my lips were stuck together with dried vomit. They cracked open enough for me to get a bitter taste of what had come up earlier, before my dive into blackness. The pain that began in my stomach was now engulfing every inch of my body, and finally my eyes adjusted enough to make out the familiar surroundings of my bedroom.

"Wha…what's…" I tried to speak, but each syllable felt like a razor that was tearing the tissue in my throat. Then the shaking began. It started in my legs as I lay helplessly on my bed, unable to move because the pain was too intense. I tried to will my legs to stop, but I could see them literally convulsing. And then it spread through my torso and up through my entire body.

I was trapped in a useless body, desperate for the shaking to stop, but it was an exhausting battle. I could feel the wet warmth of tears rolling down my cheeks, but no matter how hard I tried I couldn't even move my hand to wipe them away.

"Shannon, are you OK?"

The voice came from above me on the left side of the bed. I shifted my eyes towards it and saw Brittany, fear etched on her face.

"No," I managed through a clenched jaw.

Now frantic, she took an extra blanket from the foot of the bed and covered me up to my neck. "What do I do? Should I get your aunt?"

With all the energy I could muster, I took in a deep breath and exhaled in an attempt to calm my nerves. Brittany had taken my hand in hers and was now sitting on the edge of the bed, stroking my hair. "Shhhh, it's OK," she crooned, as if to a little child.

The last thing I wanted her to do was get Aunt Debbie out of bed, because that would mean the end of my social world. "I'm…" I took in a deep breath, and blew it out. "I'm—OK," I finally managed, as my grip on her hand tightened enough to make her cringe.

I don't know how long Brittany sat with me that night, but it was long enough to calm my nerves just enough to pass out again.

I woke up the next morning to the sun sending laser beams of light through my eyes, into my brain, and scorching what nerve endings I had left. "Ooohhh, God," I moaned from the pain. I tried to swallow, but it felt as if a wad of cotton had been jammed into my esophagus.

Brittany came into the room with a radiant smile, fully decked out in her best attire. "Hey, you're up! Mom's going to pick us up in an hour to go to that mall modeling audition."

"NO!" I thought. This time, the adrenaline coursing through my body was from the threat of sheer stupidity, and the realization of how late I was to something that was very important. I sat up, and the room did a "180."

"Ohhh," I moaned, and I lay back down.

"Oh, come on!" Brittany pleaded and grabbed my hands, pulling me back up. "You've bounced back better than this! You have to do this with me, Shannon!"

Letting out a deep breath, I managed to sit up straight. My eyes still squinting from the rays of sun flowing through the room, I caught a glimpse of myself in the mirror on the dresser next to my bed. My eyeliner was smudged, and black veins of mascara covered my cheeks. But that wasn't the worst of it. My skin was as translucent as the best sci-fi ghost ever created on television. Had I not personally lived through the hell that caused my reflection, I would have sworn that we had been invaded by the living dead.

"Come on, get in the shower, and go drink some milk."

This thought came as clearly as if it had been spoken into my ear. I looked at Brittany, but she was already heading for the door. "I don't like milk," I said.

Brittany turned around and furrowed her eyebrows. "I don't, either," she said and hesitated. "Do you need something to drink?"

I brushed the thought away but realized I craved a glass of water. "Yeah, hey, will you help me get to the kitchen?"

Brittany nodded and came back, helping me down the stairs and into the kitchen. It was a humbling moment to be at someone else's mercy. On the island was a note from Aunt Debbie:

Glad you made it in OK last night. You guys were so quiet I never knew when you got in! I'm out doing some errands; I'll see you later this evening.
Love, Aunt. D.

Relief swept through me. At least I wasn't in trouble.

"Drink some milk."

The thought hit again, this time as if someone had yelled it into my ear. It was so clear that I looked up at Brittany, annoyed.

"What?" I asked her.

"Hum?" she answered.

As if someone had hit an on/off switch in my stomach, the all too familiar pain from the night before returned.

"Drink some milk!"

This time, I couldn't argue with whomever or whatever was telling me to do this. I turned around, reached into the fridge, grabbed the milk, and drank from the carton.

"Gross, Shannon! What are you doing?" Brittany said. "You just said you didn't like milk. You'll have to throw that out. Do you know how nasty your breath is right now?" Her eyes were wide in mock-horror.

About three gulps of ice cold milk made its way to my stomach, and then *bam!* I dropped the carton on the counter and ran to the bathroom. Before I could fumble to get the toilet lid up, I felt my body convulse in spasms. My knees hit the floor, and every muscle contracted, pushing the poison out of my system and into the commode.

Plop! Plop! Plop!

Huge chunks of curdled milk hit the water, causing bits of backsplash to come back and hit my face.

And then it was over. Spent and exhausted, I lay in a heap at the foot of the toilet, a damp towel that Brittany had thrown at me was pressed to my forehead. As I lay there, I couldn't help but think how quickly my stomach had been freed, and how normal I felt again. The milk had done the trick.

Too self-absorbed to thank God or allow the moment to soak in long enough for me to recognize the true danger I was in, I continued to lay on the floor, contemplating whether I was well enough to make it to the fashion show auditions.

"OK, that was disgusting," Brittany said as she popped her head into the bathroom. "Hopefully it made you feel better, because you only have thirty minutes to look like you are alive."

Thus began a life-diminishing cycle that not even the threat of death could stop. The self destruction continued. There were mornings after nights out when my head would hurt so badly, my stomach couldn't even take the salt of a cracker, and my mind was so foggy that I couldn't recall whether I had said any insane or stupid things to my latest crush. I could never recall important facts. Did we kiss? Did we do anything else? "Oh, God," I would pray, "I hope not!"

But my prayers to God in such an inappropriate frame of reference were all that God got from me. The more I partied, drank, and did things I was told not to do, the further I retreated from God. It kept me from saying even the simplest, memorized prayers.

Every weekend for two years, this cycle repeated. In the beginning, I was happy. The thrill of this new world kept me on a euphoric high. I had tasted what popularity felt like, and I was part of a new crowd of friends that accepted me—at least the "me" who worked hard to not say stupid things or go against what the crowd did as a whole. Like a chameleon, my outer skin morphed so that everyone would like me.

The only way I went against the flow was by refusing to smoke pot. My sister Carrie had smoked enough around me that it held no mystery, and I blamed her pot smoking for her countless fights with my parents. I was smart, a member of FCA (Fellowship of Christian Athletes), and I attended church every Sunday with my friends. On the outside, to the community, I was an upstanding youth. A Junior Achiever. An Honor Roll Student. One of the upper echelons. The cream of the crop.

I made my choices, and although I was rarely alone, living this way sure was lonely.

Interchanging through the various personalities of good daughter, honor student, loyal friend, and party buddy was exasperating. Many nights, I would lay in bed, wishing my life were different. I wanted to feel real and still be happy. Joyful happy. I wanted what I felt that others had but I did not. I wanted better clothes, or better looks, or maybe if I were nicer or smarter. But even as I dreamt of these things, that pit of emptiness remained.

# Awakenings

Beloved, let us love one another, because love is from God; everyone who loves is begotten by God and knows God.

—1 John 4:7

THEN, ONE DAY, I met a boy.

In the winter of my sophomore year, sometime in December, I sat in the passenger seat of Brittany's car as we cruised the downtown strip, shamelessly eyeing every cute boy we saw. It didn't take long to find a great spot to park. She pulled into a parking space alongside the tallest guy I had ever seen. But she wasn't after him. She knew his friend somehow and thus began our evening.

I gravitated to the tall and sporty one. It wasn't his looks that pulled me to him but his fiery personality that was as colossal and enrapturing as his height. He had a head of red hair that punctuated the aura he exuded. He could hardly stand still, bouncing lightly on the balls of his feet, and nervously rubbing the tip of his index finger across his thumb. Standing next to him, I was dwarfed by his six-feet-ten-inch frame.

"I'm Shannon. What's your name?" I asked.

"Matt," he said.

The prospect of dating someone outside of my usual crowd was exciting. "Where do you go to school?" I asked. It might be odd that this was the first thing on my mind. My first thought wasn't whether he liked me, or a daydream about whether we would date. I knew we would date. The minute I saw him, I knew.

Since I was fifteen and unable to date, the kind of relationship we would be able to have and how we would accomplish having it was an exciting mystery. It became more of a problem when he informed me that he was from a nearby small town.

How could I date a guy that I would never see during the week?

Then again, maybe that would be a good thing, since the guys I had dated and seen every day never lasted more than a month or two. They had either said something that turned me off, worn something that made me think they were a dork, or the thrill of the chase had gone away when the party was over.

That night, Brittany, the boys and I went for a ride in their car along the strip, talking about the differences in our schools. We had hundreds of kids in our graduating class, and they only had about 40. Matt also talked a lot about basketball.

We exchanged numbers, and for the following week Matt called me every evening at eight o' clock. We talked for hours about our days, likes, dislikes, families, friends, and anything that came to our minds. Our relationship went very well for the first few months. He would come over on the weekends, and Dad enjoyed having him around. At times he would even allow us to go out and get something to eat—a feat for my father, who was very strict. In fact, all of my girlfriends, including Jenny, ended up dating Matt's good friends, which offered us more opportunities to see each other. Dating him kept me out of the party scene and reopened the door to my friendship with Jenny.

About a month into our relationship, basketball season began, and Jenny's father would take us to go see the games. It was a thrill to watch my boyfriend dunk the ball in the basket with little effort and hear those around me cheer for him. For the first time in a long time I felt blessed.

I had begged God to send me someone to care for me, with whom I could have a relationship. Despite who I had become in the past year, my prayer was answered.

Before Matt, puberty had stolen my worthiness. I had gone from finding favor in God to finding favor in boys. For two years, I had gone from one boy to another—never far enough to have sex, but far enough to feel the desire. In moments of drunken stupor, I felt wanted. But I didn't need to be lost in the haze of alcohol with Matt. When I was with him, I didn't need to impress. He gave me back the security I had once felt as a young girl, confident in knowing I was in God's favor.

On Valentine's Day, Matt surprised me by coming over with two roses, one for each month we had been seeing each other, and a little white stuffed bear with two hearts dangling from its neck.

He was always doing things that made me feel special. One afternoon, he talked Dad into allowing me to go on a date. His team was meeting at a rival school to watch them play a game; this team was next on their schedule. Afterwards, we would go to dinner, just the two of us. Matt had been working on Dad for a while, until he finally relented with his rule and allowed me to go.

My body couldn't contain the excitement that coursed through my veins. Although Matt and I had had many opportunities in the last two months to go on group dates and meet each other out, on this night I needed something special to wear. I borrowed a rhinestone-studded, white button-down oxford shirt from my neighbor, and I wore a studded belt and acid-washed jeans. I curled my thick, long, blonde hair in big ringlets and then brushed it out so the curls bounced and framed my face.

Nothing was normal with Matt. When we got into his cramped Dodge Daytona, and he turned to me and winked, I knew it was going to be a memory in the making.

As we zipped down country roads, the radio belted out various old rock songs. The silence was golden. We were free, together, and it was nice.

"You look great," Matt said about five minutes into the drive.

I smiled in return, and he reached over and grabbed my hand.

The chords of Lynyrd Skynyrd's "Free Bird" ignited our excitement, and together we practically tore our vocal chords as we sang along, neither of us doing a great job, but it didn't make a difference.

> If I leave here tomorrow
> Would you still remember me?
> For I must be traveling on, now,
> There's too many places I've got to see.
> And if I stayed here with you, now
> Things just wouldn't be the same.

Matt rolled down his window, and, without letting go of my hand, he steered the car with his knee. Reaching his left hand and half of his upper torso out of the window, he belted out the chorus as if it were his life motto:

> Well I'm as free as a bird now,
> And this bird you cannot change…
> Lord knows I can't change.

Scared to death he'd wreck the car and we'd be gone for good but at the same time fueled by his vivaciousness, I rolled down my window to join him. My hand made waves in the wind and even though I had been careful to pick out the best outfit and my hair had been perfectly curled, I no longer cared what I looked like.

> For I'm as free as a bird now,
> And this bird you'll never change.
> And this bird you cannot change.
> And this bird you cannot change.
> Lord knows, I can't change.
> Lord help me, I can't change.

The freedom was intoxicating.

After the game and dinner at a hole-in-the-wall Mexican food restaurant, Matt drove us to his home, which was set apart from any remnants of civilization. As we passed by his house, he turned off the headlights but kept driving down the gravel road. At first this caused the neuroses in me to tense up, but then he grabbed my hand.

"Look out the window to the tops of the trees," he said.

He was going about thirty miles an hour, navigating simply by the moonlight shining through the tips of the trees that lined the road. "I do this sometimes when I'm on edge. It helps calm my nerves." The sight was beautiful, and putting aside my fear and worry and allowing him to be in control felt invigorating.

This simple gesture was a huge one for me because I was not a risk taker. Driving in the dark, however, wasn't Matt's only surprise of the night. He had driven about five miles down the road before turning on the headlights again and taking a detour on another dirt road, and finally he stopped at a water tower.

"Let's go," he said with a mischievous laugh.

He turned off the car, got out, and came around to my side. I honestly thought we were parked there to make out and was taken aback when he got out so fast. He opened my door. "Come on."

I got out of the car, and, hand in hand, we walked over to the water tower. "Let's climb it," he said.

My heart left my rib cage and implanted itself in my throat. Climb? "Um, that's OK," I said. "I'm fine down here." I was afraid of heights!

"No, you've gotta do this," he responded. "It is so beautiful up there!"

I wanted to go with him and experience another beautiful sight, but I couldn't get past the fear. The moonlight ride was one thing; heights were another.

Either Matt saw me shaking or he felt my death grip on his hand, because he took me into a bear hug. "Never mind," he said. "We'll get to it another time."

This first real date couldn't be topped. Even with all the surprises, Matt managed to get me home on time.

Matt was the first boyfriend that had overcome many of the idiosyncrasies that usually had me kicking them to the curb after two or three months. Many of his qualities were perfect, but our relationship was not. Far from it. Matt was nuts enough to impress on the first date, but that energy and fire would ignite something fierce between the two of us, and we would argue about anything and everything.

He had a way of getting me to let go of my control. I knew I needed to have that release, but at times I found myself scrambling to hold tightly to familiar stubbornness and insecurities. Sometimes I think we argued for the enjoyment of it! We were so alike that it felt like we were two steaming bulls in an arena, battling for the prize of being right. The aggression between us would turn into passion, but we never went too far. Matt was always a gentleman.

The months before I had met Matt, I could easily flirt and kiss other boys, but for some reason the intimacy that Matt and I shared caused me to pull away. I wanted to long for him and share what I felt should come naturally, but with each new day I recoiled inside. Subconsciously, I was saving myself from the hurt I knew was inevitable.

Later in life, after years of counseling for different issues, I learned that this was due to a fear of true intimacy. The more I loved, the less I could share of myself physically. I acted how I had learned to act from witnessing my sister Carrie's relationships, or, more accurately, her sexual encounters. The intimacy I had with Matt left me fearful and confused.

I did not have this self-healing epiphany at the time, so the fear corrupted my mind, and I felt that I was hurting Matt more by staying with him than I would have been if I had continued on. He never pushed me into doing anything I didn't want. I loved him so much that I didn't think it was fair for him to have someone who was so confused, hurt, and frustrated. I didn't know why I felt this way, but because I loved Matt I couldn't break up with him. Instead, I tortured him with cruel words and indifference, in hopes that he would get fed up and break up with me.

I knew it was working when my mother and I drove into town one day on an errand and came upon Matt's car with Jenny in the passenger seat. He and I were still a couple, and while I knew they had formed a friendship, intuition told me that, if allowed, she, and maybe even he, could feel more. That moment killed something inside of me. I trusted Matt and had years of trust in my friend. None of that had been broken. Instead, I realized my actions had worked, and I had pushed real love away.

It was my punishment, I believed, for living in constant sin. My relationship with God, despite the blessing of Matt, was nonexistent. As a child, I had felt so strongly that he had saved me from real evil that I owed him my life. Even so, I was acting out like a petulant child. I was upset, because I felt that he had let me down through people.

This troubled Matt, who was strong in his faith. He and I would often talk about his relationship with God. After a tragic accident took the life of a close friend of his, Matt asked me if I feared death.

"Yes," I said fervently.

"I don't," he said, and as he looked at me with such conviction, guilt made me look away. "I know where I'm going when I die, and I think heaven would be a much better place."

"I wish I could say that," I said. "Death seems so final. And I don't even know if I'm good enough to go to heaven."

"You are," he said. "God's given me more than I could ask for. I don't see why I would need to be afraid."

He was so certain. I was jealous of his confidence, but instead of wanting to figure out how to get to where Matt was in his faith, I felt even more lost and alone.

We managed to hang on to our relationship for Matt's prom, which, shockingly, Dad allowed me to attend—as long as we doubled with some of our friends.

When I opened the front door, Matt stood before me, looking debonair in a classic black tux. The fresh scent of his mild-musk cologne filled the air, and, despite myself, I fell deeper in love.

"You look amazing," he said as he walked in with his friend David, who had been waiting behind him.

"Hey, is Ashley here yet?" David said as he pushed past us. David and Ashley had hit it off from the beginning and were in the same boat as we were, rarely getting to see each other unless we all went out together.

"No, she's on her way," I said. "You look nice, David." He was average height and handsome, with dark brown hair, a slim face, and brown eyes. Matt and I often joked with Ashley and David because, with their distinctive long-sloped noses, they sometimes looked more like brother and sister than boyfriend and girlfriend.

Once our foursome was complete, we suffered through the picture taking in front of the fireplace, laughing as Mom had to walk all the way to the far back wall to include Matt's head in the frame.

Matt grabbed my hand and guided me to the black stretch limousine waiting outside. He opened the door and lightly tilted my chin up so that I had to stand on the tip of my toes, despite my two-inch heels, to receive his tender kiss. "Thank you for being my date," he said.

Butterfly flutters tickled my chest, and for one split second I realized the blessing I was preventing myself from receiving. When we arrived to the historical train depot where the dinner and prom were held, the energy in the room kept us on a euphoric high, dancing, laughing, and never leaving each other's side.

Toward the end of the evening, while Matt and I were outside in the courtyard waiting for David and Ashley to join us, he lifted me onto a short concrete ledge so that we were nearly eye to eye, and he took my hands in his and held them to his chest. "I've had fun," he said. For the first time in the five months we had been dating, everything about Matt was serious. What we felt was unspoken, and the only thing that had stopped me from personally sabotaging our relationship was the fact that I had never had to look him in the eyes and hear him say what I had felt.

But it was about to happen, and, as much as I longed to hear it and let him know that I felt the same way, the feeling I didn't deserve it was even stronger. I quickly kissed him on the lips and hopped down from the ledge. "Where are they?" I asked impatiently, allowing the irritable, hard to please Shannon come forward in the quest to corrupt our relationship, despite the fact that we had shared a fairy tale evening together. Dejected but also resolved to my ways, Matt shrugged his shoulders, and in his slouch I saw defeat.

About one month later, I accomplished what I knew deep inside was my subconscious goal—we broke up. A gaping hole of no more phone calls, crazy outings, spectacular arguments, and simple "Matt" moments filled my days. I ached for our relationship, but the pressure was gone. I didn't think I could be enough for him, and now he was able to find what could be.

Single again, the party scene called, and I was ready and willing to escape. I needed to get him out of my mind, but as I continued to see his crowd I was haunted by memories of him. Matt and I were no longer bound by the imaginary string that ties young unmarried couples together, but I still saw his friends, and we would run into each other on occasion. Sometimes he would appear with a new girl, and I would cringe inside.

One summer evening, not long after my sixteenth birthday, while my friends and I were cruising the strip in my gigantic, maroon Riviera convertible, we saw Matt and his friends in the same spot I had met him nine months before. It was my intention to cruise by, wave, and avoid inevitable awkward and painful conversation, but Matt darted out in my path, causing me to slam on the brakes. Once the air came back into my lungs and my nerves loosened, I allowed myself to smile, because it was such a "Matt" thing to do. He waved us into the parking spot next to his car.

"Hey, haven't seen you all summer," he smiled. "Scoot over, I want to drive this thing."

The other girls got out of the car just seconds before he started backing out onto the road with the other cruising vehicles. "Glad you feel so comfortable," I said with dry sarcasm.

He glanced over and winked. "Always did."

"Yeah, sometimes too much," I laughed, recalling the many memories of him maneuvering through my life, walking through my front door as if he had owned our house, teasing Morgan by calling her "Z-Rocker," after the popular rock station, and getting her so riled up that they would end up in a boxing match in the middle of the family room.

"Ah, come on, just because your dad loved me more than you, you shouldn't hold it against me."

We laughed. Our minds were in sync with similar memories, but we did not have to share them out loud.

"Kiss him," my mind screamed. It was what I wanted to do. I missed him so much. We were comfortable, and it was nice.

"You're an idiot," my mind scolded. "You're a little too late."

At the first onset of silence, I did the unmentionable and mentioned her. "So, I heard you're dating someone new?"

His back straightened, and he kept his eyes on the taillights in front of him. "Yeah, she's great," he said. "I really like her."

Shifting in the seat, I turned my gaze to the parked cars and clumps of teens standing around. "Idiot," I reminded myself.

"She's fun to hang out with."

I caught an image of myself in the side mirror. Eyes dulled by their own curse stared back at me from the reflection. "That's good," I said. "I'd like to meet her sometime."

"Yeah," he paused. "I'd like that too. Really, I think y'all would get along."

It was too much to witness in my own reflection, so I closed my eyes and tried to swallow my jealousy.

Neither of us said anything for two blocks. We left each other alone to our own regrets until I couldn't take the suspense anymore. Positioning myself to face him completely so that I could no longer witness any of my own emotion in front of me, but only his, I finally asked, "So what else is up?"

We passed our spot and began the drive down Main Street again. "Funny how you know me like you do," he said. "I don't know why, but when I saw you pull up I felt like I really needed to say something to you."

He had my attention, and for once I listened.

"I don't think I was very nice to you at times when we were dating, and to be honest, I can't think of why we even broke up. I wanted to say I'm sorry if I hurt you."

He was sorry? I blatantly sabotaged our relationship and now he was sorry? Who was I that I could be so cruel to him? Who was I that I could never accept the love he wanted to give or give him the love that I felt? I was crap.

"Don't," I said, reaching out lightheartedly and punching his leg. "Please don't say that. I need to say I'm sorry. I wasn't exactly nice to you all the time, either." What I really wanted to say was, "It was my fault! Save me from me and take me back!"

"Friends?" he said as he reached over to shake my hand.

I didn't want to shake his hand. I wanted to wrap my arms around him and feel the comfort of a hug. But it wasn't my place. I shook his hand and then I did what I did best: I hid behind sarcasm and buried the unexpected and foreign surge of raw emotion back into the depths from which it came. "Friends. But you're still a smart butt."

The ice had been broken, and my mind had been cleared. "Friends" was comfortable.

# I Do

Let love be sincere; hate what is evil, hold on to what is good.
—Romans 12:9

LIFE CONTINUED, AND soon, a few short months later, my family went to Florida to visit Carrie for the Christmas holidays. Carrie had skipped town two years before with a boyfriend who embodied the reckless lifestyle of drugs and partying to which my sister had grown accustomed. Our roles remained the same, despite our six year difference. I was the protector and defender against the judgments and ridicule of our family and all of the unseen enemies she felt had surrounded her in our hometown. It was a bittersweet trip —one on which I saw my niece and also celebrated a forced yet belated marriage that I knew would take place, even though I knew it wasn't what Carrie wanted.

Walking into her duplex, the faint smell of burnt weed permeated the thin walls. "Hey girl," Carrie said as she appeared from the kitchen, her once lustrous, caramel colored hair now overly bleached and hanging dead around her shoulders, weighing down the rest of her frail, five-feet-two-inch frame. As we hugged, my arms felt as if they could wrap around her twice. For once, I was glad to be the tallest woman in the family, because it meant that she couldn't see the pain I felt for her.

"Girl," she fidgeted, backing up so she could look at me. "You are getting so tall! How tall are you now?"

"Five foot seven," I said sheepishly, trying not to stare at the years that, while unlived, had taken residency in her tough skin and weary eyes.

"Wow," she said. She was always amazed, and I loved her for it. It was the one reaction Carrie would have to life that could bring back the youth she had left behind.

We weren't there an hour before the news broke that there was to be a wedding at the Justice of the Peace the following morning. They already had the marriage license ready, and even Courtney, my nine-month old niece, had an outfit to wear.

Alone with my thoughts and Walkman® in the corner of the cramped duplex, I meditated on whether there was such a gift as romance.

"Hey."

I felt my foot get kicked, and I opened my eyes. Carrie sat down.

I took off the headphones and smiled. "Are you excited?"

"Yeah," she shrugged as she reached across me for a packet of cigarettes on the shelf. "Come outside while I smoke."

Being invited into a conversation with Carrie was still exciting, especially if it meant that she wasn't yelling. But the wonder and awe of her world had disappeared years before, as I had happened upon too many situations my eyes should not have seen, and witnessed too many fights that left me cowardly praying for reprieve in the corner of my room. With Carrie, I never knew what I would hear, and lately most of it left me more and more powerless to help her.

She sat on the only white plastic lawn chair that inhabited the tiny porch, so I sat down on the concrete and leaned against the edge of the front door.

"Can you believe I'm getting married?"

"No," I laughed, being honest. "Are you excited?"

She lit the cigarette and took a long drag. Turning away from me, she blew out the smoke and shrugged her shoulders. "He's good to me and I have a kid now, so…"

Apparently, the rest of her thought wasn't as important as the next drag of her cigarette.

An invisible blanket of sadness draped Carrie's body as she sat balled up in the chair with her knees up to her chest. She continued to look off into the distance. Every few seconds, she took a drag of her cigarette, knocking the ashes off the side of the porch onto the grass below. A web of ugly, puffed-up purple scars crisscrossed her wrist and seemed to pulsate with every flick of the cigarette. They represented the first mentally abusive relationship she had entered into when we moved to Sherman.

He had been a drugged out diabetic that lived life as if there were no tomorrow. In fact, he never cared if there would be a tomorrow. She followed his every move, in a downward spiral to a drug-infested pit that ended with her fist through a plate glass window and a heart that could never be mended. And then there was the next prospect that managed to fill something inside of her. He persuaded her to run away from home and quit high school two months before graduation, and then rewarded her with two nasty black eyes, a swollen lip, and an arm in a sling.

Now, states away from home, twenty-two years old, and a mother of a beautiful little girl, I recognized the haunted look in her eyes and knew that nothing had changed.

"What are you going to wear for the wedding?"

Another shrug. "Nothing special," she said. "I don't have anything nice."

"I brought a skirt and sweater that I bet would look good on you. I was going to wear them, but I think you should." I rarely wore skirts or dresses but had brought them to wear to Mass.

"You want to be my maid of honor?"

Despite the lack of joy that usually surrounded a wedding ceremony, this simple request made me the proudest person on earth. "Sure! Thanks!"

She smiled a genuine smile and I was taken aback by her real beauty.

As soon as she discarded the cigarette, she grabbed another and lit it up. "So what's been going on with you? You still seeing that real tall guy?"

Now it was my turn to carry the torch of sadness. "No," I said. "We broke up awhile ago."

"Really? I thought you really liked him?"

"I did," I said with a shrug. "I messed that up."

"What do you mean?"

I grabbed a twig and started tracing the broken lines of concrete at my feet. "I don't know. I guess I was scared. I don't know, really. I wouldn't mind trying again, but it's over. He is with someone now, and apparently he likes her a lot."

"I'm sorry," she said. "You'll be OK, though."

"Will I?" I thought. "Will you?"

We witnessed the five minute ceremony. My sister was dressed in my best outfit, the skirt practically wrapped twice around her skeletal frame and fastened with a safety pin. She cried. I cried. We all cried.

In that moment, I believe that Carrie was happy, because it was one of the most normal things she had done in the short time of her life—marrying the father of her daughter. For those five minutes, the hope of a functional life floated between the simple gold bands that were exchanged and the binding words of the law.

Two days later, after accidentally discovering a crumpled baggie of marijuana in a collector's mug, the irritation in Mom and Dad's voices indicated that they had had enough, and we left them to their own corrupted devices.

# A Little Too Late

For I am convinced that neither death, nor life, nor angels, nor principalities, nor present things, nor future things, nor powers, nor height, nor depth, nor any other creature will be able to separate us from the love of God in Christ Jesus our Lord.

—Romans 8:38–39

AFTER WE RETURNED home, the woman watching our house said that a tall man with beautiful red roses in his hand had come to visit. She couldn't recall his name, and he didn't leave the flowers. Matt came to mind. Who else could it have been? But why didn't he leave a note or tell her who he was? And why did he come see me when he had a girlfriend?

Every day, I found myself standing with my hand on the phone, ready to call Matt and ask. It would have been a simple call, but I didn't have the guts. If it was important, I reasoned, he would try again.

Three and half weeks later, a late-night phone call changed the course of my life. A friend of Matt's called to let me know that Matt and David had been in a car accident. I was anxious to get to the hospital to see how he was doing, but Jenny convinced me there was nothing we could do until the next day.

It was the crack of a stormy dawn. Rain came in sheets, and then suddenly it stopped, as though God had turned the valve to "off." I was dressed in the tackiest, bright purple leotards for Drill Team, and their matching iridescent pink skirt. Jenny's parents had driven us to the hospital, not trusting either one of us to drive our own cars. We walked in just a few minutes after the lights had malfunctioned and left everyone in the building in darkness, with only a few emergency lights illuminating the hallways. We walked through the door and found the circular information desk in the center of the lobby.

A woman appeared from a doorway behind the booth.

"Can you help us?" I said.

"I'll do the best I can," she answered. "The computers are down."

"We're here to see Matt Beasley."

She flipped through an index file, searching the names with a pen light. When she reached the end, she got frustrated and flipped through the cards again. "I'm sorry, who are you looking for?"

"Matt Beasley," I said again.

She flipped through the index file a third time and pulled out a card. She looked at me again. "Are you family?"

"No." Jenny and I said, shaking our heads. "But we're close friends."

"He's dead," she said.

Just like that.

Dead.

Not, "I'm sorry, he's passed," or, "Would you like to sit down? I'm afraid I have bad news."

Just, "He's dead."

Dead.

No more Matt. No more life. No more vibrancy.

No more smart comments.

No more basketball.

No more dreams.

No more risk taking.

No more talks.

*No more chances.*

No more.

Just dead.

Matt had left basketball practice to take David to the hospital. David's mother had cancer and was undergoing extensive chemotherapy that kept her hospitalized for weeks at a time. It was early on Monday evening, about two miles from the high school, when Matt, in his compact Dodge Daytona, approached a curve, and encountered a large log in the road. He swerved to avoid it, but to no avail. He collided with the log and hit an oncoming truck head on.

It was too surreal. When the receptionist dropped the news, my world became a cheap carnival fun house. Everything was distorted. Objects before me were misshapen and out of place. Jenny's voice, her cries, were distant, and then earsplitting. My thoughts were frozen on the word "dead." Jenny's face came into view, and her eyes dripped with the anguish I felt inside but couldn't release.

"And David Thompson?" Jenny's voice was shrill with desperation.

Mommy. Daddy. I needed Mom and Dad.

Again, the woman behind the booth flipped through the index cards, and, finally, she said, "He's in room 325."

Jenny brushed past me, the contact jolting me back to clear thought. I turned and watched her go out the doors to her dad's car. My mom! My dad! My tears finally broke free, and I rushed to the nearest pay phone.

I fumbled frantically in my purse, as though my life depended on the speed at which I could call my parents. Finally, the tips of my fingers found the zipper to my wallet and retrieved a quarter.

The line rang, and as I waited for someone to answer, I thought that maybe this was a joke. But the irrational thought calmed me down.

"Hello? Mommy!"

The cries strangled my voice.

65

"Hello? Shannon?" my mom answered. "What's wrong? Talk to me, honey. What's going on?"

"He's dead," I managed to say in a raspy whisper. Then a pocket of air got caught in my chest, and my cries turned into exaggerated gasps.

"Oh, Honey," my mom said. I could barely hear her response. "I'm so sorry."

"But they told me he was fine!" A wave of sorrow washed over me so quickly that the tears that so desperately needed to fall got backed up in the undertow, leaving my face frozen in anguish.

Jenny walked up to me with her mom and touched my shoulder. "Who are you talking to?" she whispered.

I couldn't move my mouth to speak anymore. Instead, my eyes stared back at her, wide and wild in response.

"Shannon," her mom said as she stroked my hair. "We're going to take you to school."

"School?" I thought, as my eyes shifted in her direction.

"Shannon? Shannon?" My mom was still on the line.

"School," I thought, finally blinking back some recognition of the present day.

My voice came out raspy and small. "Mom, Jenny's mom is taking us to school."

"Are you sure? Do you need me to come get you?"

I shook my head before answering into the receiver. "No," I managed.

"I'll see you this afternoon then. I love you, Shannon."

I nodded and hung up the phone. Jenny grabbed my arm, and we fell into each other, relying on each other's bodies for stability.

"My mom thought we should at least go to school and check in," Jenny said. "And then later we can leave, so it's not an absent, especially now that we'll have the funeral and stuff."

At that moment, I wasn't thinking at all. I didn't know where to go, what I wanted to do, or who I wanted to talk to. The only thing I wanted I couldn't have, and that was one more chance to see Matt so I could tell him how I really felt.

Like a zombie, I went through the motions of the day, never thinking to call Mom and take the day off. Many friends heard the news and offered condolences, but I was too numb to hear them. Ashley, David's ex-girlfriend, stuck by me through the day and offered to take me to the hospital so we could visit with David.

I had forgotten all about David, and when she offered I broke down again. How selfish could I be? I didn't even ask to see David! I knew he wasn't dead, but was he OK? Matt was his best friend. The anticipation to be near someone that loved Matt as much as I did kept me going.

Jenny, Ashley, and I received permission to leave school after sixth period. Together, we walked through the swishing hospital doors that would forever be engraved in my memory of that morning. Arm in arm, we walked purposefully to the elevator, and waited in silence as it took us up to the third floor.

When the doors opened and we got off the elevator, we were surprised to see a floor that was packed with what must have been Matt and David's entire high school. Students were everywhere. Most of them we recognized, but some were new faces. We got a few nods of recognition, but otherwise we received a chilling welcome. They did not like us very much. We were the girls who had taken their guys. We were the outsiders, and we didn't belong.

Ty, another close friend of Matt's, who also happened to be Jenny's ex-boyfriend, came up to us, and we each gave him a hug. "I know David will be happy to see you," he said. "I'll go tell him you're here. He can only have two or three people in his room at a time."

I grabbed Ty's arm before he could turn around. "Is he OK? I mean, we don't even know what injuries he has or anything."

"He…" Ty paused, and I felt the anguish that was reflected on his face and in his voice. "His shoulder and leg are messed up, but the doctors said it's nothing too serious that can't be fixed." He shrugged.

"And his face is cut up. He has some stitches across his nose where his face met the windshield."

"I'm sorry, Ty," I said.

His eyes mirrored my own.

"I'll go tell David you're here."

A moment later, as we entered David's room, I caught the stare of one of the girls as she was leaving. Had I been breakable, her look could've shattered my bones. Instantly, by habit, I put my guard up. I didn't have time to react to David's broken body and battered face.

"Hey!" he exclaimed, once he realized who was now occupying the tiny room with him.

Ashley went over to him, sat on the edge of the bed, and held his one good hand. Jenny and I stood awkwardly at the foot of the bed.

Small talk ensued, and it was obvious that everyone was trying to skirt around the boulder of evidence before us. There had been an accident. Matt was dead. And not only did David witness his best friend in his last moment of life, but he, too, would now face months of recovery.

What were we to say?

I wanted so badly to sit where Ashley was sitting and hold David's hand to let him know that I loved Matt, too. I understood his loss. I needed him to know how much I cared. But then again, I was a little too late.

Laughter broke me out of a reverie, and I heard Jenny say, "Matt would've loved that."

My heart sped up, and I looked at David's face, startled by his intense stare.

"Would you guys mind leaving Shannon and me alone for a minute?" he asked.

Ashley and Jenny looked at me, eyebrows raised. "Sure," Ashley said as she squeezed David's hand. She put her hand through the crook of Jenny's arm, and they walked out together.

"Come here," David said, patting the bed where Ashley had been sitting.

The beat of my heart couldn't get any faster. Could he read my mind?

In such close proximity, I could finally see his wounds. A nasty gash tore across the bridge of his nose, and dozens of lacerations covered his forehead and cheeks. I couldn't stop the tears. Embarrassed, I turned away to hide my face.

"You can cry," he said softly. "I cry every chance I get to be alone."

I turned back to him, laid my head on his chest, and sobbed.

With his free hand, he stroked my hair. "I know how much you cared for him," he said. "And I want you to know that he loved you."

There they were—the three words I could read in Matt's eyes, that he had tried so many times to tell me, but I would never let him, and now they came at me from the grave.

"No," I whispered into his chest.

"Matt told me when y'all broke up that he loved you and knew you needed time. He was giving you that time."

Suddenly I sat up. "No, please," I pleaded. My chest was too tight to speak. "Please don't say that," I managed between breaths. "He has…" I shook my head with my mistake. "He *had* a girlfriend. And he liked her a lot. He loved her." I brought my hands to my face in shame. "I just wish I could've told him that I loved him."

David reached out and touched my arm. "Yes, he cared for Natasha a lot. Maybe he loved her, too. But he knew you loved him. And he told me about going over to your house over Christmas. He wanted to see if there was a chance."

My heart shattered, and I crumpled over onto the bed and buried my face in the sheet. "No, no, no!" My inner voice was stuck and kept me in the nightmare.

The days that followed were like a never-ending tunnel with walls that were threatening to close in and crush my spirit. My memories of Matt and the many conversations we'd had, especially the night we talked about dying, were on a continuous loop.

Did Matt know he was going to die? Did he have some kind of sixth sense of how short his life would be? Why did he come to see me at Christmas when he had a girlfriend? Why would David say that to me after Matt and I had been broken up for over six months?

Matt's death and my inability to allow my emotions to fully succumb to the pain caused me to recoil like a frightened animal. Nothing could sooth me, least of all the mechanical phrases, like, "He's in a better place." "It was just his time." "I'm sorry." The last thing I wanted to do was pray to God. He could punish me, but this was too much.

The only person that kept me from becoming a recluse was David. He was the closest person to Matt. David and I drew strength from one another and soon began to heal.

The desire to be up front and real with our emotions was heightened by Matt's death, and many of us clung together after school and on weekends, not only to speak of our good memories of him, but also to create new ones and feel normal and alive again. It was only a few weeks after the accident when Jenny, Ashley, Ty, and I got David and his wheelchair into the car and took him to a Japanese hibachi steakhouse. For the first time, we were able to laugh, and see David, as scarred and battered as he was, genuinely smile and have a good time.

At every outing, kisses were given in greeting, and we kissed one another when we said our goodbyes. The words "I love you" flowed freely off of our tongues, in case it would be the last thing we ever said. It was as if we were all holding on to a ledge, and our fingers were barely able to sustain the weight, because we knew that at any moment, just like Matt, we could take our last breath.

Soon David and I separated from the group and spent every free moment together. We went to Matt's house, relaxing with Matt's mom and dad and filling them in on our day-to-day achievements and adventures. On occasion, a word or two would be said about Matt. It was inevitable, considering that his pictures were up everywhere. The eleven by ten inch picture of us from prom night stared back at me from the fireplace mantel, constantly reminding me of the moment we had shared that night.

Two months after the accident, David ditched the wheelchair for crutches. In celebration, he asked me to his senior prom, and I was glad to accept. It was surreal. I had been to the same prom the year before with Matt, when he was a junior. Natasha, Matt's girlfriend, was there as well, and even though that could have been awkward for me, being with David kept me secure, open to get to know Natasha, and realize why Matt fell for her as well. She was beautiful and had a natural wit that I'm sure kept Matt on his toes.

"Take My Breath Away" came on, and everyone filed onto the dance floor. For the first time, without tears and arms full of pity and sorrow, David and I held each other, allowing the dance to open a door that neither of us had ever expected to walk through.

"You are amazing and beautiful," he whispered as his arms tightened around my waist.

Exhilarated by the familiar feeling of attraction and ready to submit to any emotion other than despair, my body relaxed in his embrace, and we swayed as one to the music. When the night was over, however, a greater reality surfaced.

In my car, parked in the middle of nowhere, David moved in closer, and we allowed the once simple kisses to explode with an aching need. It was intense, fast, and too much for me to handle. It wasn't right.

"Sorry," I whispered, breaking free.

He adjusted in his seat, took my hands in his, and looked me in the face. "What for?" he asked.

His gentle brown eyes, full of intensity, love, and hope, kept me silent. It didn't feel right. We had crossed that invisible line between friends that can either erupt into an amazing love or destroy a relationship.

"Hey," he said as he reached over and stroked my face with his hand. "I love you, remember?"

My shattered heart turned to dust. I was a witch. Who was I to get us in the predicament we were in? Who was I to do nothing but take and take from him, stealing his strength and courage in order to move forward without Matt, only to lead him to another path of disappointment and heartache?

Finally, I nodded. Tonight was not the night I needed to bring us to the ugly truth. "I love you, too," I whispered through my tears. It was not a lie. I did love him, but not in the way that I loved Matt.

The following day, David came over to my house, driving himself for the first time since the accident. The air between us was different, uneasy, and thick. When he limped in, he handed me a folded note. "I couldn't sleep last night so I needed to write down what was on my mind."

"OK."

"If you don't mind, read it now and then we can talk about it."

If my heart could have beaten any faster, it would have burst out of my chest and already been a mile down the road. I unfolded the note, and David carefully hobbled into the living room and sat on the couch.

David's note was raw, full of clarity and went into detail about his true emotions. When he said he loved me, he had meant it, with all that he was. He wanted to know my feelings and if I would be able to reciprocate them. It was beautiful, a treasure, but not meant for me. I had fooled him, and in that moment, if I could have twitched my nose to wipe myself off the face of the earth, I would have done it in a second.

Sitting next to him on the couch, I carefully refolded the note and tried to search for the courage to be honest. "I love you. I hope you know that."

His smile faded. He knew.

"But," I continued, "I just don't love you like that. And I'm afraid that if I were to even give it a try I would only be lying to myself and hurting you even more."

As quickly as he could manage, David got off the couch, avoiding direct contact with me and not speaking until he was at the door. "I kind of had that feeling," he said. "But I hoped what we had this past month was special."

"It was," I interjected, desperate for him to realize how much he meant to me. "I do love you, David. Please know that. Please, let's be friends. Don't stop being my friend."

But he was already out the door and getting into his car. I followed him out, crazed to make sure he knew I wasn't lying. I did love and care for him. I was losing him right before my eyes, and I couldn't stop it from happening.

"Please, David, please. Don't go. Let's talk. Please."

The red brake lights glared in answer: "Go to hell!"

All of this—the death, love, lies, fear, and friction of emotions—sent me over the edge. I didn't want to feel anymore. Once awakened with excitement and energy, I was now bitter and cold, and my spirit was hibernating.

I kept my distance from David and the rest of his crowd. Even when I heard that David's mother had lost her battle to cancer just a few weeks after he sped away from my home, I couldn't muster up the courage to face him. I had let him down, just like I had done with Matt, and there was no way I could retrieve the pieces and snap them back into place.

Drinking was my refuge. It was the only thing I knew could mask the disdain I had for myself. New friendships surfaced with people I had known for years but with whom I had never had the time to foster relationships. They weren't really Bible beaters, but they weren't druggies or troublemakers, either. It was a good group who offered what I was searching for at the time—acceptance and fun.

Whenever I spoke to Jenny, she caught me up on David's whereabouts. He had begun to hang out with a new crowd as well—the kind that wore a lot of black and demonstrated their frustrations through extreme music and heavy drinking. With each tidbit of information, I withdrew more and more. I didn't have the strength to go to him, and I was certain he didn't want me near.

Summer was over when I received the phone call.

"Shannon? It's Jenny."

"Hey, what's up?"

"It's David," she said, breaking into tears.

The tips of my fingers tingled and went numb. "I don't want to hear this," I thought.

She calmed down and tried again. "He tried to kill himself last night."

Silence.

*What?*

My mind screamed. Was she kidding me?

"Shannon?"

No tears. No outward emotion. I was numb. I couldn't do this.

"Um, yeah," I whispered. "How is he?"

She blew her nose and answered, "I guess OK. I don't know much about what happened except that he and his dad got in a fight and someone found him later."

"Well is he in the hospital?" I snapped, irritated with the lack of information.

"I don't know. I don't think so. Should we go see him? Can't you talk to him? I heard he's not only drinking but doing drugs now, too."

"He doesn't want to see me," I said.

"How do you know that?"

"Jenny," I said, my frustration at its peak. But I wasn't frustrated with her—only with myself. "We haven't spoken to each other in almost three months. I don't know what I could do or say that would make a difference."

"Fine," she said. "I'll let you go then."

"Yes, let me go," I thought. "I'll bring you down, too."

The tears came as I hung up the phone, and I crumpled to the cold kitchen floor. Jenny had been my best friend since the sixth grade, and now, six years later, I was forcing her love away, too.

"Oh God!" I cried. The tears stained my cheeks and fell to the floor. I had nowhere else to turn. "Oh God, I'm sorry."

# Taken

Void of God's love they [Adam & Eve] no longer experienced sexual desire as the power to be a gift to one another. Instead, they desired to grasp and possess one another for their own gratification. The relationship of the gift is changed into the relationship of appropriation. To "appropriate" in this sense means to "take hold of" (Theology of the Body for Beginners. A Basic Introduction to Pope John Paul II's Sexual Revolution, pg. 37.).

I FELT THAT since God hadn't been pleased with me before, he couldn't be pleased with me now. I was sixteen years old, and any semblance of faith had slipped through my young fingers like sand in an hourglass. Inside, there was a dark struggle with my belief in God. If he did exist, he was indeed to be feared, but any hint of a relationship with him had been completely lost the moment the pain of Matt's death settled into my heart. I wanted to be angry with God for allowing me to feel such anguish and guilt. At the same time, I didn't feel good enough for his blessings, and that led me to believe there was nothing I could do to get into his good graces.

At work was something—or someone—evil and false, but I didn't know, nor would I have recognized who or what it was.

On the outside, to my parents and friends, it was easy to put on a front of cheerfulness and control. It was a game of dramatic proportions. Which character could I be today? Even though I was sane, I created my own schizophrenic world in order to survive.

Because I was the middle child and Carrie and Kyle were lost in the world of drugs, I had always felt an obligation that I put on myself, to be the "good girl," to fit into the "right" crowd, wear the "right" clothes, make the "good" grades, and uphold the family name in the public eye.

Witnessing the chaos, torment, and sheer sadness that dominated the relationship between Carrie and my parents split me in two. I loved my sister no matter what she was involved in, but I couldn't stand the evil that surrounded her. The rage she displayed wrecked our home and the relationships we had with Carrie. It was enough to keep me from ever wanting to struggle down that same path. On the other hand, my parents were consumed with Carrie's wrath, and it drove them to respond in ways that kept me from ever wanting to be in her shoes for fear of them heaping that same punishment on me if I were to act out in the same way.

Witnessing these events as a young adolescent kept me from many dark paths, and I am thankful to have learned from that troubled time in our family life. Because these gloomy times were never discussed, they left me in a state of fear. I didn't want to make the wrong move and end up in my sister's position, whether in her personal one or even that of the one experiencing the punishment.

At school, I yearned to feel accepted. I wanted everyone to like me. I could see a beauty in every person at school, and I wanted to receive the same respect I had for others. Getting every single type of person to like me, however, created a schism in the invisible lines that divided us. To belong in a group, there were unspoken rules on how to act or behave in a certain manner, and to try to belong in all groups meant that the lines would cross and clash.

One day, I might have chosen to like country music and date someone who wore Wranglers® and was in Future Farmers of America.

The next day, I would find myself at the latest exciting party, where there was no room for cowboy types, and I would switch masks and leave friends behind in the dust.

Through this time, if I would have realized how many people I was hurting by my actions, I might've seen that, instead of getting everyone to like me, I was becoming my own worst enemy.

I was in desperate need of feeling loved. My hormones raged, and all I wanted was a very cute boy to notice me. There was someone in every class I could have set my eyes on, but one boy in particular had all of my attention.

Aside from the fact that he was athletic, like Matt, and comparable in his ability to make wise cracks, Paul, who played lacrosse, was Matt's opposite. He was not a colossal giant, like Matt, but he stood at least six feet tall with hair the color of a scrumptious Hershey's® Kiss™. His broad smile caused my stomach to flounder. He and I had known each other since the sixth grade. From day one, I had a crush on him, but every time I would come close to building up the nerve to see if he liked me, he would end up with another girl. As time passed, he and I became pretty good friends—not the "let's share every secret" kind of friends, but we hung with the same group and would flirt with each other at birthday parties. Once we reached high school, I never gave him a thought. And then Matt and I were together for my entire sophomore year.

By the end of junior year, all that had changed. I was running away from Matt's death, from David and the pain he was suffering, and from anything and everyone that I associated with that time in my life. The poison of hatred bubbled deep in my soul, and beneath it all was a good, young woman who was anxious to be validated.

I felt that Paul could be that validation. It would be a prize won. I was determined to get him to not only like me but love me. In my very feeble, adolescent mind, I thought I could make Paul fall in love with me. The innocent flirtations turned into a stream of inexperienced advances. I didn't want sex. I was a virgin and despite my anger towards God I felt that if I could remain a virgin until marriage it would be my ticket to heaven. At the time, however, the only way I knew to get love was to be sexy. Paul had always been out of reach, so getting him to like me meant that I could be in control again.

Winning was all I cared about. I never took into consideration that my hollow words would be put to the ultimate test of authenticity.

"If we go out, what will you do for me?" Paul asked one day, sitting in his desk beside me in class.

For three months, Paul and I circled around the subject of sex.

"Going out with me is enough," I retorted with a wink.

"Is it?" he said as he broke into a smile that brightened the deep sea green of his eyes.

I flipped my hair back and turned in the seat to get closer to him. "If you'd ask me out on a real date, not a hook up at some lame party, then maybe you'd find that out."

He reached across the aisle and grabbed my hand. "You know I've been busy with lacrosse. We'll go on a date, I promise."

It was all about timing.

But the summer came, and the phone did not ring. It was par for the course. Again, I felt punished by God, but I did not take into consideration that each choice and decision made was mine. Weeks into the summer, I submerged myself into a series of long days at the lake, lying lazily on the beaches of the islands. At night, we partied at various hangouts. If we were brave enough to use fake IDs, we would go dancing. We were headed into our senior year, and on the outside we were all perfectly content.

On occasion, Paul would join up with our group, and we would flirt like crazy but never take it outside of those comfortable boundaries. At other times it would just be us girls, free to do and say what we wanted, and leaving behind the need to impress.

I was content to allow the days and weeks go by without dates, because Paul would show enough interest to keep me hooked on the dream that we might one day become an actual couple.

Two weeks before my seventeenth birthday, the call came.

"Hey Shannon, it's Paul. Come over."

"Why?"

"I haven't seen you in awhile, that's why."

"You've never asked me to come over before."

"Well that's my mistake, isn't it?"

"You know it."

"So are you going to come over or what? Bring your yearbook, and I'll finally give you the note you've always wanted."

"Ohhhh…can't wait."

Dressed in short white tennis shorts to show off my legs and a modest white tank top with a pink Polo® emblem embroidered above the left breast, I went over to Paul's house with the full understanding that our time had come to be a couple.

He wanted to date me, and the game was over. He really cared about me, and there was no need for other people to muddle our lives.

The game was over, but not in my favor. Although the words came out of my mouth that I might be up for sex, I didn't want it to happen, at least until I knew we were meant to be together for a long time.

On that day, however, sex was all that Paul had on his mind. I could see it in his eyes when he led me through the house to his room.

"Are your parents home?" I asked.

"No," he answered, "but my brother's in his room."

"Oh, I didn't know you had a brother." My eyes darted around the nondescript living room, soaking in the environment he called home. He moved as fast as he was talking so there wasn't much I could take in. I realized I knew nothing of his family, or even of him, and it woke me up from the fantasy game.

Who was he? What did he like and dislike? What were his aspirations? What did he fear?

When we got to his room, he took my free hand and ushered me through the door. He pointed to the yearbook in my other hand, pointed to a bookshelf, and said, "You can put that down over there."

He held onto my free hand as I leaned over and set the book down.

Pulling me into him, he took both of my hands, pressed them to his chest, and leaned forward so we could kiss. At first it was a nice, but eager, kiss. When I pushed back to catch my breath and regroup, however, his hands tightened around my wrists.

He fell backward onto his bed, taking me with him.

"Ah!" I cried out in surprise. My hands jerked, jutting out to catch my fall, but he held onto them so that my full weight was on his chest.

He kissed me again and let go long enough to flip over on top of me.

"Hey," I mumbled through our pressed lips, his forced kisses, and our clashing teeth. "Slow," I said, trying hard to get the words out. "Slow down…please…wait."

This wasn't how I had envisioned our first romantic experience would be, and I know I wasn't expecting my first sexual experience that day. He sat up, and I was free to speak.

"What are you doing?" I asked. I tried to sit up under his weight, but he still had his hand wrapped around my right wrist. He pressed it down on the bed. "I don't want this," I said frantically.

Paul, the boy whose smile had made my knees weak for six years, the boy that I thought had cared about me, wouldn't even look at me when he spoke. "Shut up!" he yelled. "You know this is what you wanted."

His tone, his avoidance, and even the physical pain he was inflicting wouldn't register. I begged him to listen. "No, Paul. Not now. Not like this."

"Shut up!" he yelled, and he pressed his lips so hard against mine that I could have sworn I heard them crack from the pressure.

What followed was a nasty and violent physical battle of wills, emotions, and animalistic desires that stripped away any innocence that remained within my soul.

He was spent. I was battered on the outside and dead inside.

"Get up," he said as he walked into the adjoining bathroom.

Ashamed that I had brought myself to this, I struggled to sit up and claim my dignity. "That's it? That's all you're going to say?"

I don't know who looked at me, but it wasn't Paul. What I saw in his eyes piled goose bumps upon the tremors that were already coursing through my body. "You need to go," he said. "I have lacrosse practice."

Twenty minutes after gliding into Paul's home, I stumbled out into the bright afternoon, sore, bruised, and unable to feel the warmth of the sun, but only the chill within. The anger toward God in my heart over Matt turned into a heavy loss. Even with the anger, there had still been a sliver of hope that resided in me—a hope that maybe God would take me back, despite my sin. That afternoon, in my defeated mind, I felt that I had erased that hope by playing with the Devil.

# Bittersweet

The sexual embrace is meant to image and express divine love. Anything less is a counterfeit that not only fails to satisfy, but wounds us terribly. (Theology of the Body pg. 33).

I DIDN'T TELL.
I got in my car and inspected the damage in the rearview mirror. I was thankful the only evidence that could be seen on my face was the faded area of red where his hand pressed over my mouth. Otherwise all the bruising was where no one but me would ever see. I drove over to my friend Brittany's house, and sat on her toilet, staring at the bright red streak of blood that had transferred from my white panties onto my white shorts. It took only a breath to decide my fate. I knew I couldn't tell her the truth because I still couldn't believe it myself. The fear of being called a liar was worse than telling the actual ugly truth.

Brittany was busy in her room, packing and getting ready to leave town with her family.

"Paul and I did it," I said, the flat words swimming before me and the reality of no longer being a virgin breaking through the shock.

"You what?" She stopped and stood in the doorway of the bathroom. Glimpsing the red on my shorts, her hand flew to her mouth. "Shut! Up! No, you didn't!"

The butterflies that once fluttered in my stomach for Paul were now dead and rotting, their decay threatening to well up and overflow, but my will to be accepted kept it down.

"Not lying," I said, forcing a smile. "Can I borrow some shorts?"

"Only if you tell me what happened?" She skipped to her dresser and came back with a fresh pair of panties and some athletic shorts. "Tell me all about it," she said. "Did you enjoy it?"

Only then did I dare to tell the truth. "No, not really." The smile faded, and I swallowed the urge to cry. She giggled and handed me a pair of gray cotton shorts.

"Thanks for the clothes," I said as I hid in the bathroom and changed. "I need to get home. I'll call you later." I grabbed the soiled evidence and ditched it in a trashcan once outside.

There was no time to dwell in the sorrow of losing my virginity or to fester in the pain of the brutality in which it was taken. As a defense of shielding myself from reality, and from the truth of the part I played in the chase with Paul, I locked the experience behind a steel iron wall.

It was rape, yes, but a thick layer of guilt and shame covered any desire of speaking out. At the time I felt I couldn't put all the blame on Paul. Even though there was no arguing that what he did was unthinkable and criminal, I felt, however, that my actions and decisions had fueled his unscrupulous desire.

I should have gone straight to the hospital and not to Brittany's. I should have never gone to Paul's house or even pretended I could give him what he wanted when we were flirting. I should have known better.

Of course, none of that mattered. What happened was wrong, and I needed help. I *deserved* help. So strong was the disgust I had for myself that if I did speak to a close friend about being with Paul, I referred to the experience as "sex."

If I had had more self-love and worth I would have turned him in. Then again, if I had had what it took to be so bold, the choices I had made before things got out of hand would never have put me in that position. Had's and should have's only lead to more pain and undue shame. The reality is I fell into the Devil's intricate web of lies, which led me to make a choice to stay hidden in the dark.

He never called, and I never spoke of him again. Thankfully, Brittany stopped asking, and there were only a few close friends I felt obligated to tell in case he was out spreading the word. But if we did see each other, it was as if nothing had ever happened.

Until my mother threw a kink in my wheel of denial.

"Shannon, I made an appointment for you to see Dr. Sutherland," she hollered from the kitchen as I was walking up the stairs. We had just begun school, not even two weeks into the first semester of my senior year, and Drill Team was in full swing. What did I need a doctor's appointment for?

"Why?" I hollered back.

She wiped her hands on a dish towel and came around the corner into the dining room where she could see me on the stairs. "Because you're seventeen now, and you need to get checked."

I shrugged and began my ascent again. "Whatever."

"Besides, if you're sexually active, then you definitely need to have a check up."

I wanted to throw up. Did she know?

She looked up, not with a look of condemnation, but with curiosity. "Are you?" she asked.

How sad it was that my mother couldn't sit me down for a decent talk on chastity, or even offer experience from her past mistakes. I looked at her from the stairs, fearing she could read through my face of disgust. I wanted her to call me down and talk to me. I wanted to tell her the truth. Had I told her the truth, the future course of my life would have been dramatically different.

"No!" I denied the truth.

"Well, it'll be good for you anyway," she said as she walked back into the kitchen.

In my room, which was decorated with high school banners, homecoming mums, theatre posters, and picture collages that covered the hideous magenta walls, I sat on my bed and cried. What would the doctor say? Would he tell my mom? Did I want him to tell my mom? What if he found something?

A month had passed, and this was my first time facing the repercussions of having sex. I knew I wasn't pregnant because Mother Nature had come to visit the week before. I wanted to thank God for the gift, but I didn't dare thank him for a gift I didn't deserve. God was now tucked securely away from my sights, locked away by keys of shame, guilt, disgust, and anger.

The doctor's visit wasn't as dreadful as I had anticipated. Mom remained in the waiting room until the end, when he needed to inform her of a cyst he had found on my ovary. Because of this cyst and other menstrual issues, his medical advice was to start me on low dosage hormones. Birth control.

Because it had already been established between my mother and me that I was not sexually active, this seemed to be the best form of treatment for the cyst. Miraculously, by the time of my next six-week visit, the cyst had popped and was gone.

But I remained on birth control.

My days became monotonous.

Get up. Dress up. Smile.

Get up. Dress up. Smile.

*Who was I?* Did it even matter, as long as everyone else was happy?

Get up. Dress up. Smile.

Fall became winter, and the one-year anniversary of Matt's death loomed over Christmas. I still hadn't spoken to David, and the incident with Paul wasn't as easy to ignore because I saw him every single day. There were no rumors, at least to my knowledge, and if he could act like nothing had happened, then I would muster up the courage to do the same.

Dating wasn't important anymore. I tried to be safe and date docile guys who would treat me with respect, but it didn't work because I had no self-respect. When a guy showed respect, I ran. I felt that I didn't deserve a good guy, and I was like a time bomb that would bring harm to anyone who wanted to show love.

No one knew who I was anymore, especially me.

I looked forward to parties to keep me focused day to day, hoping that the next buzz would break my hard shell and allow me to laugh again. During Spring Break, a few of us girls decided to take a senior cruise. It was an amazing adventure, but it was the boy I met the day we got back that really took me for a ride.

As seniors, three days of our final Spring Break remained, and we were still high from all of the college boys we'd danced with on the cruise until all hours of the night. Feeling lucky, we gathered our fake IDs and headed out for more dancing.

While on the dance floor, in a line with Brittany, Mandy, and Allison, learning to dance the Four Corners, a giant of a man bumped into me.

"Oh, excuse me, beautiful." He was tall, about six feet five, and his husky size would have intimidated me, were it not for his baby face and fair blonde hair that appeared to glow in the club's dimmed lights.

"Oh," I smiled, shamelessly taken in by this stranger.

He grabbed my hand. "Let me help you out," he said, guiding me through the dance, keeping his eyes on me the whole time.

When the song was over, he asked me to dance again, but this time he guided me along the dance floor in a two-step. The songs continued playing, and we continued to dance. As we did, I found out more about this man, making my heart pump life once again.

His name was Keith, and he was a freshman in college. He was a lineman for his college football team and was home for spring break. Gentle, kind, and not afraid to look me in the eyes, he caught me, hook, line, and sinker.

A tug on the elbow sucked me back into the reality of curfews and my own mundane life. "We gotta go. It's already midnight," Brittany said, grabbing my hand and dragging me off of the dance floor.

"Can I get your number?" Keith asked as he took my other hand and followed us to the front door.

"Sure," I said with a smile. Despite our night together on the dance floor, I was shocked that his interest would go any further. Letting go of both of their hands, I went to the bar, asked for a pen, and then wrote my number on a napkin.

The sun hadn't fully ascended above the horizon before he called.

"Hey, it's Keith."

I could feel his smile through the line. "Hi," I answered, desperate to keep my voice steady.

"I have the day free, and I was wondering if you wanted to spend it together?"

"OK," I said. "I don't have anything going on. What do you want to do?"

"It doesn't matter as long as I get to look into those eyes of yours."

He was so sweet! "Well, you could come over and hang out here if you want."

"Let me know where you live and I'm there."

After I gave him directions and we said our goodbyes, I realized that I would now have to explain who he was to my parents. Dad loved to embarrass me in front of my boyfriends. With any luck, Dad would be gone all day. I ran down the stairs to check.

"Mom!" I called out, almost running into my father at the foot of the stairs as he came out of his study.

"Whoa, where are you going?"

"Nowhere," I said. "Where's Mom?"

"She had to go run some errands."

"Shoot," I thought, beginning to rehearse a call to Keith to delay his arrival.

"Why?" Dad asked. "What is it Mom can help you with that I can't?"

"Well, there's this guy I met, and he's coming over today. I wanted to make sure Mom was going to be here."

"A guy? When's he coming over? I'll make sure I'm here."

I rolled my eyes. "Dad, he's a freshman in college. Please don't embarrass me."

"Have I ever embarrassed you before?" he asked, sarcasm dripping from each word. He laughed as I huffed and turned to go back upstairs.

After spending an hour inspecting, pondering, and discarding every article of clothing in my closet onto the floor, I collapsed onto my bed and moaned. I had nothing to wear.

The dogs barked, declaring the arrival of a guest.

"No!" I sat up and flopped to the floor, crawling about frantically to find the cut-off shorts I had worn a few days before. Once I found them, I grabbed the first tank top in my reach and put it on. The adrenaline rush felt good. I hadn't been this excited since Matt took me on our first date!

The doorbell rang, and I rushed downstairs before Dad could give Keith his "Hurt My Daughter and I'll Kill You" greeting.

Keith's shadow seemed endless behind the stained-glass door. When I opened the door, he was looking down at me and holding a single daisy in his hand. "Beautiful flower for a beautiful girl."

"You are so sweet!" I took the flower and moved aside to let him into the house. He followed me into the kitchen and leaned against the island, never taking his eyes off of me. Normally, it would have made me uncomfortable to have someone so intent on my every movement, but, instead, I felt flattered and special. I was, however, uncomfortable with awkward silence, so I chattered incessantly, warning him about my father, and how strict he was when it came to boys being in the house. They weren't allowed upstairs, or in the house without an adult home, and they always had to come to the door to pick me up before I could go out on a date. Honking the horn was not allowed. I didn't mind the rules. I liked a gentleman, even though I would never fall for one. The other rules, however, I lived to break.

I was getting us something to drink when Dad walked into the kitchen.

"Oh!" he bellowed, standing up straight with an exaggerated sway in his back, and wiping his hands on the front of his shirt. He extended a hand to Keith. "Tom," he said, his voice deeper and more deliberate than normal.

Keith didn't flinch. He took Dad's hand and shook it firmly, shifting his direct eye contact from me to my father. "Keith Seisemore."

"Well, Keith, you're a big guy. You play football?"

"Yes, sir, lineman."

"Did you get a scholarship?"

"Yes sir, I did. Full scholarship."

Dad began the bombardment of personal questions, asking everything short of his Social Security number. I tuned them out at this point and handed Keith a glass of tea.

Dad reached over and squeezed my shoulder, pulling me into a bear hug. "Shannon told me not to embarrass her," he said, laughing, "so I guess I can't say what I'd normally say."

My cheeks burned like hot coals. If they reached over to touch me, they would have been sent to the ER with third degree burns.

Keith laughed. "Oh, I think you should embarrass her."

My eyes widened.

"Really?" I could see the thrill come across Dad's face. "You must really like her then, over here on a Saturday before lunch. Where did you meet her?"

Dying of humiliation, I bent over in exaggeration, as if crippled in pain. "What are you doing?" I moaned.

The room filled with boisterous laughter.

"Oh, sir, I met her last night and just had to meet her again to make sure I wasn't dreaming."

Dad raised his eyebrows. "Really?"

"Your daughter is very special, sir."

Keith couldn't detect it, but it was there, on Dad's face, the look that only he could give—the "I smell bull" look.

"She seems stronger than any other girl I've met," Keith continued.

As quickly as the look appeared, it was washed away by Keith's save. "She is a tough girl," Dad said as he reached over to pound me on the back. "Which is why I don't ever have to worry about her."

This time, my stomach churned. I forced a smile of agreement in Dad's direction.

"Well, I'll leave you two alone. I'll be on the mower. Mom will be home in about an hour. Nice meeting you, Keith."

"Good to meet you too, Sir," Keith said as he shook Dad's hand.

"I guess that wasn't so bad," I said with a laugh, covering the guilt that had been exposed.

"Nah, he was nice."

We walked into the game room and set our drinks down on the bar. "How about some Nine Ball?" I walked over to the pool table and picked up a stick.

His smile widened. "Are you sure about that? Because you're going down."

Every weekend for two months, Keith and I were inseparable. He would come home on Friday and pick me up to go out to eat or see a movie. Sometimes we'd park at an old Air Force landing strip or find a random country road. Other times, we'd come home, and Keith and Dad would play some pool or talk about school and Keith's future. I adored him. Dad adored him. He was the sweetest guy, and although at times he seemed to be hovering over me, I felt as if I was everything to him.

Keith was always complimenting me, giving me little gifts, bringing me flowers, and making me feel special. It was a different feeling than I had with Matt. After Matt's death, I had become only surface-deep, and

I offered no real substance for Keith to get to know. Our relationship was surface, too, which meant that it was safe.

Two months later was my senior prom. I anticipated the evening with disdain. It was exciting to be at the pinnacle of my high school career, but the expectation of consummating our relationship weighed heavily on my shoulders. Keith wasn't pressuring me, but the subject came up often. Because we never spoke about anything in depth, I did not feel comfortable telling him that I wanted to wait. Instead, I subconsciously did everything I could to put him off, including buying a hideous sequined dress that covered nearly every inch of my flesh from my wrists up to my neck.

Everything Keith did that night irritated me. His obvious anticipation of the evening only fueled the anger I held inside.

"What's your problem?" he asked when we were finally alone on the dance floor and away from the others.

"Nothing," I snapped. I had no valid reason to be irritated at everything he said or did, but he was getting on my nerves.

I wasn't sure if the disconnect between us was because I had no other way of saying I wasn't ready for sex, or if it was because I was not interested in him.

In the car on the way to the after party, we sat parked in front of the house, arguing because I wanted to go inside and he wanted to stay outside and make out.

"This is my prom night," I whined. "I want to be with my friends and have fun."

Scooting over the hump in the middle of the old Cadillac he had borrowed, he wrapped his arm around my shoulder. "Being with you is fun," he said. "We can do both."

"Come on, Keith," I said. "Let's go inside, just for a little bit. We have all night, and we don't have to be at my house for breakfast for another four hours." I was pleading with him, which made me angrier. Why did I need to plead with him to do what I wanted on my prom night?

He unwrapped his arm from my shoulder and reached down and grabbed a beer from the case he had picked up on the way. In the hours between dinner and sneaking out to the car at the dance, he had consumed an entire twelve pack. "You go inside," he said. "I'm going to stay out here for a minute."

Mortified to walk into the party without my date, I opened the door and stomped out into the cool night air, slamming the car door behind me. If I went in by myself they would want to know where he was, and I didn't want them to know we had been fighting. I walked over to the curb, sat down, and waited for Keith to feel sorry for me and take me to the party.

Five minutes passed, and I could barely make out his shadow in the front seat. Believing he was looking at me, too, I turned my head and looked up at the stars. A few more minutes ticked by, and my patience was gone.

I walked over to the car and peered into the passenger window, only to find him passed out, his head lolled to the side, mouth agape, and an open beer poised in his hand.

He had fallen asleep.

Humiliated, the only action that seemed logical was to get into the back seat and lie down. I was not going to attend a party by myself because my drunken boyfriend didn't care enough about me to stay sober and awake! I knew that everyone would think we were having sex, but at that moment, I could handle that more than the rejection.

The world had succeeded, or, rather, the Devil's influence had gotten the best of me. I had excused Keith's behavior because I cared more about what others thought of me than I did about myself.

We sailed through the next month, swatting away the memory of prom and our argument. Keith went back to school, deep in finals, and I immersed myself in the many senior parties that were held in our honor. Every weekend, there were at least three, if not four, parties to attend. We seniors were a close-knit group, and, even though our surface relationships were based mostly on drinking, we were constantly floundering, and we needed one another to hold each other up.

None of them were aware of the pain I had been harboring over Carrie and the life she was throwing away in Florida. None of them realized that my brother's homecoming from the Navy was due to a dishonorable discharge, and therefore was not one that should be celebrated, leaving the air in our house thick and intolerable. None of them knew that Morgan, who was only a freshman at the time, was swimming in her own pool of angst and woe, mad at me for being an insufferable preppie and mad at my parents for not accepting the gothic style she had adopted.

None of the girls knew that, at night, I wished I could be any one of them, living in their homes, wearing their nicer clothes, looking in their mirrors, and resting their eyes upon their prettier faces, with eyes that shimmered, free of dark secrets. None of the boys knew that I longed for them to see me as a catch—someone they could hold on for the long term, just like they swooned over the others. None of the boys knew that I detested being the buddy, the "friend with benefits," or the odd one out. And none of them knew that one of their own had violently stolen my most precious gift and left me hollow inside.

I told myself it didn't matter. We were graduating, and soon we would move to separate towns, attend separate universities, and begin separate lives. We would never know each other's truths.

I guess that was why, on graduation night, when Keith declared that it was time to consummate our relationship and that he had a hotel room waiting, it didn't bother me to leave the final graduation party to be with him.

Somewhere along the way, I began to feel that it was my duty to take care of his needs. If I wanted to keep a boy, I needed to take care of him, like feeding a dog or maintaining a car. He had stuck with me for months and never forced me into sex. At least, this time it would be better than it was with Paul. I talked myself into it by imagining the way I would really want my first time to be—with emotion, romance, love, and tenderness.

Before Paul, I had imagined that all these things would happen with my husband on our wedding night. If I had been told the truth that since my virginity was not freely given that spiritually I remained a virgin, I'd like to think I would not have given up the fight to have my special wedding night. However, that is a truth I had not learned till years into my adult life. Had I been told that I wasn't tainted and could start over, I might have felt some hope resurface. But no one knew my predicament, and my friends had already been sucked into the same evil deceit—that in order to keep love, you had to have sex.

As a young girl, I watched my sister fall into a similar trap of lies and deceit, and, even then, I would cringe as I recognized that she was a puppet who did for others and pleased others, no matter how demeaning or demoralizing the request. It was odd that, when she fought with my parents, her strength could move mountains. I never understood why she wouldn't stand up to these guys the way she would to my parents.

Here I was, no longer that clever little girl, unable to see for myself the puppet strings that were now attached to me. I told myself that Keith had earned it. I owed it to him to give him what he needed. After all, he had stayed with me when he could have had any other girl.

I left the party and headed to the hotel by myself. Keith had refused to go to the party, because he did not want to repeat prom night. I made it to the Holiday Inn at midnight, about an hour before we were supposed to meet. My heart was heavy with uncertainty, and my stomach churned the one wine cooler I had consumed hours before, threatening to release it at any given second. My fingers tingled with anticipation.

Did I really want to do this? I would lose him if I didn't.

I wanted to go home, but I feared I would never see him again.

Did he love me?

A key rattled in the lock of the hotel door, and my eyes popped open. The red iridescent numbers on the nightstand read 3:00 A.M. Except for the strip of light coming from the crack in the bathroom door, the room was dark. I had waited in the bed, in the dark, with just a T-shirt on, too nervous to undress in front of him.

He stumbled past the foot of the bed and stopped in front of it. Through the tiny slit in the bottom of my eyelids, I could tell that he was swaying, and a wave of stale cigarette smoke and beer hovered over the bed.

"He's drunk!" I yelled inside. How dare he come here drunk when this was supposed to be a romantic night? For all he knew, it was my first time.

"Shannon, are you awake?" he whispered. I could hear the spittle fly from his mouth.

I was frozen and felt trapped like a caged animal. What had I gotten myself into? I couldn't get out of there. How could I get up and walk out? I didn't even have pants on.

Ashamed to admit it, I felt trapped again. For months I had fended off his advances by promising that, once I graduated, it would happen. And that time was now. Did it matter that he hadn't been waiting for me with candles and roses when I had arrived? Did it matter that he'd had too much to drink? I was supposed to be living it up with my friends, too. Did it matter that I was smothered beneath his weight and in a precarious position I would come to regret?

Did it matter?

I couldn't get this love thing right.

I didn't fight, and I didn't say no. It was over in a flash, and before I could say goodnight he was snoring like a muffled mule.

It was done. There were no fireworks, fabulous explosions, or any emotions of any kind. Maybe that was how sex worked. I had done the deed, and there was no turning back.

# Used

Lust is not always plain and obvious; sometimes it is concealed, so that it passes itself off as "love."…Does this mean it is our duty to distrust the human heart? No! It only means that we must keep it under control (Theology of the Body pg. 51).

K EITH COULDN'T GET enough of me. It was as if every part of me had been taken over by some unexplainable force. Not even my thoughts belonged to me. I was giving him what he wanted, which made him happy and kept him around.

There was nothing left of my old spirit to break through the muck that now clouded my judgment. I felt nothing. I got no enjoyment from my actions and deeds. The occasional hush of a gentle whisper, however, chilled my bones enough to remind me that I was not a robot.

In mid-June, my parents left on a week-long trip and entrusted me to stay home with Morgan. They knew I wouldn't have a party and compromise our property. What they didn't know was that I would compromise myself.

"So, Mike and I are meeting up tonight, but I thought I'd come by later," Keith told me on the phone the first Tuesday afternoon my parents had left.

Disappointed that he didn't make plans to spend the time with me, I chastised myself for being selfish. "Oh sure, have fun," I said. I wanted so badly to ask where they would be going or what they would be doing, but I did not want to be a nag.

"I'll see you later on tonight then," Keith said. "Leave the door open for me."

He hung up. How late was he going to be?

An hour later, Brittany called. "Let's go out!" she said. "I'm bored!"

"Well, Keith said he was coming by later. I don't want to be rude and not be here when he comes over."

"Well, what's he doing? Who's he with?"

"I don't know, but I'm sure he'll be here early."

"OK, well, I'd come over, but I really am bored, and I wanted to go dancing or something!"

Ten o'clock came and went. Eleven o'clock came and went. Morgan came in the door at midnight and went up to bed. I followed behind her but made sure to leave the front door unlocked.

A two o'clock, I heard the front door squeak open. I was still awake, lying in bed, allowing the blood in my veins to boil with anger and frustration. As quiet as a three-year old sneaking a piece of candy from the forbidden top shelf, Keith snuck upstairs. When my door opened, I closed my eyes and pretended to be asleep.

"Shannon," he said, attempting a whisper.

I wanted to sit up and snap at him. I had a lot to say, but I didn't have the courage.

He came to rest on the edge of the bed at my feet. "Shannon." I felt his hand on my side. "Shannon, wake up."

I had no strength to continue my charade. I turned over and opened my eyes. The stench of stale smoke and beer hit me. "Why are you so late?"

"I'm sorry," he said. "Mike kind of got in this fight and, well, you know. I had to back him up."

Playing on my sympathy and curiosity, I sat up. "What happened?"

And so went his tale of contrived heroism. Sucked in like a dust bunny into a vacuum, I fell for it. He slept over, got what he wanted, and then left the next morning before my sister could wake up and catch him.

Wednesday came and went—same scenario, different story.

On Thursday night, I insisted he spend time with me. He came over and we watched a movie, but then he went out with Mike. Mike had been having troubles at home, and Keith needed to be there for him. Who was I to keep friends apart?

He showed up again, early in the morning, but this time he was so drunk that he couldn't even cash in on what he wanted.

On Friday night, Keith called and said he had plans with the guys, so I decided to go out dancing with the girls.

The front parking lot was full, so Brittany pulled around to the back lot. She and I were supposed to be meeting some of the other girls inside. We walked through the lot towards the back entrance.

"Hey," Brittany said, slowing down. "Isn't that Keith's truck?"

I stopped walking, looked a row over, and saw the university sticker on the back window of Keith's truck. "Yeah, it is."

"But I thought you said he was with the guys tonight?"

Curious but not wanting to admit it, I made light of it. I didn't want Brittany to think our relationship was anything but perfect. "He is," I said, "but I didn't know where they were going."

I heard Keith's boisterous laugh as we got closer to the truck, even before I saw him. Then I took two more steps and saw the tall blonde hanging on his arm.

"Oh, uh-huh," Brittany said, voicing my disbelief. "Who the heck is that?"

"I don't know," I said through clenched teeth. "But let's find out." I stomped over to the open passenger door.

"Out with the guys?" I said, sweet venom dripping from every syllable.

"Goldilocks" turned in my direction with confusion in her eyes, and Keith's face fell. "Shannon. Hey, Babe." Quick to recover, he shut the passenger door before the unnamed girl could get in and walked over to me. "What are you doing here?" he asked, stopping within my personal space, but for once not bothering to cross it with the usual kiss or hug.

Brittany, who was ten steps behind, tried to coax me into delivering my own clever inquisition. But I didn't need clever. I wanted answers. "Who's the girl?"

The girl stood with her hands on her hips as though something was brewing and ready to spill forth from her lips.

"Oh, she's just a friend who needed a ride home."

"Really?" I said. "It's not even ten o'clock. Why so early?"

"Uh," he faltered, "her car had broken down and so I'm going to take her home."

What I said next I don't even want to repeat. Since the rape had happened, my language had caught up to my attitude on life: foul.

After screaming some expletives at Keith, I went with Brittany, who finally grabbed me and pulled me in the direction of the back door.

I didn't know what the other girl thought, but I didn't care. I could still hear Keith apologizing over my tirade, swearing it wasn't what it looked like. As pissed as I was, I held on to that, because I still needed to believe he was telling the truth.

Inside, Brittany managed to sneak us a few free drinks from some of our older friends. With a broken heart and carefree tipsiness, I set out to dance with anyone who would do me the honor.

An hour later, I sensed an intense stare, so I turned my head to search for it. My eyes fell upon Keith, who was leaning over the rail that surrounded the dance floor, his arms resting on the wood, and his hands clasped together. When I caught his eyes, his gaze didn't move.

My heart quickened, and, even though I wanted to be mad, I began rationalizing his actions, putting Band-Aids® over my wounds. He *did* come back, and he looked so sad. He was being nice.

The dance was over. I thanked my partner and made my way to the railing. He stood up, but his gaze never faltered.

Like a dejected little boy, he put on his best pout. "Are you still mad?" he said.

"Where did she go?"

"I took her home, just like I said."

"And where are Mike and the others? I thought you were supposed to be out with them?"

He leaned down. "I can't hear you," he said. "Let's go outside."

I nodded. He reached out to take my hand, but I wanted him to suffer and kept it to myself. "Hold on," I said. "Let me tell Brittany."

I found her on the dance floor and explained that Keith had come back.

"You think he was telling the truth?" She asked, raising her eyebrows.

I shrugged. "I don't know. We're going to talk outside."

"OK, but let me know if you're leaving."

"We'll see," I said, and I went to find Keith.

"I can't believe I caught you with another girl," I said. My anger was gone, and tears of betrayal began to fall, one by one, clogging my throat.

Keith moved in, wrapped his arms around my shoulders, and pressed my head into his chest. "Oh. Babe, it's not what it looked like. I swear. You're too good to me. I wouldn't do that to you."

"Then why was she holding on to you like that?"

"I…" There was a slight catch in his train of thought. "I don't know. I guess I said something funny. Really, she's a friend I've had for a long time."

"If she's such an old friend, how come she didn't know who I was?"

"She did," he said. "She was just surprised. I mean, you were screaming at me. You scared her to death."

"Good," I thought, hiding a smile.

"Come on, let me take you home," he said, leaning down and pulling me away from him enough to reach down and kiss me. "I love you."

By Saturday evening, I was sick—runny nose, tight throat, and churning stomach sick. Keith called to see if we wanted to watch a movie at the house.

"I don't know," I said. "I don't want you to get sick." I said this, but what I really wanted was for him to come over, anyway, and bring me soup, wipe my forehead, hold my hand, and be with me.

"Oh, well, what if I come by later on tonight and see how you're doing?"

I wanted to ask what "later" meant, but instead I said, "OK. I'll be here." Then I hung up the phone, went into the study, curled up on the couch with Dad's old army blanket, and watched movies with Morgan.

Two movies and a box of Kleenex® later, Morgan went up to bed, and I moved into my parents' bedroom. They had a TV, and I needed to prop myself up with pillows to breathe. Plus, I wanted to finish a movie I had found on Lifetime®.

Lost in the welcoming arms of sleep, I didn't hear the front door open or Keith enter my parents' bedroom. I was startled awake as he lightly touched my lips.

"Ah!" I screamed and jerked, reflexively punching Keith on the arm.

He doubled over on the bed in laughter to the point that he couldn't even catch his own breath long enough to speak.

Adrenaline pumped through my heart, and the deep sound of every beat echoed in my clogged ears. "That wasn't funny."

"Oohh, man, yes it was!" he said, sitting up and putting his arms around my torso. "Hey babe. You sound horrible."

"Thanks," I said, my voice muffled with sarcasm and phlegm.

He pulled back the covers and began to caress my legs. "You know, tonight is our last night to be free without your parents here."

"I don't feel good, Keith. My stomach hurts, I can't breathe, and I'm sure I look awful." I grabbed a Kleenex® and blew.

Ignoring me, Keith moved in closer and allowed his hand to travel further up my leg. "We don't have to kiss."

"Keith, come on," I whined. "I don't feel good." I wanted to cry. Why was he insisting? I didn't feel good!

"Shannon, come on. It won't take that long. You don't even have to do anything."

And so I didn't. I did nothing.

The following week, I buried myself into preparing for the trip that Mom and I would be taking to my university's orientation that weekend. I was excited to see what my dorm would look like and really get a taste of what the school would offer in a few short months.

Our family was also expecting a German foreign exchange student from the Rotary Foundation Group's Study Exchange program by the end of the month. She was supposed to stay with us for four weeks and then I would fly back with her and the rest of the exchange students and stay at her home for four weeks. It was a graduation gift from my parents, and I looked forward to getting out and experiencing a new life.

Many changes were taking place, and, after that last night with Keith, I felt that none of them should include him. He had demeaned me beyond repair. Instead of doing something about it, however, I always chickened out and let things ride, allowing our busy schedules to help me ignore confrontation.

We went out on a date before I left—the first real date we'd had in nearly two months. During dinner, my feelings wavered. He was polite, called me "Babe," and didn't seem like the uncaring oaf who had had sex with his ill girlfriend.

After dinner, he drove out into the country and parked alongside a water reserve. As soon as the vehicle was in park he was on top of me.

"Wait!" I yelled, pushing on his chest with my forearms.

He sat up. "What?"

"I don't know, let's talk or something. We don't always have to go right into sex."

Dejected, he huffed and sat back, leaning his head against the seat. "OK, what do you want to talk about?"

"Us," I said. The adrenaline in my veins picked up.

He turned his head and looked at me. "What's wrong?"

"I don't know," I said, shrugging my shoulders. "You know, I'm about to go to Germany, and then to school, and we'll be seven hours apart."

"So?" he said, leaning forward to grab my hand.

I looked down at my lap and picked at the hem on my shorts with my free hand. "I don't know, maybe we should break up. You know?" I looked him in the eye and saw his face fall.

"What? Are you serious?" Like a surprise shower on a clear summer day, his eyes filled with tears. "I love you, Shannon."

He looked sad. I couldn't speak. All this time, I had wanted someone to love me the way I once had, but had given up. Although this wasn't the same type of love I had with Matt, maybe I was making the same mistake and sabotaging everything. I didn't realize how desperate I had become.

Keith pulled me to him and kissed my neck and my face, all the while chanting, "I love you, Shannon. Don't leave me."

I was weak.

I couldn't do it.

I resolved to be his physical comfort.

# Spoiled American

For the whole law is fulfilled in one statement, namely, "You shall love your neighbor as yourself." But if you go on biting and devouring one another, beware that you are not consumed by one another.

—Galatians 5:14–15

THE UNIVERSITY CAMPUS was located in a small town, nestled deep within a forest. As we drove through the pine tree-lined streets I knew that this was my opportunity to figure out who I was, what I liked and disliked. This was my one shot to be real.

Mom and I took our things into the dorm I would call home once I moved away in the fall. We unpacked and then checked our schedules and maps to see where we needed to be. I was due for a new student orientation meeting, and my mother was supposed to go to the parent meeting. We walked together across the campus.

I entered a large room that was set up like a mini-theater, with cushioned, stadium-style seats that ran all the way up to the nosebleed section. There was no platform or stage on the floor, just a large screen, rolling chalkboard, and a podium with a microphone. The place wasn't full. There were many seats available, so I looked around and spotted a girl my age that was by herself. Ready to make friends, I sat down next to her.

"Hi," I said. "I'm Shannon."

As soon as she smiled, I cursed my decision. She was beautiful. She reminded me of the beauty in our school who had mesmerized all the guys, leaving me feeling inadequate and useless.

"Hi, I'm Lauren," she said in a gentle, unassuming voice. Her eyes were green and kind.

The curse of regret disappeared as quickly as it had come. "Where are you from?" I asked.

"Here," she sighed. "I didn't really feel like going anywhere else."

"Really?" I said. "Funny, I wanted to get away from everyone and everything having to do with my hometown."

She shrugged. "Yeah, well not a lot of my high school friends are going here. They are leaving to go to A&M, UT, or Louisiana."

I nodded. "Yeah, mine, too. I couldn't go to A&M or UT because they are so big. I'm not sure I could make it as a number."

"Exactly," she said, smiling. "What dorm did you request?"

I told her, and then asked, "Are you going to still live at home?"

"No, that was the deal," she answered. "If I stayed, then I would get to live on campus in the dorms. I wanted to make sure I experienced this as if I were going away. I want to meet new people."

"What dorm did you choose?" I asked.

"The same," she said. I'm not sure I could do the community bathroom thing."

It was fun getting to know someone new, feeling comfortable and not worrying about what she thought. As the room filled with more incoming freshmen, she told me she had been a cheerleader and considered trying out for the team but decided against it. We realized we were both going to rush a sorority in the fall and had other things in common as well, such as music and books.

After the overview of the weekend, we were escorted out and divided into groups for a campus tour. Lauren and I stayed together, and, as we were walking, she asked if I had a roommate.

"No, I went potluck," I said. "I don't really know anyone from my school that is coming here."

"Really? Wow, you are really starting over."

"Yeah," I said with a smile.

"Do you want to room together? I was going potluck, too."

"Wow!" I thought. "What luck, I found a roommate and we got along!"

"Oh my gosh, that would be awesome! Who do we tell so that they don't assign anyone else to us?"

We set about getting our living arrangements in order. Later, I introduced Lauren to my mom, and I could see she was relieved to see that I had found someone compatible.

The weekend flew by, and when it came time to leave campus for the three-and-a-half-hour drive home, I was filled with dread. The only thing that kept me from begging to stay and attend summer school was my upcoming trip to Germany.

Roselyn arrived from Germany the next week, and I was disappointed to find out that she was only fifteen years old. Her English was good, but she was shy, and our personalities clashed. I was hoping for a girl that would want to go to parties, hang out with my friends, and maybe even double date with Keith and his friends so I could continue to keep my distance from him.

She was nice, but my attitude overshadowed her feeble attempt to mesh with our household. We had frequent gatherings with the rest of the Rotary exchange students in the Dallas County area. We took expeditions to the state capitol in Austin, to Six Flags in Arlington, and to various barbecues at famous Dallas ranches. The group formed a bond, and Roselyn was able to relate to some of the other German students her age.

In the first week of July, our family took a road trip to some family-owned land in the mountains of Pagosa Springs, Colorado. We were attending a family reunion and giving Roselyn a chance to see more of the United States. The trip helped her open up to our family, and I was able to shed the tough exterior long enough to begin viewing her as a younger sister—one who needed a lot of guidance because of her obvious gullibility.

In the mountains, it was freezing, both at night and in the morning, but warm during the day. There was no television—only radio and a variety of games. We washed our hair in the creek and laughed about how numb we were from head to toe, because the water was beyond freezing. I was able to forget about Keith and everything else at home that had me in knots, until my parents began telling Aunt Denise about him.

"How long have you guys been dating?" Aunt Denise asked. "How come you haven't said anything?"

"Oh, it's not a big deal," I said. "I'm about to go to school, and we'll be too far away. I don't know. We've been dating almost five months—not that long, really."

I went into the camper to avoid any further conversation. In fact, I avoided Aunt Denise all weekend. She kept asking about my faith and wondering if I had remained faithful since the weekend I stayed with them when I was nine.

She reminded me who I should be, and I was certain she would see that the light was gone. Aunt Denise represented God—not the part that made me angry, but the part that had once loved me. I was certain that God was disappointed in my actions and decisions.

Roselyn and my cousin Nikki, who was now sixteen, entered the camper behind me.

"Why you look upset?" Roselyn asked, her English getting better every day. She sat down on the other side of the laminate table where I was shuffling a deck of cards.

"I'm fine," I said. "It's cold, and I don't feel like standing out there anymore."

"So tell me about your boyfriend," Nikki asked, and she sat down in the captain's chair across from us.

I thought about Keith and what I could share about him that was most important. I never had to think about it before because all of my friends knew him. "Well, he plays football," I hesitated. There wasn't much else to say about him. He didn't have a job, I didn't know much about his family, and our relationship was mostly about sex. I wasn't sure what else I could share.

"Well, I have a boyfriend too," Nikki said in a conspiratorial tone. Her eyes lit up, and a slight hint of color rose from the nape of her neck to her cheeks. "His name is Jack. We've been dating for almost a year now. He is amazing! He takes me to all these neat places. We don't just go to the movies; we see plays, go to museums, and neat places for dinner." She stopped and took a breath. "We go to church together, too, and he brings me flowers and little gifts all the time."

Envious of the mutual adoration she and Jack shared, I withdrew from the conversation and chose not to share any more information about my relationship with Keith.

I suffered through various stories of intimacy, grandeur, and absolute friendship. With each story, I nodded in feigned agreement, as if I understood, but, in truth, each story only revealed more and more about how much my own relationship lacked.

I could not define my relationship with Keith. Not even "friends with benefits" would cover it—unless you took out the word "friends" and simply tagged us "benefits." We were buddies who had mistaken heightened sexuality with being in love.

"Jack takes care of me, and that's what I love the most," Nikki said, leaning back in the chair, content to rest her thoughts on the love she had left at home.

I wanted to be taken care of, too, and my heart fell to my stomach. Listening to Nikki stirred something inside of me that I had felt long before I had even met Matt. I didn't want to feel like I had to be sexy, look sexy, or dress sexy to get a man's attention. I wanted to be respected, to have someone love me for me without expecting anything from me in return. Most importantly, I wanted to love myself, to look in the mirror and acknowledge that I still had purpose, the purpose that I once felt had been given to me by God when I was a child. I wanted to go back to being in his favor.

My heart couldn't handle the flood of emotions that followed our conversation. Before anyone could read it all over my face, I excused myself. "I'm going to bed," I said. "I don't feel good."

"Are you okay?" Nikki called after me as I went to the back of the camper and climbed onto one of the bunk beds.

"I'm fine," I answered. "It's probably just the hot dogs or something. Good night."

Lost in my own despair, I welcomed the blackness of sleep.

As soon as we got back from Colorado, Roselyn and I began packing for the trip to Germany. Loaded with excuses, like packing, shopping, and saying goodbye to family, I managed to dodge any of Keith's attempts at getting me alone on a date.

Between Nikki's nauseating "Jack talk," my aunt's constant encouragement to be strong in my faith, the crisp mountain air, and the freezing creek water, the family reunion had cleared my mind. I realized I deserved better than Keith. But I still did not have the courage to break up with him. Instead, I figured that, once I was in Germany for four weeks, he would get sick of being alone, and break up with me while I was gone.

On the plane to Germany, I felt free of any cords that tied me to Keith. With each hour, I could feel them snap *Snap! Snap! Snap!* — until there were no more thoughts of him and his betrayal of our relationship. I settled in and made friends with some of the other exchange students. We had known each other from our little excursions all over Texas, but there was nothing like being stuck on a plane for nine hours, off to a foreign land, to get the friendships sealed.

When we reached Frankfurt and took another short flight over to Hanover, we had to say our goodbyes to each other for a few days. Each of us was picked up by our new family and told we would meet up again in Hanover for a Rotary function and some sightseeing. Roselyn and I did not speak on the flight. We had overcome our awkwardness on the trip to Colorado, but we still didn't have a whole lot to talk about. She was still innocent and, in many ways, intimidating. She knew more than one language and had enough courage to go to the States and live with complete strangers at the age of fifteen! Her attitude was positive, and she never complained. Being around Roselyn had forced me to see my flaws, but I wasn't ready to change.

When we turned the corner to the baggage claim area, a husband and wife in their late fifties rushed up to us, gushed over Roselyn, and hugged me as well. I don't know why, but I was shocked. They were older than my parents! Mrs. Von Aiken was stunning, with silky gray hair that flowed past her shoulder. She was tall, like Roselyn, and had warmth about her that set me at ease. Mr. Von Aiken was a few inches shorter than his wife with a round face and thin wire glasses perched on his nose. He seemed full of life and very happy to see us. They escorted us outside. Roselyn's father, the true gentleman, tried to manage both of our bags and struggled the whole way to the car. I asked to help, but, with the little English he knew, he insisted on getting them himself.

The airport was my first view of another country, but it wasn't much different than any airport in the States. When we reached the car, however, I got a taste of Europe. It was the tiniest vehicle I had ever encountered. Then I looked around and realized that at least ninety percent of all the cars in the garage were the same! They looked like little matchbox vehicles! The Von Aiken's was red and square. Mr. Von Aiken barely managed to fit one suitcase in the trunk. Roselyn and I had to squeeze the other in between us in the back seat.

Jet lag kicked in on the way to Lehrte, the quaint town near Hanover where the Von Aikens lived. It felt like I was in a vacuum-sealed tube. When Mrs. Von Aiken would turn around in her seat and speak to Roselyn in German, Roselyn would translate and ask me various questions about my parents, siblings, and the States. That was when I realized how much I would have to rely on Roselyn for the next four weeks. They did not speak English, and I did not know German.

Desperate to stay awake on the ride to their home, I kept my eyes moving across the landscape and scenery, which reminded me of the vast countryside in Texas. A small farming town came into view, and I was transported into the setting of the "Sound of Music." Then I saw a sign warning that we were entering the Autobahn. With my eyes wide, I watched as the Von Aiken's little red car chugged its way onto the entrance ramp and into a main lane. Instantly, a car whizzed by, and then another, and another. These cars were flying!

As we exited the Autobahn, I saw a sign that read "Ausfahrt." It made me giggle and lightened a weight on my shoulders I didn't realize existed. In the town of Lehrte, the streets were narrow, and the houses, while beautiful, were old. We passed the town and went about five minutes down a road that led us deeper into the country. We pulled through a gate and up a long drive to a historic, two-story brick home. There was a smaller cottage to the right of the house that was an extension of the original home. We pulled along the circular drive and parked.

As we unfolded out of the car, we stretched our cramped limbs.

"Welcome!" Mr. Von Aiken said as he stretched out his arms and gestured toward the house.

I smiled. He seemed to have a sense of humor and was trying so hard to make me feel at ease. I headed for the front door, and he opened it for me. There was a staircase to the right going upstairs and a staircase to the left that led to a main room downstairs.

Roselyn passed me and said, "We're up here. My grandmother lives downstairs."

Confused but too tired to figure it out on my own, I obediently followed Roselyn.

She was waiting for me on the landing. The wood floors, a deep mahogany, creaked with each step. "This is nice," I said, taking a few steps to look around. It was. It was simple but tasteful, with fresh flowers on every table.

Roselyn opened a door in front of us. "This is my room," she said, "but you will sleep here." She stepped in and motioned for me to follow.

We stepped into what we in the States would have considered the equivalent of a narrow walk-in closet. There was a window in front of us, and to the left of it, coming out to the middle of the ledge, was a long and narrow twin-sized bed with a thick, white, down comforter. At the foot of the bed, against the wall, was a tall, narrow set of drawers, and, across from that, on the wall to my right, was a full-length mirror and electrical outlet. There were only a few things on the wall that might hint to Roselyn's existence, but otherwise there was no room.

Realizing my silence was rude, I spoke up. "This is nice, but where will you sleep?"

"On the couch in the other room," she said.

"Are you sure?" I asked, feeling bad. She'd been gone from her own room for a month, and for another month, she was going to forfeit it to sleep on the couch? I wasn't so sure I'd do the same.

She smiled. "Yes, I'm sure," she said. "Here, let me show you the bathroom. There is only one." Before we stepped back into the open landing, she stopped and said, "My parents get mad when I take too long in the tub. Hot water goes fast. You can't take a bath every day like at your home."

I scrunched up my nose in disgust. I was on her turf, and I had to follow their rules. "Where is the bathroom?" I asked.

We took a few steps across the landing and opened another door. Inside another tiny room was an antique, claw-foot bathtub with a long spout that had a spray nozzle attached to it. No shower.

"Nice," I said, politely covering my disappointment. I followed her out of the bathroom and through a door that was to the right of the room I would be sleeping in. The room, identical to the long and narrow walk-in closet, but just a little bit wider, was their kitchen. To the left was a tall, narrow refrigerator, stovetop oven, and small pantry. To the right, in front of a window overlooking a beautiful garden in a vast expanse of yard, was a square, bar-style table with four bar stools.

"That's my mother's garden," Roselyn offered. "She works in it every day."

"It's beautiful," I said. It was as if it had been placed there by Martha Stewart's perfect touch.

We heard Roselyn's father calling out to us, and we found her parents in the living room, the biggest room of their upstairs space. In it were a couch, recliner, small coffee table, and television set. On one side of the room were built-in bookshelves that were filled with various novels and hardcover books on photography. I scanned the shelf briefly before taking a seat on the couch.

Not sure of what anyone was saying, my eyelids betrayed me and closed. I tried to stay awake and not be rude, but they caught sight of my slumber and ushered me to bed.

I slept through dinner and didn't wake up until the next morning.

The first few days in Germany were nice and relaxing. Mr. Von Aiken was excited to have a more alert visitor to whom he could show the one part of the estate that I did not get to see the day before. I briefly saw the bottom half of their house, and met Roselyn's grandmother, but I could sense that it was not really a place we should go into any time we pleased. Her grandmother was a sweet woman, but she knew no English, and I did not see her for much of the visit.

What got Mr. Von Aiken excited was the little cottage adjacent to the main house. Inside was an impressive photo gallery, showcasing his work. There were many pictures of Roselyn as a child running in fields and picking flowers, and of Ms. Von Aiken, working in her garden or resting on a swing. In some were other people, maybe friends or family, all captured in moments of work or play.

The pictures were amazing, and I felt like a voyeur in their private world. As I walked around the room and took in each photograph, I noticed an intriguing theme. Some of his photos showed his subjects' eyes as they laughed at an unseen person, or a hint of a smile or gesture, caught and frozen in time. Aside from that, his subjects never looked at the camera.

Mr. Von Aiken captured life in its rawest form, not posed and contrived but vulnerable and real. The effect surprised me. It was my first experience of appreciating art. I looked over at Mr. Von Aiken and smiled. "These are amazing," I said.

Pleased, but unaware of what I said, he looked to his daughter for clarification. She repeated what I said in German, and his smile broadened. "Danke schöen."

During those first few days before we were scheduled to meet the rest of the exchange students in Hanover, Roselyn and I explored Lehrte. She taught me the train system, which was impressive. I was envious of how simple it was to catch a train a few blocks from home and take it into the city. Because there was no traffic, the danger of tragic accidents was considerably less, and on a train you could read a book, listen to music, or take a nap. The most extraordinary things about Germany, that I loved so much, were the ice cream parlors that seemed to be on every corner.

Germany had me under its spell. It was amazing to go into the busy city of Hanover, in the middle of the city square, surrounded by ancient architecture in a modern, bustling world, and feel safe. Crime was low, and people put more responsibility and trust in their youth, which seemed to create a much more pleasant atmosphere.

We shopped, and, just because we could, we went to every pub around. But we didn't really get drunk. Drinking beer was like drinking tea. In fact, at the Rotary meeting they served it to all of us without option. Because it was so readily available, it tamed the need to rebel and drink as much of it as we could just to prove a point. Instead, we behaved like adults, enjoying good conversation and beer.

There was a break in the group's gatherings to allow us to spend time with our host families. I was not looking forward to the loss of communication with the group. They were my only means of sanity, because I didn't speak German, and they had no issue speaking to me in English and wanting to show me around. Up to that point, the few moments I'd had with the Von Aiken's were pleasant, but I could sense Mr. Von Aiken's agitation when I was in the bathroom too long or used the phone. He would be visibly irritated with me and then have Roselyn tell me we weren't in America. Everything I did cost money.

I was the typical spoiled American, and the more agitated Mr. Von Aiken became, the more I egged him on out of spite. I didn't want to hurt him, but it was easy to take all of my frustration, anger, and disappointment, both in Keith and myself, out on him.

When Roselyn informed me that we were going to Copenhagen, Denmark, to see her cousin, I was thrilled. The drive was a simple four-hour stretch, not unusual for a Texan, but, to the Von Aikens, who had to stop and stretch every half hour, it was one of the longest trips they had ever driven. Each stop fueled my disdain for elders. Every time they urged me out of the car to stretch, all I wanted to do was drive.

At one point, I didn't care whether they understood me or not. At about the fifth stop, with two hours still to go, I squeezed out of the back seat and did an exaggerated stretch of my arms and back. "There!" I snapped. "Are you happy? Can we please go? We only have two more hours to get there!"

Mr. Von Aiken's face fell. Mrs. Von Aiken looked at me, and I could read the disappointment in every feature of her merciful face. As irritated as I was, I knew I was the biggest irritation. I was a teenager who would rather face the Devil on a bad day than admit her own faults.

For the remainder of the trip, the air in the car was thick with despondency. Only when we crossed into the picturesque, enchanting land did I allow my spirits to rise. Copenhagen was breathtaking.

Roselyn's cousin was in her late twenties and married with a young child. She was also my savior for the trip. From the moment we met, our eyes connected, and, despite the obvious language barrier, it was as if she could read my mind. For the first time with that family, I felt comfortable and understood, and we never even spoke a word. It was the understanding in her eyes that put me at ease.

Two days later, when we left to embark on another four-hour trip that threatened to be a full day's excursion, Roselyn's cousin hugged me and whispered something into my ear. I don't know what she said, but in my heart she was telling me I would be OK.

# Breaking Free

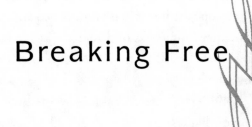

O God, you are my God—for you I long! For you my body yearns; for
you my soul thirsts, like a land parched, lifeless, and without water.

—Psalm 63:2

DURING THE LAST week of my trip, Roselyn and I met up with
the other exchange students in their hometowns, visiting their
houses, shopping, and enjoying one another's company. I managed to
stay clear of the phones, speaking to my parents only when I had to,
and I missed American food. I lived off of Movenpick® caramel and
chocolate ice cream, and tons of tap water—but not the bubbly kind.
The beer flowed more readily than the tap water I craved, but I didn't
care for it. It was liberating to go out and not have to catch a buzz to
enjoy myself. In Germany I enjoyed myself "waste free."

Near the end of my trip, my parents insisted that I call Keith. They
said he was anxious to hear from me. I found that interesting—getting
the reaction I had craved—but I didn't give in. What I found even more
amusing was that one of my best guy friends, Daniel, took the time to
get the Von Aiken's phone number from my parents and call me at seven
o'clock in the morning, which was midnight his time.

"Hello," I mumbled, my mouth covered by the down comforter.

"Shannon! It's Daniel!"

I smiled. Daniel was one of those friends that could always make you feel special just when you needed it. Hearing his voice across the ocean after four weeks of distance was a treat. "Hi," I said. "What time is it there?" I tried to sit up and squint at the small clock on the shelf above the bed.

"Midnight," Daniel said. "I wanted to call a few hours ago, but I thought that'd be rude to get a 5:00 A.M. wake up call."

I laughed. "Yeah, I'm not sure the Von Aikens would've appreciated that."

"So, when do you come home? I want to see you. I'm dying to see you."

His exuberance was out of the ordinary, considering the nature of our friendship. I was thankful that someone wanted to see me. "Wow, I'm lucky," I said, giggling. "I leave in four days. We leave here on Saturday evening but get back to the states Saturday afternoon."

"Cool! OK, well, then I'm going to be at your house when you get back."

"OK, why?" I said. "I mean, that'd be great, but is everything OK?"

"Definitely. There is a lot I want to talk to you about. It's all come clear to me since you've been gone, and I can't wait to see you to tell you all about it."

He had piqued my curiosity. "OK, you can talk to me now, you know? You have me worried."

"Nope!" he said, adrenaline shooting from his voice. "Don't worry! It's all good. Trust me, it's all good."

I giggled in the covers. "Whatever you say, Daniel. I miss talking to you, and I'll see you in a few days."

"I miss you too, Shannon. I do. I'll see you in a few! Bye!"

I hung up the receiver and replayed the conversation, breaking it down, bit by bit. I had met Daniel when I was a freshman and he was a junior at one of the biggest parties of the year. He was one of the popular guys in high school, and his girlfriend, Stacy, a sophomore on drill team, had taken Brittany and me to the party. We didn't become good friends until he was a senior, and I got a job as a hostess in the restaurant where he waited tables. Daniel remembered me from the party, took me under his wing at the restaurant, and did not allow anyone to hit on me. I always felt protected, as if he were the big brother Kyle would never be. Daniel and I hadn't seen each other since I had been dating Keith. He had been away at college for the past two years, so our friendship only consisted of phone calls and holiday parties. But when he was home, it was clear that Daniel couldn't stand to be around Keith, and Keith felt intimidated by our friendship. I had always assured Keith not to worry, because Daniel and I were so close that we were more like brother and sister.

But something was different in his voice this time. It seemed like he really missed me. I shrugged it off to the fact that we hadn't seen each other in two months and thought that maybe the connection had made his voice sound anxious. I was certain it was nothing more, and I went back to sleep.

I spent my last few days in Germany trying to see all of my new German friends and spend quality time with them before saying goodbye. Traveling two continents with a group of people for eight weeks in tight-knit living quarters had created a bond I couldn't find in the friends I'd had since elementary school. Even though I was often tactless, irritable, and downright spoiled, this group of people had seen my true colors and they still accepted me for me.

On the morning of my departure to the States, while packing my carry-on, Mr. Von Aiken came into my room holding a photograph in his hand. "I'm sorry if I was too strict," he said, struggling to find the right English words. "I enjoyed your visit very much."

I wasn't one to cry. Over the course of the last year I had built up a tough exterior so that no one would know how much my heart ached. At that moment, however, tears betrayed me and filled my eyes. With each irritable exchange I had caused with Mr. Von Aiken, I would walk away with a huge boulder of regret and guilt on my shoulder. I had taken anything and everything that went wrong on the trip out on him, just to cause grief. He hadn't deserved it, and I didn't deserve his apology.

I shook my head. "No, I'm sorry. I—"

"No, please," he interrupted, thrusting the photograph towards me. "I take this. You in garden with Roselyn. You have it."

It was a headshot of me, just my face, looking to the side and smiling. I had never seen a picture of me that was this revealing. It was a genuine smile, and it caught my eye first because it wasn't a planned grin or a tight-lipped "get this over with" sort of smirk. It appeared that I was laughing or agreeing with something that possibly Roselyn or her mother had said. I had heard smiles described as warm, but I had never understood that description until I saw that picture. It was as if I was staring at someone other than myself. Someone less pessimistic. Someone friendly.

Then I saw the sunlight that filtered through my thick hair, causing it to shimmer and appear ethereal. Finally, I looked at my eyes. Their edges crinkled with the smile, giving the impression of joy. At first glance, the intensity of their clear blue color took me by surprise. For the first time, my reaction to my own qualities was pleasurable. But as I admired the two-dimensional appearance of my biggest and best feature, I saw something else—something that no one else would probably ever see.

I saw sadness.

As I witnessed it, I shoved the reality away. I looked up at Mr. Von Aiken, realizing I had never said a word since he'd handed me the photo, but he had already left the room. Without another glance, I put the picture in my carry-on and gathered all of my belongings. I was ready to go home.

The entire Rotary group gathered at the airport. We took pictures of our farewell, gave final hugs, and exchanged addresses.

When it came time to say goodbye to Roselyn, I was flooded with remorse. We hadn't bonded like the others and I had. I had been too busy ignoring her and she had been too busy taking care of me. When I hugged her, I wanted to tell her I was sorry, but my pride overruled my intention. My goodbyes with Mr. and Mrs. Von Aiken were about the same. I was a spoiled American girl who had been hurt to the core, and I refused to appreciate the gifts that God had given me in this family.

It was my loss.

Back in the states, Mom and Dad picked me up from the airport. The goodbyes with the American group were just as emotional, mostly because we knew we would not keep in touch. Our lives had meshed for two months, and now we were free to go our separate ways.

On the forty-five minute drive home, Mom prepared me for what was waiting.

"You have two young men waiting for you at the house," she said, giving Dad one of those "if she only knew what we know" looks.

"Two?" I figured Keith would be there, despite our lack of communication. He had tried to reach me several times at the Von Aiken's, but I had managed to avoid his calls.

"Keith showed up just before we left, and Daniel was already there talking to Morgan."

"Daniel?" I knew he had missed me, but he wasn't supposed to be in town until the following week.

Dad craned his neck to look at me through the rearview mirror. "Is there something we should know about you and Daniel?"

"No!" I answered.

"Are you sure he knows that?" Mom quipped.

My eyes widened as I looked at her. "What are you guys talking about?"

"It's obvious Daniel has a thing for you," Dad laughed. "But how does Keith feel about that?"

I was shocked. A "thing" for me? Wouldn't that be like incest? There was no way he had a "thing" for me. "There is nothing going on between me and Daniel," I said. "He probably had to come home and help his mom."

Mom looked at me and smiled. "OK. Well, tell us about Germany."

When we pulled into the driveway, I was overcome with an overwhelming feeling of comfort and familiarity. It was good to be home. Before I could even get my foot out of the car, Keith was at the passenger door, giving me a hand.

"Hey, Sweetie!" he said as he gathered me into a bear hug. "I missed you so much."

My eyes caught Daniel's as he walked up behind Keith. "Hey, I'm glad you're back," Daniel said.

Keith let go and turned around to glare at Daniel. He didn't say anything, but if his eyes could have done damage, then damage was done. He let go of my waist and went to help Dad with the bags.

Daniel stepped forward and gave me a hug.

"What are you doing here?" I whispered, careful not to let Keith hear.

He stepped back and smiled. "I wanted to see you."

"Oh," I said, my eyes wide with surprise.

He smiled and turned around to help Dad with the last bag.

My jet-lagged mind couldn't grasp the situation at hand. There were two guys waiting for me inside—one for whom I had no feelings, and, in fact, whose very appearance made me ill, and another who was familiar and comfortable, but for whom romantic thoughts seemed unusual.

I dragged my feet inside, not wanting to carry on with the crazy evening, but only wanting to crawl into bed and sleep it off.

Everyone was waiting in the formal living room. Daniel and Keith sat on the couch, leaving the middle spot open. I sat in between them. Keith reached over to grab my hand, but I moved it away. I could feel his hurt, but I couldn't bring myself to look at his face.

For the next half hour, I felt like I was on display. I answered questions about where I had been, what we had seen, and what the Von Aikens were like. Desperate to get up from the testosterone-dominated couch, I went to my bag for the gifts and souvenirs.

Tired of the entertainment my callers had been providing, my parents excused themselves and went into the study. I thought Daniel would be next, giving me the space I needed to deal with Keith, but he was determined to remain. It was obvious that Keith was troubled by Daniel's persistent presence and my constant denial of his affections.

At last, Keith stood up and announced his exit. He looked at Daniel as if expecting him to follow suit, but Daniel stayed on the couch and waved goodbye. Despite my confusion at Daniel's behavior, I had to laugh at his arrogance.

Keith and I walked outside. "What's going on between you and Daniel?" Keith demanded before the patio door could shut behind us.

"What do you mean, 'what's going on?'" I said, crossing my arms in defense.

"Don't act stupid! Why is he here? Why won't he leave? Why is he looking at you like—like…"

"What?" I jumped in. "He's not looking at me in any kind of way. He's a good friend, and you know that. There is nothing wrong with him being here. Besides, I've been in Germany for a month! What do you think could be going on with us?"

Keith looked as if he wanted to cry, and he reached out to grab my arms. "Shannon, why are you being so cold?"

My heart froze. At that moment, all of the guilt that had built up over the summer, and the degradation I had experienced in my many nights alone, waiting to be Keith's toy, collided.

His touch repulsed me.

"Keith, I can't see you anymore."

"What?"

I turned back to the house.

"Shannon! Wait, I don't understand."

Before I opened the front door, I turned back to Keith. "Please don't call me again," I said. Then I stepped inside and shut the door.

Daniel got off the couch and came over to me. "What's wrong?"

With dry eyes and a weightless heart, I looked up at Daniel and smiled. "Nothing. I broke up with Keith."

Daniel smiled. "Good!"

I laughed. Yes, it was good.

"OK, well I want to see pictures and hear all about what you did," Daniel said, walking towards the game room like he always did when he came over.

I laughed some more. It was Daniel, my friend Daniel, and nothing more. I followed after him and smiled.

# Girl Gone Wild

Turn away your face from my sins; blot out all my guilt. A clean heart create for me, God; renew in me a steadfast spirit.

—Psalm 51:11–12

AFTER THREE WEEKS of being home from Germany, sixty phone calls from Keith begging me to come back because he was a changed man, and a multitude of shopping trips to gather last-minute dorm room necessities, my mom and I filled my 323 Mazda and Dad's Dodge Ram truck to their limits, and we set off for my new home in east Texas.

Once we had unloaded, made the bed, settled in, sticky-tacked pictures to the walls, and stocked the mini refrigerator with a week's supply of yogurt, pudding snacks, and Gouda cheese, there wasn't much left for my mom to do. So we said our goodbyes, and she left me to my first exam: living on my own.

That night, Lauren and I took it easy. We had dinner together, took a trip to Wal-Mart for a few knickknacks, and, at about eleven o'clock, the phone rang. It was a call for Lauren, and her face lit up.

"It's Scott," she said. "They're having a party at his place. Want to go?"

My first reaction was that it was eleven o'clock and too late to go to a party. Then freedom slapped me in the face. "Sure!"

It didn't take long to get the adrenaline flowing, as I madly dashed to change clothes and refresh my makeup. We were out the door and on our way by 11:30.

Lauren's friend Scott was already a senior, and everyone at the party was at least three, if not four or five, years older than us. It was exhilarating to be at a college party and mingle with people who actually wanted to carry on conversations with substance. At the same time, the consumption of alcohol made the sloppiness of our high school parties pale in comparison.

Alcohol wasn't the fix of choice, either. At one point, late into the morning, while I was sitting on the couch in deep conversation with (and in awe of) Scott's roommate, Trent, who was a clone of Freddie Prinze, Jr., Scott walked out of the bathroom. He was sniffing his nose and wiping it with the back of his hand. He walked over to us, and as I caught a glimpse of the remnants of white powder under his nostril, Trent shot up off of the couch, blocking my view of Scott. He said something to him in a hushed whisper and then sat down again. When I looked at Scott, his face was clean, but his eyes were glassy.

I guessed it was cocaine, but I never asked. Instead, I allowed Trent's deep voice to hypnotize me until the sun shone through the window. I looked at my watch, shocked to see that we had stayed there until 6:00 A.M. I had been too into Trent to realize the other partiers had left, and Lauren and Scott had crashed out on the couch next to us. I was about to get Lauren so we could head back to the dorm, when she woke up.

On the drive home, I told her about what I had seen on Scott. I wanted to know if she was into that scene or at least warn her that he was if she didn't already know.

"Yeah," she nodded. "He does a line every now and then, but he never asks me to join him. He knows I don't do that kind of thing."

I sighed with relief. Alcohol was one thing, and I could admit that I didn't have a handle on it myself, but drugs were another story. They had ravaged my sister's life, and at that point I wanted nothing to do with them.

For the next few days, we were busy registering for classes and buying books. Lauren took me around to familiarize me with the town and campus. At night, we would go over to Scott and Trent's. There wasn't always a party. Sometimes we'd just sit and watch TV. By this time, Trent and I had moved into a more intimate stage of our relationship. Everything about him was mesmerizing: his voice, his six feet six inches stature, his looks, and his gentleness. He was not demanding or controlling. He did not push sex and was fine with cuddling.

We continued to double with Scott and Trent, and, during the week of my eighteenth birthday, two weeks after moving into town, Trent, Scott, and Lauren threw me a surprise birthday party. I was stunned. They had only known me for a few weeks, and they went through the trouble of cake, balloons, and even gifts. Of course, there were also a few kegs and many people I didn't know, but the effort and thought were heartwarming.

That night, I stayed with Trent in his room for the first time.

I have no excuse for my sexual escapades at that point of my life, but that night, my first overnight with Trent, began a short period of absolutely inexcusable behavior.

My relationship with Trent lasted about six weeks. He was quite a gentleman, and he never asked me to engage in anything I hadn't heard of or wanted to try. School began, and, rather than break up, we simply faded away. It felt very grown up to not attach any kind of emotion to the relationship. Besides, Keith continued to call and beg me to take him back, reminding me that I did not want to get caught up in that again.

I felt nothing.

The new me, the real me, had become more removed from the old church going, purpose-filled Shannon. I lived for drinking and partying. I did not know how to care, and I did not want to go home to visit my family. Going home would have meant that I had to define a character for myself, and, at that point in my life, I didn't have it in me to try. I no longer attended Mass to appease anyone. Living at school made it easy to live in the void without God, since I felt that he had given up on me anyway.

Not long into the semester, Lauren and I met Derek and Jason, two roommates from the men's dorm across from ours. We met them in the cafeteria one day when we couldn't find an empty table. The one thing we had in common was that we were all Catholic—except for Lauren, who was Protestant. Although I had no regard for my faith at the time, it still felt nice to have a connection. They both had girlfriends, too, so it was easy to become close friends without expectations, and soon they were like my brothers.

Whether we went to a club or party, they always seemed to be the ones picking me up, heaving me over their shoulders and depositing me on the steps of my dorm. Sometimes I would let my wall down and cry, and they would sit with me, listen to me babble, and allow me to lean on them. They gave and gave without ever expecting anything in return. Despite the fact that they were both very attractive, I did not have physical chemistry with either one of them.

If I could have been mature enough to look beyond myself at the time, I would have seen God's hand in our friendship. He was still looking out for me, even though I had denounced him from my life. I was spiraling out of control, drinking everything in sight. Playing quarters with Mad Dog 20/20®, guzzling liters of Purple Passion (a concoction made with Everclear®), doing keg stands with cheap Keystone® beer. Every night, I blacked out, waking up in my own vomit, and barely recalling bits and pieces of the evening. Some of my actions were too embarrassing to admit. I would pass out in some stranger's apartment, only to wake up and throw up all over their couch or floor, or worse. But some memories are better left unsaid.

It was Jason and Derek who would look for me the next day, worried to death that I hadn't come home. It was Jason and Derek who went over the various scenarios with me to reassure me that I was physically

OK. It was also Jason and Derek who sat me down one day and told me to slow down.

They even convinced me to attend Mass with them one Sunday, opening a door that I thought had been bolted shut.

Derek and Jason saved my life.

Slowly, the binge drinking came to an end. I was spent. After Mass that one Sunday, I felt a faint tug of recognition—not like the meaningless kind I had felt at home, where Mass had become part of the background of family life. This recognition was more like the kind I felt in the rare moments I had with my grandmother, my dad's mom, sitting in the back pew of the church, as she told me what God had done for her in her life. I wanted to know why she would say the rosary every day and why I would find her mumbling prayers from a tattered prayer book. When my grandmother spoke of her faith, it gave my heart a jolt. But I hadn't felt that in years.

Sitting in Mass in east Texas, far away from home, gave me a nostalgic feeling. This was something I had to make an effort to attend, and, by taking that step, I cracked open the door.

Daniel would call, and he was jealous of the fact I had two new male friends to keep me straight. Every weekend, he asked me to come visit, and, finally, with Lauren willing to tag along, we made plans to go to the south part of Texas, where he was attending college.

Getting into the car and driving four-and-a-half hours to an unknown place was a new experience. Lauren and I made the most of the drive, talking about our lives, mistakes, and dreams. We talked about the upcoming spring semester, going through rush week, and which sororities we were interested in. She and I clicked in many ways and were respectful of one another. Because she was around me day in and day out, she was the first person who truly knew me, and not as the "multi-personality" I had been at home.

Daniel's home was in the worse location imaginable, which was probably why those homes were rented to college students. It was on the very edge of the airport. If you were outside when a plane headed in for a landing, it felt like you could reach up and touch its underbelly. It was loud, and it shook the small wood frame of the house.

Lauren and I were greeted at the front steps. Daniel ran up to me, grabbed me, and lifted me up into the air. At that point, I realized that Dad may have been right. Maybe Daniel did have something for me. But the thought was too alien to grasp, so I shook it off and let it go.

"It didn't take you long to get here," Daniel said as he took our bags from our hands and carried them into the house.

"Nope," I said as we followed behind. "It wasn't as far as I'd thought it would be."

Daniel's roommate, Nate, who had also graduated from our high school one year after Daniel, came into the living room from the kitchen. "Hey, Shannon!" he yelled. "Man, I haven't seen you in, what, a year? You look great!"

"Lauren, this is Daniel and Nate," I said, introducing her.

She smiled. "Hi."

"Where do you want our stuff?" I asked, assuming that she and I would sleep on the couches in the living room.

"You'll sleep in my room," Daniel said, "and Lauren will sleep in Nate's. We'll take the couches."

"Oh, no, you don't have to," Lauren said, jumping in. "It's OK, really."

Daniel smiled, "Nope, it's how we want it."

Lauren looked at me and shrugged. I knew what she was thinking. Why not just put us in the same room, and they could share the other? The thought crossed my mind as well, but I had known Daniel for years, and there was no need for me to second guess his hospitality.

"Are y'all hungry? Let's go eat!" Daniel said, ushering us out of the house for lunch.

Later that night, after a small party Daniel and Nate threw in our favor, I had had enough to drink to go beyond a buzz to feeling extremely good and tired. There were no pretenses about what might happen later that night, so I felt no need to continue drinking.

Daniel stayed by my side for most of the evening. He didn't drink much because he was more into smoking pot. It relaxed him and made him content. In the beginning of the night, I contemplated whether to try it or not. Nate offered, but Daniel jumped in. "No, she doesn't need any."

Glad he spoke for me but confused at his firmness, I gave him a puzzled look. "Not that I want any, but that doesn't make sense," I said.

He pointed to my wine cooler and said, "Hey, I think smoking pot is safer than drinking that crap. But if you're going to get caught up in it, I don't want it to be because of me or with me." He had no idea his future actions would one day cause me to eventually give in to the one evil I swore I would never do: drugs, mainly marijuana and one bad night with LSD. Thankfully, after one night of a bad trip I walked easily away from the horror of the fix and stuck with drinking as my drug of choice.

I was used to him protecting me, but this had a different flavor. My heart did a little jump, and I looked at his profile in a new light.

Later on, after I had gone to bed, and was snug and under the covers, Daniel came in and said, "Do you mind if I sleep with you?"

"That's fine," I mumbled, half asleep and trusting.

The next morning, as the sun filtered in through the blinds, stealing away the coveted darkness. I lay next to Daniel, on my side, with our backs touching and my eyes wide open. It was an odd feeling to stare at his bland, white wall, feel his body so close to mine, and not have to think, "What are my parents going to think when I get home so late?" I was free to do as I pleased, to pick up on a Friday afternoon and drive for hours to visit a friend. I had no curfew, and no regulations.

It scared me. My spirit was restless.

I felt Daniel stir and turn over. He inched closer and draped his arm over my waist. It shocked me at first. He and I were so close that even sharing a bed was no big deal. But for him to spoon and hold me was odd.

Not certain of where I wanted this to go or what my feelings were toward Daniel, I shut my eyes and acted like I was asleep. I could sense that he was awake, waiting for me to roll over, but I was determined to stay on the fence and not make a decision.

I felt his hand move up from my waist and caress my arm and neck. Daniel was no longer the good ole buddy I had known for the past few years. He had made the decision for me.

As we crossed the line between friends and lovers, I felt a new hope that maybe he and I could have something deeper than anything I had experienced before. This was my first time beginning a relationship as best friends. He already knew everything about me, including all of my faults and quirks. He had seen me at my worst and was still holding me with gentleness that morning. I turned onto my back, and we locked eyes. Not a word was said. He kissed me.

That was all we did that morning. It was nice. It was safe. It was comforting.

For the rest of the weekend, it was obvious that Daniel was happy. I was happy because he was happy. He took care of me. He loved me, and that was all that mattered.

# Friends With Benefits

CAMPING HAD ALWAYS been a fun pastime for my family, so
when Daniel and I decided to go camping in the woods of east
Texas, I thought it would be a great way to be alone and focus on each
other. It had been three weeks since we had seen each other and crossed
the line of friendship into a relationship. We spoke on the phone every
day, but I still felt like Daniel was more of a brother than a boyfriend.
We had agreed to keep our relationship open and date other people.
Daniel didn't want me to feel bound by him in my first year of college,
and I figured what I didn't know wouldn't hurt me.

But after three weeks it was obvious that we needed to see each other.
We set out to meet before Thanksgiving. Although we would both be in
our hometown for the holiday, we knew we would never get the chance
to spend quality time together.

Daniel came prepared with a tent, food, and plenty of beer. The
weather was nice—not an extreme bitter cold, but the air had a bite to

it that kept us huddled together in a sleeping bag that night. It was nice to be close to him and feel the security in his arms. It had been three weeks since our first kiss, but I couldn't fathom kissing Daniel. There were no fireworks. It felt comfortable and safe.

That night, in the tiny one-man tent, an urgent need erupted in Daniel. I was now experienced enough to know what he wanted, and, without a second of hesitation, I allowed him that satisfaction. It was Daniel, I rationalized. But there was no passion or desire, just his fulfillment and my emptiness.

He rolled over and was snoring within seconds. I didn't move. Instead, I spent the rest of the night in self-pity, making excuses for his sudden rude behavior, until I was overcome with sleep.

Our relationship continued over the holiday season. My parents were pleased to see that we were dating, and we began to attend parties together in our hometown. Over the long Christmas break, I prepared for Rush Week, the Panhellenic system of entering a sorority. Daniel wasn't too keen on the idea of me becoming a sorority girl because it didn't mesh well with his liberal beliefs. We didn't fit together well at all. We were truly an odd couple.

Rush took place the week before second semester classes began. But the dorms opened for those of us rushing. It had been a few weeks since Daniel and I had been alone, so he suggested meeting me at a hotel the night before I was due back at the dorms. Feeling the old pressures of hometown life, I was glad to get out of town a day early. I told my parents I was staying at Lauren's parents' house before the dorms opened, and they never let on they believed differently.

I arrived at the hotel before sundown. Daniel had already checked in, and when I entered he had the bath water running.

"Hi!" His smile was wide and welcoming. He gave me a hug and kissed my forehead.

I laid my bag on the king sized bed. Then something in my stomach flipped and turned sour. I was in a hotel room with Daniel. This wasn't right.

Daniel turned and headed toward the bathroom. "I'm going to take a bath. You're welcome to join me," he said as he shut the door.

Moments later, he called out, "Is everything all right?"

Away from the door and safe on the edge of the bed, I let out a long sigh. "Yeah, I'm fine," I said. "Really." For the first time since I had left home for college, I wanted to be home. I wanted to feel safe and secure, but here I was, out of my element and over my head.

The water drained from the tub, and Daniel whistled as he dried off with a towel. Desperate to appear as if I had been doing something during his bath, I grabbed for my bag and dug out a Danielle Steele novel. I scooted to the headboard and propped myself up, opening the book on my lap.

"You want to go out for dinner?" Daniel said as he came out, the towel wrapped around his hips, accentuating the bulk of his torso, which was not as defined as it was in the glory days of his high school football career.

"Sure," I said, a little too fast. Anything to get me out of the hotel room was a relief.

We had dinner at a Mexican restaurant that was pleasant and allowed me to take my mind off of what had happened in the hotel room. The feelings and emotions had taken me by surprise, and I didn't know what to do about them.

Later that night, we flipped on the TV and waited for Saturday Night Live to come on. They had a new bit on sorority sisters that broke my stark mood and made us both laugh.

"I can't believe that by this time next week you're going to be one of those girls," Daniel said during the commercial.

Hearing the disparagement in his voice, I defensively shot back, "Well, I might not be in that sorority. There are other sororities."

"What difference does it make?" he said. "They are all the same. You're buying friends."

I inched out of his arms. "That's not true. There's a lot more behind it than just the social."

135

Daniel leaned back and laughed. "Oh, come on!"

"What? They do a lot of service projects, you have to stay on top of things academically, and you can get a lot of contacts for jobs after school."

He reached over and patted me on the back. "Tell yourself whatever you want," he said. "You're still buying friends."

He was being condescending. I rolled over in a huff and settled myself for sleep.

"Not to mention the frat boys you'll meet."

I turned to look at him. "Oh, so that's it! You don't want me to date any frat guys!"

"No," he said. "You can see whoever you want. We don't need to be tied together."

"So you'll be fine if I date as many frat guys as I want?" I said, chastising him. I wanted him to offer a sense of permanency in our relationship. I needed him to give me a reason to feel that I was more than just the whore I felt I was becoming.

"If that's what you want to do, go right ahead. They're a bunch of egotistical jerks, but whatever floats your boat."

"Whatever you say, Daniel," I said, deflated and dead inside.

The next morning, he dropped me off at my dorm, and we kissed goodbye.

"Call and let me know who you bought," he said, playfully slapping my butt before getting into his car.

"Shut up," I mumbled as I watched him drive off.

Used to switching gears, I pushed the night with Daniel out of my head and focused on rushing. Lauren was also rushing sororities so we spent the next four days comparing notes, laughing about the forced conversations in some of the houses, anguishing together about the possibility of being cut, and ultimately realizing we were headed in separate directions. She was becoming more enchanted with the Tri-Delts®. I liked them, but they weren't for me. Our conversations made me feel too much like I had stepped back into high school.

I was searching for a sorority where I could feel comfortable, wanted, and welcomed. Chi Omega® was my first choice, and in the end Lauren and I both got what we wanted. On bid day, when it was revealed who got what, Lauren and I pretty much already knew the outcome.

"I have a lot of friends that are Chi Omegas®. You're going to like them a lot," she said, sitting on her side of the room as we waited to be picked up by our new sisters.

"I know," I said, nodding and smiling. "It would've been fun to be in the same one, but that's OK."

"We're still roommates, though," Lauren said. "We'll still do stuff together." Her face looked hopeful.

I giggled. "We sound like we're about to be carried off to different worlds or something. Of course we'll still do stuff together."

Chants and cheers began to fill the hall, and then a knock at the door announced our induction into the Greek society.

With being a pledge and classes beginning, there was not enough time in the day to think about Daniel or our issues. The calls subsided, too, because the long distance bill from before the holidays was atrocious. Despite the fact that the relationship I held with Daniel wasn't becoming the desired fairy tale of unconditional love my spirit longed for, I still considered him a best friend. When we did speak I communicated my issues with school and my insecurities in being a pledge. The latter made him chuckle, but although he was condescending, he didn't always trash me for being in a sorority.

After a month had passed, we still hadn't seen each other since he'd dropped me off after Christmas break. Kaitlyn, a pledge sister of mine, also had a boyfriend that went to Daniel's university. Late one Friday night, after realizing that for once we had no major commitments the entire weekend, we took off to visit them, popping NoDoz® and Mountain Dew® to keep us awake. On the way, I called Daniel, who seemed pleased by my surprise visit.

The sun peeked out from above the rocky hills as we drove into town. I dropped Kaitlyn off at her boyfriend's dorm, and, finally, with my eyes wide in caffeine shock, I made it to Daniel's. As I stepped out of the car, my knees buckled, and I could barely hold myself up. I hadn't slept in twenty-four hours. Apparently, my nerves weren't used to the caffeine high, because I was shaking like an addict in need of a fix.

Daniel ran outside to greet me and put an arm around my shoulder. "I can't believe you did that." His voice was firm but gentle.

"What?" I asked, unable to clear the fog from my mind to figure out what had made him upset.

"Driving so late like that. Your dad would kill me if he ever found out."

I laughed at the irony. "He'd kill me for more than just driving to see you."

Once inside, he carried me to his bedroom and helped me undress. I crawled under the covers and closed my eyes. Maybe he did really care for me. Maybe I was too picky and expected too much. He was so gentle and kind.

Rays of sunlight pierced through the bedroom window through a thin white curtain. When I closed my eyes, the light illuminated my eyelids. I needed darkness. I tried to hide my head under a pillow to block out the light, but delirium had already taken over.

I couldn't sleep. I needed to sleep so I could enjoy the visit. I was frustrated, and tears began to fill my closed eyes. The door to the bedroom opened. I wanted to move so I could lift the pillow off of my face and wipe my cheeks, but I didn't want Daniel to think I was silly for crying.

The bed sagged with Daniel's weight. He lay beside me, reached over, and pulled me in closer. With my head still under the pillow, I managed a smile, and relaxed with a sense of security. He sat up enough to lightly rub my back with the tips of his fingers, and my fatigued muscles began to settle down. The tension left my body, and, for once, sleep seemed possible.

Until Daniel's hands began roaming.

My eyes popped open. "What are you doing? I'm tired!" I screamed inside. My heart beat quickly with anger. I reached up and grabbed the pillow off of my face so I could see him. "Daniel," I said, trying to keep my voice calm because I knew that most of the anger and emotion had been brought on by lack of sleep. "I'm tired," I said, whining like a little girl.

"Ah, come on, Shannon, I haven't seen you in forever. Let's be together, and I'll let you sleep all day if you want."

"Why can't I sleep now?" I thought, but I couldn't say it out loud. I didn't feel it was my right to deny him. He loved me, cared for me, and he wasn't trying to take anything from me. Maybe if I hadn't been so sleep deprived, I would have found his need endearing. Rationalizing had become my new faith. It was the only vice that kept me from being eaten away with guilt.

I allowed him to fulfill his need, wishing that one day my needs would be met—not my physical needs but my needs for nurturing and gentle care.

After Daniel left the room, I still couldn't sleep.

# Find Me Somebody To Love

Many deceivers have gone out into the world, those who do not acknowledge Jesus Christ as coming in the flesh; such is the deceitful one and the antichrist.

—2 John 1:7

A CRISP SPRING breeze rustled the needles on the giant pine trees that clustered around the pond. The bright afternoon sun poked holes through the branches, shedding much needed light and warmth on the benches that had been strategically placed on the man-made paths through the trees. This made the pond a famous spot to daydream. It was the perfect place to forget that you were a student who needed to study.

Books were splayed in front of me and lay opened on the ground as little ants marched across their pages. Their cadence was mesmerizing, keeping my mind empty of everything, including my mid-term exams. There was a rustle in the water, and I looked up in time to catch a graceful white swan arch its neck and rustle its feathers. Water formed in droplets and rolled off of its back. Then it settled back into position, and, with its neck arched into a perfect "S," it slowly swam away from the shadows of the trees and into the sun.

"Ow!" I jumped up and swatted my bare foot. The cadence of ants had made its way to the tempting flesh under my feet. I picked my feet up, sat with my legs crossed on the bench, and sighed.

The reverie had been broken, and all that had clouded my mind returned. I didn't know what to do about Daniel. He had just left to go back to school after attending my Chi-Omega Southern Formal. We doubled with my big sis in the sorority, and she and her boyfriend had let us stay at her boyfriend's house.

I shook my head as I remembered the night before. Daniel had been rude and obnoxious. After having too many Crown and Cokes, he decided to bash the Greek system at the top of his lungs. When we got him back to the house, he passed out on top of the pool table. He made a fool of me, and when I confronted him about it in the morning he rolled his eyes, offering no apologies.

Before he left, we were in my dorm room alone. Lauren was at the library studying, and Daniel lay on the bed. I sat down on the edge.

"Daniel, what's going on with us?" I asked, my heart hurting. Daniel was my best friend, the one I had gone to for years, able to tell him anything without being judged. But now I felt like I was continuously messing up, not living up to his ideals, and deeper still the hurt ached because he wasn't fulfilling mine.

He closed his eyes and mumbled, "I don't know what you're talking about."

Defeated, I stood up and sat down at my desk. The cassette tapes of songs he had compiled for me for Christmas were stacked neatly by the telephone. Not all of them were cheesy love songs, but they all meant something to us as a couple. A few of them had lyrics that proclaimed the bond of our friendship and love.

That bond wasn't there anymore. I wanted to feel secure with him again and not a constant disappointment. He had fallen asleep, and when he woke up he gave me a hug and kissed me goodbye. "I'll call you in a few days," he said. "Be good."

"Yes, Dad," I thought with disdain.

I shuddered at the way he tried to control me. Sighing again, I relented to the fact that I would not be able to get any studying done, and I gathered my books.

A plus of being Greek was the great social life. The monthly socials were the biggest hit. A social was when a fraternity would throw a party for a sorority. Because there were twice as many fraternities as sororities, each semester fraternities would make bids to a sorority to have a social. If the sorority accepted, they would set the date, and the fraternity would come up with a theme for the evening. There were many themes, such as Food Fight, Rodeo Roundup, Groovy Night, and so on. We would dress up accordingly, and then two to three pledges would rotate as designated drivers for the entire chapter.

I was excited for this month's social. Ever since Daniel had left a few days before, I wanted to get out and let it all go. I wanted to have fun. I had been a designated driver for the Food Fight extravaganza the month before, which was probably the worst one to have to drive everyone home, because they were not only filthy but filthy drunk. Despite the constant stops to allow the pledge sisters to upchuck on the side of the road, it was a very bonding experience. Taking care of another person was humbling.

The theme of this month's social was psychedelic, and it was nice because we didn't have to dress up in funky clothes. The group of pledges I had bonded with the week before had been invited to a pre-party with one of the active sisters. She was the "big sis" of one of the girls and was dating a guy in the fraternity. When we went over to the pre-party, a group of guys and some of the older actives were drinking beer and lounging around a pit fire.

The temperature had dropped as the sun went down, and all I had brought with me was a light jacket. I sat around the pit with Sarah, Leslie, and Kat, one hand holding a beer and the other jammed into my pocket. Some of the guys came over to talk, and one in particular caught my attention. He was the best looking guy there, in my opinion, and also my type—knee-buckling handsome, tall, around six feet five, with a football player's physique and a smile that numbed my mind.

He was my type but out of my league.

Our eyes connected for a brief moment, and this time he directed his smile my way. When I say that his smile was mind-numbing, I mean that I could not even think to respond. Like a prepubescent fool, I sat there in shock. Then one of his buddies called him away, and the moment was lost.

I convinced myself that he was just being polite. He really was out of my league. I looked around to see where he had gone, but he was no longer outside. Certain there would be no other opportunity I rejoined the conversation with my pledge sisters.

"Aren't you cold?" asked a baritone voice from behind me. The other girls glanced up over my head, so I turned around. It was him. He was standing directly behind me, and there was no mistaking that he was talking to me.

"A little," I said with a smile.

He came around the bench, sat down beside me, and put his arm around my shoulders. "Here, does this help?"

"Sure, thanks," I said, my eyes widening as I looked over at Sarah. Sarah raised her eyebrows.

"What's your name?" asked the stealer of my senses.

"Shannon." A quick shiver coursed through my spine.

He tightened his arm around my shoulder and scooted in closer. "I'm Nick," he said. "You're a pledge, right? Freshman?"

"Yeah, what…"

"Hey Nick!" interrupted one of his brothers, poking his head outside and breaking up our introduction. "You gotta come see this!"

The warmth of his arm was gone. "Nice meeting you, Shannon. I'll come find you at the lodge later."

"Wow! He is so cute!" Kat said as she quickly occupied Nick's empty space. "What did he say?"

"Nothing, really. He just offered to keep me warm."

"Yeah, right," Sarah rolled her eyes and poked me in the side.

"What year is he?" I wondered out loud.

"You don't know who that was?" Sarah asked, her eyes growing in mock horror. "That was Nick Ferrante. He's the fraternity's vice president and captain of the university football team."

"Really?" My face dropped. I was being played for a fool. Why, then, would he want to talk to me? That was probably why he asked me if I was a freshman.

"Yeah, girl, he was in to you!" she laughed, grabbing my arm and pulling me off the bench. "Come on, let's get to the lodge!"

The lodge was packed, the lights were off, and the guys had spray-painted glow-in-the-dark, neon green signs, words, and Greek letters everywhere. One disco ball hung in the middle of the lodge to designate a dance floor, and near the makeshift DJ area was a trash can full of punch. The fraternity pledges were busy serving every girl a full glass of this mysterious and potent concoction, and making sure our glasses were never empty.

By the time I had two glasses I was feeling no pain. My pledge sisters and I enjoyed dancing in a small circle, arms raised above our heads, entertaining ourselves with shouts of "Wahoo!" and nearly peeing our pants from laughter for reasons no one else could or would understand.

I needed a break and rushed to the bathroom, only to wait in a line. Leaning against the wall, I stared into an open room that doubled as a makeshift dance area, squinting to make out the faces.

"Having fun?" an unmistakable male voice asked.

I turned and looked to my left. Nick took the extra step to stand next to me, his face disguised by dark shadows, and his extreme white teeth glowing in the black light.

"Yes!" I answered, standing up a little straighter and losing the insistent urge to pee. "That trash can punch is toxic! Did y'all set out to kill us?"

His laugh, shy and soft, accentuated his otherwise colossal exterior. "Maybe harm, but I wouldn't say 'kill,'" he laughed again.

"Well, it's working!" I laughed, realizing I had moved to the front of the line. "Oh, I'm next." I had become a babbling idiot.

"I'll wait," he said as he walked over to the other side of the hallway, leaned against the wall, and put his hands in his pockets as if he didn't have a care in the world.

When I came out, he was still standing there in the same position, until he saw me, stood up, and reached out to take my hand. "Let's go outside. Do you want to?"

"Sure!" The alcohol had numbed my insecurities. I was still ecstatic that he was interested, but now I was able to enjoy it rather than wonder why.

He led me out to the deck area where some tables and chairs had been set up. The temperature had dropped a few degrees as the night had progressed, and my jacket was no longer cutting it.

"Here," Nick said as he took off his jacket and put it around my shoulders. "If you're too cold, we can go back inside. I wanted to talk to you for a bit."

"Oh, no, I'm fine," I answered. "Are you sure you're not too cold?"

He smiled. "I'm good. So, talk to me. Tell me about yourself."

We spent the rest of the evening outside, away from the overbearing music and claustrophobic dance floor. He talked about football and graduating, and all I could talk about was my life at school. If I had talked about home, it would bring up the embarrassing age difference between us, and I didn't dare do that.

Promptly at eleven o'clock, the actives started gathering the pledges and reminding them of their curfew. Pledges were only allowed to stay at the socials until eleven. Once you became active, there was no curfew. Liz Rowland was the active walking the outside premises. When she found us, her eyes were wide with surprise.

"Shannon, your ride's about to leave," she said abruptly.

I felt busted, but I was not sure why. We had only been talking. "OK," I stammered, getting up. "It was nice meeting you, Nick."

Nick looked at Liz with a smirk on his face, and she turned and walked away. When I said his name, his expression changed back into a sincere smile. "Oh yeah," he said, jumping up and giving me a bear hug. "Can I call you tomorrow?"

I couldn't hide the smile on my face even through a brown paper bag. "Sure!"

"I'll get your number from one of the actives."

"Shannon!" Sarah hollered from the parking lot.

"OK," I said, careful not to stumble. Then I rushed back to my sisters.

True to his word, Nick called the very next day and asked me out to a movie. Unable to contain my excitement, I ran up the stairs in Steen Hall to Kaitlyn and Meg's room.

"I'm going out with Nick Ferrante tonight!" I screamed. "He just called!" I sat on the bed and hugged a crimson and gold Chi-Omega pillow to my chest. "He's so good looking," I breathed as I fell back in a faint.

"That's awesome, Shannon!" Meg said. She and Kaitlyn sat on the bed across from me. "Where is he taking you?" she asked.

"I have no idea. A movie, I think. It can be McDonald's for all I care." The memory of his smile made my stomach flip. He was too good to be true. Handsome and polite, he reminded me of Matt.

"Maybe we can double one night," Kaitlyn said, covering her sly smile with her hand. She had just broken up with her long-term boyfriend.

I sat up, eyes wide. "Come on! Tell us," I prodded, reaching out and playfully slapping Katilyn's leg. "Who did you snag?"

"Chad, Nick's best friend!" The smile on her face said it all, and we giggled like elementary schoolgirls.

For the rest of the afternoon, we exchanged stories from the night before, and then they came up to my room and helped me pick out an outfit to wear.

"Did you and Daniel break up?" Meg asked, looking at the pictures of us on the pegboard above my desk.

Daniel. For a split second, I felt a tinge of guilt that maybe even talking to Nick was a betrayal. But the way Daniel had left things, I knew I would be a fool not to play the field. Maybe we would sort things out in the long run, but for now, the excitement and newness of Nick was too much to pass up. I didn't even want to think about Daniel.

"No, we haven't broken up," I said, "but we've always been open to date other people. I haven't yet until now."

"Is he dating other people?" Kaitlyn asked, handing me a different top.

Despite my resolve to be grown up about the scenario, the thought of Daniel dating others had never crossed my mind. In that moment, despite my excitement to move forward, it hurt. "I don't know."

"Well, if you ask me, I think Nick is a better catch," Meg offered.

"Maybe," I said. "Daniel and I have been best friends for years." I sat down on the bed; my spirits dampened. "Maybe I shouldn't do this."

"What!" Kaitlyn interjected. "There is nothing wrong with you going out to dinner with someone else!"

I looked over at the clock on the desk. I had an hour to shower and get ready. I didn't have long to dwell on it. "You're right," I said, smiling. "Thanks for helping. I'll call y'all tomorrow and tell you how it went."

Nick arrived promptly, well dressed, and bearing one single red rose. Romantic, charming, and good-looking, Daniel was forgotten at "Hello."

"You look amazing," he said. His eyes sucked me in and savored me like a fine mint.

Flattered, and a bit uneasy, I giggled to release my nerves. "Thanks, so do you."

We went to a movie, and afterwards, the evening drifted by without missing a beat. Nick was a natural at everything. There was pleasant conversation, flirtatious banter, and enough compliments to make me feel special but not overworked.

At the end of the evening, he drove me back to the dorm and walked me up to the door. "Can I see you again?" he asked.

We stood there, inches apart, and my face lifted up to his. "I'd like that," I said and smiled.

He leaned down, kissed me gently on the lips, and said softly, "What about tonight? Come stay with me."

I smiled in response, afraid to speak and ruin the moment, but I knew that staying with him would ruin the beginning of something that could be normal and good. "Not tonight," I said.

"Tomorrow night then. We'll do a movie at my place." He backed away. "OK, then, I'll call tomorrow to make sure it's still on, but plan on me picking you up about 6:00 P.M."

"OK, sounds good," I said as I walked into the dorm. I turned back around, on impulse, to see if he was gone, and I caught him turning back to look at me. This gesture sent sparks of excitement through my heart. He was into me. I felt wanted again, and so far it wasn't all about him.

"I'll take this one slow," I thought. I wanted him to respect me and to get to know me.

Lauren was up reading a book when I floated into the room. "I had the best date ever."

She put the book down. "Really? Who'd you go out with?" She'd been staying at her parents' house for the past two days studying for a biology exam.

"Nick Ferrante! We met at the social last night."

Her forehead creased in a frown. "Really?" she said, sitting up. Her facial expression deflated like a balloon that had been popped by a needle.

"What?" I asked. "What do you know?"

She shook her head. "Oh, nothing, really. I thought one of our actives was dating him. Or at least she'd dated him for a long time."

"I didn't think he was dating anyone at all. He didn't say anything, and none of his friends seemed to act like it."

Lauren's face softened, and she smiled. "Oh, I'm sure they've broken up. Don't worry about it."

But the damage was done. What if I was being played? "No," I thought. "He was too nice." I told myself not to let one comment ruin my moment. I deserved a good relationship. This might be the one.

# Once...Shame On You.
# Twice...Shame On Me

If the body and sex are meant to proclaim our union with God, and if there's an enemy who wants to separate us from God, what do you think he's going to attack? The enemy is no dummy (*Theology of the Body pg, 12*).

THE NEXT DAY after lunch, Nick called to confirm our date for the evening. "I'll cook you dinner, and we can relax at my place."

Cook me dinner? He couldn't be real. "Sounds great!" I said. I was starting to feel like a windup doll: "Sounds great!" "Awesome!" "OK!" "Whatever you say, Nick, whatever you say."

Nick was prompt, dressed more casually than the night before, in jeans and a long-sleeved polo. I had guessed well with my choice of sweater and jeans and was pleased how easily we locked hands as we walked to the car.

When we got to the apartment, his roommate was in the kitchen. "Mike here was keeping an eye on the stove for me." He winked at Mike. "I hope you like spaghetti."

"Love it! But who really made it? You or Mike?"

Mike threw up his hands in surrender. "He's a good friend," he said, "but I'm not his personal chef."

Nick laughed. "My cooking would put his to shame any day. Trust me, you'll be glad I'm the one who actually cooked." He dished out two helpings of noodles onto two plates and then smothered them with sauce.

I took a seat at the small, round, glass kitchen table, and Nick set the plates down and sat across from me. "Oh!" he said, jumping up. "Would you like something to drink? Beer? Water? Coke?"

He went to the fridge and grabbed a beer for himself.

"A beer is good."

The noodles dangled from my fork before my first bite, threatening an embarrassing moment. How could I eat? I didn't want to slurp noodles in front of him! Then Mike diverted Nick's attention, so I took my chance and sucked in the first bite.

"Hey, man, forgot to tell you she called again," Mike said.

Nick's face fell. "Are you kidding? What did she say this time?"

Mike paused, glancing at me.

Caught eavesdropping, I looked down at my plate, wanting to be invisible.

"It's OK," Nick said. "You can talk in front of Shannon. That girl is psycho anyway."

"Well," Mike continued, "I think she's still thinking y'all have something going on."

My appetite was gone. Did he have a girlfriend?

Nick saw the expression on my face. "Oh. No," he said. "This is my ex-girlfriend. She'll try to get me back by saying anything. I heard the last thing she tried was to say she was pregnant."

*Pregnant!*

Nick reached across the table and squeezed my wrist. "But she's a freaking liar."

Mike laughed. "Yeah," he said. "He can't seem to get rid of 'em."

My vision cleared. There was no such thing as perfect, after all. "Are you sure she's not pregnant?"

Nick lost his smile. "Yeah, I'm sure. I'm not a complete jerk. I would've helped her out. You see, girls always try to make the guy look bad, you know? Turn things around to make it seem like the guy's fault?"

Mike cleared his throat. "OK, I'll leave you guys alone. I have to work all weekend, and I have an Eco test on Monday, so I'll be holed up in my room all night. Nice meeting you, Shannon."

"You too," I said, looking back at Nick. The air had changed, and it was my fault that it had. I should have kept my mouth shut.

"I wasn't trying to say you were a jerk," I said softly, looking down at the untouched spaghetti on my plate.

"Oh, I know," he said, reaching across the table to squeeze my hand. "All of that is just, well, it bugs the crap out of me. Let's forget it. Are you done?"

Dinner had been ruined. I nodded, biting my inner cheek and smiling to keep from tearing up.

Nick took our plates into the kitchen and then led me into the living room where we sat down on the blue-striped, L-shaped couch. "So what kind of movie do you want to watch? Comedy? Romance? Horror?"

"Whatever, I'm not picky."

He got up and began rummaging through a stack of movies by the TV, but then he hesitated. "I forgot this VCR is broken," he said. "I have one in my room, though. Do you mind if we watch a movie in there?"

Gullible, so gullible, I replied, "Sure."

We went into his bedroom and decided on an old romantic comedy, *When Harry Met Sally.*

His queen-sized bed was the only place to sit, so he propped some pillows up against the headboard for us to lean against. About ten minutes into the movie, Nick discarded the gentleman reverie, leaned over, kissed me, and pulled me into a prone position on the bed.

He was a good kisser, but the increasing urgency of his roaming hands lit my nerves with fear. I struggled to sit up. "Nick, wait," I said. "Can we slow down? I..."

What was I to tell him? I was far from being a virgin, and I was in his room. What was I to say? I released a frustrated grumble. "Ugh."

Quickly, he sat up. "What? Did I do something wrong?"

Embarrassed, because I was certain he was beginning to see me as a little freshman girl, I shook my head. "No! No!" I pleaded. "I don't know. I'm sorry. Can we just go slower? I don't want to do so much, you know, so soon. I'm dating someone out of town, and I wouldn't feel right."

His award-winning smile returned. "Sure," he said. "We don't have to do anything you don't want to. I just wanted to kiss you. But you know that guy doesn't live here. He doesn't need to know everything." He leaned over and kissed me again. "But, whatever, we can watch the movie."

So we did, for about another thirty minutes. Then he made his move again.

This time, I let my guard down. "He knows how I feel," I thought, "I can trust him. All we are doing is kissing." I tried to make myself feel comfortable about the situation. The next thing I knew, I was flat on my back again, and he was lying on his side next to me.

Then his free hand started roaming under my sweater. The all-too familiar vice of control overwhelmed me. I pushed up on his chest. "Wait," I said.

He stopped and leaned on his arm. "What's wrong?" He leaned down and kissed me again. "I know you're enjoying it. I'm not going to hurt you. I wouldn't do anything you don't want to do."

What was my problem? Why couldn't I enjoy this? Why was I suffocating? "I'm sorry," I said, looking up at his beautiful face. I was stupid. I laughed a quiet laugh, that sounded more like a hiccup, and said, "Never mind, I'm being stupid." Then I continued kissing him.

As the minutes progressed and Nick earned my trust by staying in my boundaries, I felt the tug of sexual desire arouse the need to which I was no stranger. Sensing the rise in chemistry, Nick felt comfortable to explore previously restricted areas.

Before long, the moment of affections and embraces had swirled into the likeness of the Tasmanian Devil, my pants were down, his pants were coming off, and cold, dense reality slapped me across the face.

"Wait!" I pleaded, buckling my knees together. "Wait, I'm so sorry." Breathing rapidly, I tried desperately to save face. "Nick, please, I can't do this. I'm sorry. I know I brought you to this, but I can't."

I could tell he had heard me, but he didn't stop. Instead, he went on about his mission.

Nearer to target, Nick's face was now close to mine. "Shannon, you want it. Just two seconds ago, you were more than willing."

Despite the voice inside my head that screamed, "Stop this! Stop this now! Wake up and do something, Shannon!" the fight in me had vanished. He was there. It was too close. I didn't want to be slapped again and forced to keep quiet. I didn't want to feel demeaned. He wanted me, but I needed it to be different. I was desperate to find the love that would make me whole again instead of this broken soul. My spirit was gone. In that moment I knew I had made another mistake and I had been making them all along. I was worth more than being treated like an object, but I was too defeated to fight back.

In the end it wasn't any different than it was with Paul except less violent. I did nothing. Nothing. I could've been a corpse and he didn't even notice. After he had finished, he kissed me on the mouth and then sat up to look at the clock. "I guess I should be getting you back."

Deflated, I lay on the bed, summoning life back into my useless body. I nodded in response.

He held my lifeless hand on the way to the car and on the drive to my dorm. When we arrived, he kissed me goodbye.

"Can we see each other tomorrow?"

Did it matter what I wanted? Did *I* matter? "Sure," I said, my voice flat.

He reached over and touched the bottom of my chin. "You OK?"

The gentleness in his eyes contradicted the insistent desire that had coursed through him. I nodded, afraid that I would cry if I tried to speak.

Later that night, I crawled into bed, closed my eyes and went to God for the first time in over four years. "God," I prayed, "I know I have not been the best person in the world. And I know I've let you down, but I am sad and I don't know what to do. I want to be happy. Please let me be happy."

Something stirred deep inside the very essence of my soul. It wasn't clear, or loud, and it was barely detectable, but it was raising me from death.

At around noon, the shrill ring of the telephone snatched me out of the deep recesses of numbing sleep. It was the front desk informing me of a delivery that was waiting for me in the lobby.

I stretched and looked out the window at the overcast day. A slight spatter of raindrops fell to the sidewalk below. The day matched my mood.

Down in the lobby, I tiptoed to the front desk on bare feet. "You have a delivery for me?" I asked.

The resident assistant behind the counter smiled and turned behind her for a single red rose. She picked it up and handed it to me.

"Are you sure?" I asked without hesitation.

"It says your name," she laughed. "You can read the card."

I set the rose back down on the counter and opened the card.

*"Looking forward to seeing you again."*—Nick

Poised for a free fall without a harness at the top of the world's tallest bridge, I was pushed into an unclear abyss. Was I happy? Was I flattered? What did I feel? Couldn't someone tell me how to feel?

"Ah, how sweet!" one of my less familiar sorority sisters said as she came into the lobby and ran over to me. "Who is it from?"

"Nick Ferrante," I muttered.

She did a mock full-body shiver. "He is so adorable! You are so lucky!"

Lucky?

"Thanks," I said, heading back to the elevators. "I'll see you Monday at the meeting."

Instead of going to my floor, I went to Kaitlyn and Meg's room.

After reading the card, they looked at me with wide eyes, ready to hear about the night. There were many firsts for me that day that led to my next fatal step.

A guy like Nick, who was popular, well known, and apparently well liked, had never taken an interest in me before. To be on the receiving end of such interest, awe, and envy from my friends tinged the dread in my gut with a bit of excitement and confusion.

I did not tell them about our sexual encounter because it did not mix well with the romantic tale of the home-cooked dinner and simple movie. I wanted to forget that moment and allow myself to relax in the seat of admiration.

When Nick called a few hours later, I tried to ignore the fire that smoldered in my stomach. He asked if we could go out again, but, despite the enjoyment of admiration, I surprised myself by turning him down.

The next day, Kaitlyn came up to my room, bubbling over with excitement. "Chad and Nick want to go on a double date!"

I was stunned.

"Shannon! What's wrong? I thought you'd be excited!"

"I am," I nodded, forcing a smile. "When? When are we doing this?"

"Tonight! We'll go bowling. Doesn't that sound like fun?"

"Definitely," I said, forcing another smile.

After she had left to get ready, I sat and deliberated the situation. We would be with other people, and maybe I could get a better idea of who he was and how he felt about me. Maybe I was wrong about him. Maybe I was paranoid that night, and had given him the wrong signals.

Bowling was fun. I laughed without feeling judged in the way that Daniel made me feel. Kaitlyn and Chad were a nice distraction as well.

That night, back at the dorm, Nick hugged me and kissed me on the lips. "Thanks for coming tonight. I feel bad about the other night and want you to know that I would never do anything to hurt you."

I wanted to believe him. It would be easier to recreate the night in my mind than carry around the humility of falling prey to another person.

Two days later, I went home for a weekend visit. The drive home cleared my mind and helped me rethink my situation with Daniel and Nick. Before the formal, Daniel and I had gone from talking nearly every day to a few days a week. Now, just one month later, we only talked about once a week.

I had no plans to meet up with Daniel at home, so I seized the moment and spent the time reconnecting with some high school girlfriends who were in town. It offered me a short break from the drama at school.

On the day I returned to school, the sorority had a chapter meeting to discuss that week's Greek Week activities, and everyone wanted to know my status with Nick. With all of the comments, like, "You are so lucky," and, "He's so awesome," it was easy to ride on the coattails of admiration. It was a feeling I'd longed for but could never quite obtain.

I decided that I was a fool for making that night into a horrific memory, and I was certain there was something wrong with me.

When I got home from the meeting, there was a message on the machine from Nick, asking me to go out on another date the following evening. He didn't mention what we were going to do or where we would be going, and, despite the euphoria that had surrounded me all night because of his admirers, the pain of uncertainty in my gut returned.

"I'll go out with him, but I won't go to his apartment," I told myself. "He deserves a chance, but I have the right to be cautious."

The next evening, he picked me up from the library where I had been studying, and, to my surprise, we didn't travel far at all. We drove across campus to the football field and pond.

"Let's go for a walk," he said with a smile.

I looked around the parking lot and was pleased to see other cars there as well, and a spatter of people walking, sitting by the pond, or studying on the bleachers. It was safe and comforting.

As we walked through the stadium and down the concrete stairs to the field, Nick told me about his family. His father passed away before he entered middle school, and he rebelled all through middle school and high school, because he hated his stepfather who abused his mother. He admitted that he had an anger problem, which was why he enjoyed football so much. It helped relieve him of his pent-up frustration.

He was so sad, and my heart ached for him. I could see the pain in his face and the weight on his shoulders. We stayed on the field in the middle of the stadium for a long time, talking about our families.

I told him about my sister Carrie and how worried I was for her because I hadn't heard from her in so long. But then again, I never called her, either. Sometimes it was easier to avoid communication with her so I did not have to deal with the disappointment of hearing her drug-induced, paranoid statements. She would whine about how everyone had it better than she did, despite the fact that Dad had given her everything, including an education, a car, and sometimes even rent money. It was her misuse of what Dad had given her that left her with nothing.

It felt good to talk about Carrie and the responsibility I had put on myself for my older sister. After a few hours, we were both exhausted from sharing, mentally drained, and not once did he try to make a move to kiss me. That was redeeming.

On the way back to my dorm, he took my hand in his. "Will you stay with me tonight?"

The warmth from the evening drained out of every pore in my body. "No," I answered with new confidence. "I'm sorry. I'm glad we did this tonight, but I'm not ready to be alone with you."

"Shannon," he pleaded, "I'm sorry about that night. I am. I won't ever make you do something you don't want to do."

"Nick, I can't," I said. "It's not you, not really." I felt tears brimming behind my eyes, but I refused to cry. I bit my lip. I wanted to be strong.

We were at the door to my dorm. "OK," he sighed. "I'll be patient." He leaned down and kissed me gently on the lips. "Goodnight."

The following day was the Greek Week tennis tournament. As I sat on the sidelines with all of my pledge sisters, Nick walked up.

"Shannon, wow," someone said behind me. "He's hooked."

I smiled. He came and sat down next to me and stayed for the entire match. Nick was a genius with women. He included all of them in conversations and said things to make them feel important. And on that sunny day, having to sit and watch an uneventful match of tennis, my pledge sisters welcomed the diversion.

After Nick had left, over an hour later, I went deaf from the squeals of approval. "He's so nice and cute!"

"Isn't he dating that Tri-Delt®, Amanda Barnes?" Liz Rowland, the active who had found Nick and I talking at the social, questioned.

"They broke up a while ago," answered Courtney, another active. "I'd heard she was pregnant, and then they broke up."

"Yeah, he told me about that," I said. "She wasn't really pregnant. He didn't seem to be too happy with her because the pregnancy was something to keep him around. I mean, that's what he told me."

Liz rolled her eyes and then got up and walked away.

I wanted to get up and follow her to find out why she was the one person who seemed to be against Nick, but I didn't know her well enough. She was two years older, and that intimidated me.

Two days later, I had another date with Nick. We had spoken on the phone every night for the past week, and he would end every night's conversation by asking me out. This time, I accepted. He was trying to prove he was a changed man, so I took the step and trusted.

He picked me up from the dorm to go to a movie. Dressed in jeans and a new cashmere sweater I had bought the weekend before, I believed there was nothing about me that marked me as "easy."

Past actions never crossed my mind.

"You look amazing, as usual," he said, leaning down for a kiss. At the car, he opened the door, and once we were inside he took my hand. "Is there a movie out that you want to see?"

I thought about it. "Uh, I'm not sure. Let's see something funny this time, though."

He drove east, away from the dorm and in the opposite direction of the movie theater.

"Where are you going?" I asked.

"Oh," he said as he brought my hand up to his lips and kissed it. "I need to go by my apartment. I forgot my wallet."

My cheeks burned. I was a fool.

When we reached his apartment, I wouldn't budge. He got out of the car, came around to my door, and opened it.

"I'll stay in the car," I said, mustering up a smile.

"Oh, come on. We can go inside and figure out which movie to see."

Either I *was* a fool, or I *looked* like a fool. Not sure which.

Despite the voice that screamed inside my head, I wanted to trust him and believe that he had changed. "OK," I said, reluctant to get out of the car.

We walked into his apartment, and my heart dropped more when I realized that Mike wasn't home. "Where's Mike?" I said.

"Oh, he's not coming home tonight. He had to go home. Something to do with his family, I don't know." Nick walked down the hall to his bedroom.

I remained in the living room, perched on the edge of the L-shaped couch.

"Hey, I forgot that Mike rented this movie," he said as he came back into the living room, holding a video in his hand. "What if we watched this here?"

I stood up. "Well, what about the movies?"

"I didn't think there was anything you were dying to see."

He had me. I didn't know what to say. I was torn between running out the door and giving him a second chance.

"Shannon," he said as he came closer and touched the tip of my chin to lift my face up to his. "I said you could trust me. I won't do anything you don't want. We'll sit here on this couch and watch the movie. That's it." He smiled and turned away. "I'll even sit on this side of the couch, and you can sit on that side."

I laughed, but inside my gut was wrestling with my pride. "Shut up. I'm sorry," I said. Pride had won, and I sat down on the couch. "I want to see that movie anyway."

"You want anything to drink? Beer? Coke?"

"I'll take a glass of water," I said.

He went to the kitchen, got himself a beer and my water, put the movie in the VCR, and sat down next to me on the couch.

Once we were engrossed into the plot of the movie, Nick slumped down on the couch and reached over to grab my hand. I welcomed the contact, and, for the first time that night, I allowed the tension to seep out of my shoulders. It was nice sitting there, watching the movie and holding hands.

When the movie ended, Nick sat up just enough to kiss me.

I welcomed it.

Then, in the midst of making out, he got up from the couch and picked me up.

"Hey!" I cried out.

"Don't worry," he said. "I'm tired, and I want to lie down with you." He carried me to his room.

The tension came back, and my limbs went rigid. "No, let's just stay on the couch."

"Shannon," he sighed, "I'm not going to do anything. I'm tired. You never want to stay with me, and all I want is to sleep next to you." He put me down on his bed.

I sat up, but he turned around and grabbed my shoulders. His fingers dug into my skin as he looked me in the eye. It had been a long time since I had seen that look.

The look of the Devil.

His eyes were coal black and empty, and his brow creased into a sharp V. "I'm not going to do anything," he said pointedly, thrusting a T-shirt into my lap. "Put this on."

"But…"

His fingers tightened so much that I thought I could hear the bone crack in my shoulder.

I was stuck.

What would he do if I didn't? What would he do if I did?

With trembling fingers, I began to unbutton my sweater. He let go of my shoulders and turned his back to get something out of the dresser. I looked toward the door. Could I run?

I prayed to God, asking him to help me, but in my heart I didn't expect him to listen. I had put myself in Nick's bedroom. I had put myself into every bed I had been in for the past two years. I had walked away from God, and I couldn't blame him for not helping me then.

I was frozen on the bed. I could have run. I should have run. I didn't run.

*Keep yourself alive*, my spirit whispered to my soul.

He watched me finish undressing and slip the T-shirt over my head before he turned the lights off.

I gathered the courage to try and reason with him again. "Nick, don't be mad," I said. "I just don't feel comfortable." His silhouette moved in the darkness, and I could feel his breath on my neck.

"Lie down, Shannon. I'm tired. All I want to do is go to sleep."

"OK, but why do I need to be here? I have class tomorrow. I'll call my roommate, and she can come get me."

He grabbed my wrist with so much force that it felt as if he could snap it with one simple squeeze. "What, and go change things around? No, come on, Shannon! Go to sleep."

I scooted to the other side of the bed, and he lay down and put his arm over my chest, forcing me into a prone position. A few minutes passed, and I lay stiff as a board under the weight of his arm. It seemed like ages, but with each second I began to feel hope that maybe that was all that would take place. Nick would sleep, and I would keep watch.

Then his arm moved, and he began to touch me.

"Nick," I begged. "You said you wanted to sleep. I really don't want to do this." I tried to push his arm away, but he sat up and grabbed both of my wrists.

"Why are you teasing me!" he yelled. "If I wanted to have sex I'd go get it from Amanda!"

Fear gripped my soul. He was hurting my wrists, and even in the darkness I could see the wild, manic look on his face and hear it in his voice.

Fear, raw and exposed.

Fear rendered me frozen.

Fear for my life. "God, help me! Daddy help me!" I screamed inside. "I don't want to be here anymore!"

"OK, I'm sorry," I said, as calmly as I could, as though my life were at stake. "I didn't mean to hurt your feelings."

"You frustrate me, Shannon."

"I'm sorry."

He leaned in and kissed me hard on the mouth.

*Leave,* a voice in my head told me.

I lay there, but I wasn't there. He did things to me, but I did not feel them. My spirit had left. I felt as if it had risen from my body and no longer had to inhabit the filth that was occurring.

*He's talking!* The voice said. *Go back! Go back!*

"What's your problem?" he huffed. He leaned on his side and put his hand where he shouldn't have. "You don't even look like you're enjoying yourself. Are you mute?"

*Do what he wants so he'll be done.*

"I'm sorry," I whispered, trying to smile.

*Give him what he wants so he'll be done.*

He was pleased I had spoken and grinned like the Cheshire Cat.

I wanted to claw his eyes out.

When it was over, I couldn't stop the tears. The levy had been broken. I curled into a fetal position and wailed into the pillow.

He tried to hug me, and the gesture made me laugh with hysteria through my tears.

"I love you, Shannon," he said.

I cried harder. He was insane.

"You don't have to feel guilty because I love you. I know what your problem is. You don't want to be thought of as easy. I know, but I love you. It's OK." His voice dripped with honey, so thick and sticky that the words stuck to my brain.

"I want to go home," I said, lifting my head off the pillow. I thought that, maybe, since he was satisfied, he would finally listen.

"Why?" he demanded, pain contorting his face.

"He is crazy," I thought. Stark, raving mad.

"Because, Nick, I just do. Please take me home. Let me get my clothes on and take me home. I want to be home. In my own bed. I want to sleep by myself. Please take me home." I was rambling, but the worst was over. My fear was gone. He couldn't do anything worse to me, even if he killed me. My spirit was dead, so it didn't matter.

"Stay the night," he said. "I'll take you in the morning." He was pleading now. The demand was gone.

"No, Nick. Please take me home."

He moved off the bed, and I scrambled off to search for my clothes on the floor.

"Fine," he said. "I'll take you home." His shoulders drooped as if he had been defeated.

On the ride home, my hand held firm to the door handle, and my body hugged the side of the door. Not a word was spoken until we made it to the dorm.

"I'll call tomorrow," he said as I jumped out.

I didn't look back.

My roommate was asleep when I barged through the door. She sat up in alarm.

"What's wrong?" She mumbled, barely awake.

*Tell her!* My spirit screamed. *Tell her! Tell her!*

No, she's Amanda's sorority sister, my pride reasoned.

*Tell her!*

What if she doesn't believe me?

*Tell her!*

"Are you OK?" she asked again, rubbing her eyes.

I hesitated. "I…"

"Oh hey," she said as she pulled the covers back, got out of bed, and grabbed a note off of my desk. "You had a few calls tonight. Daniel called, and he said to call him as soon as you got home."

She handed me the paper. I couldn't speak.

"I have a test tomorrow, so I'm going back to sleep. It won't bother me if you call him back though." She crawled back into bed and pulled the covers up over her head.

I stood there, holding the paper, surprised that my trembling wasn't making the entire dorm room quake.

Suddenly, I felt dirty. Dirty. Dirty. Dirty. Dirty.

The bathroom we shared with our suitemates was empty. In less than two seconds, I was in the shower. *Hot* water only.

I scrubbed my body with a bar of soap, desperate to cleanse away the force of his hands, the remnants of his evil, and the stench of my stupidity.

Desperate to be clean.

Desperate to forget.

I fell, cowering in the corner, tears flowing out until all of my pity and self-implication had been exhausted. At some point, the hot water became very cold. Finally, I stood up, turned it off, and stepped out to dry off.

"Tell Daniel," I thought. I needed to tell someone and thought Daniel should be the one. He loved me, he was my best friend, and he would know what to say and do.

I opened the bathroom door, tiptoed into the bedroom, grabbed the phone, and pulled it into the bathroom for privacy. Sitting on the seat of the toilet, wrapped in a towel, I called Daniel.

"Hello?"

I heard the strumming of a guitar in the background. "Hi," I managed to say.

"Hey, where you been?"

I started to cry. My body shivered uncontrollably.

"Shannon? What's wrong?"

I had really let him down. "Daniel, I'm sorry."

"Sorry for what? What happened?"

"I went out with this guy, Nick." I said, pausing to gauge his reaction.

He remained silent. The guitar music stopped.

*Tell him, he'll understand,* said the voice inside me.

"Daniel, we had sex. But I didn't want to! He forced me!" The tears turned into racking sobs.

Silence.

"Daniel," I sobbed. "Please talk to me. I promise you I didn't want to. It was horrible. He made me. He was horrible, and I was afraid."

When he finally spoke, his one word dripped with sarcasm. "Really?"

I froze. My sobbing ceased. Now I was frantic.

"Yes! Daniel," I pleaded, "please believe me. I didn't want to do anything with him."

"Then why did you go out with him?"

Dry. He was so dry.

"What do you mean? We said we were going to date other people."

"Yeah, but not have sex with them."

167

"I didn't want to have sex with him! He made me!"

Then it hit me: he didn't believe me. He didn't believe that I didn't want to have sex with Nick.

"OK, well, I guess that's it."

Panic.

"Daniel," I pleaded, "I'm being honest. I didn't go out with him wanting to have sex."

"I need time to think about this," he said. "I'll call you when I'm ready."

My mouth remained open, my eyes widened, and my fist wrapped so tightly around the receiver that my knuckles turned white. I couldn't think. I couldn't move. I couldn't even breathe.

"Eegh, eegh, eegh. Please hang up and try your call again. Eegh, eegh, eegh. Please hang up and try your call again." The recording mocked me from the receiver.

The fog of dismay faded. I came to and hung up the phone. Sitting up straight, I heaved a big long sigh. That was how it was going to be. No one would believe me if my own boyfriend wouldn't.

My lips were sealed.

# The Devil's
# Last Chance

Then war broke out in heaven, Michael and his angels battled against
the dragon. The dragon and its angels fought back, but they did not
prevail, and there was no longer any place for them in heaven
—Revelation 12:7–8

LIKE A TODDLER with a lollipop, I held onto anger, resentment,
abandonment, and pain as if they were the only emotions that could
sustain my existence. Nick tried to call and carry on as though all that
had transpired between us was normal. I refused to talk to him, which
caused him to ask obvious questions. My roommate didn't understand
my sudden loss of interest in him, and neither did my sorority sisters.

Eventually, my lame excuse that I "just didn't like him anymore"
held its weight. The phone stopped ringing and my friends stopped
asking.

My message never changed, but my attitude did. I refused to go on
dates with any new prospects, stayed close to my friends, and the only
guys I trusted were Jason, Derek, and their fraternity brothers, because
I was a little sister for the fraternity. My pessimism reached new levels.

There was no way around it: life sucked.

My sense of self-worth had been beaten to a pulp and left barely alive on pride's cold tile floor. My confused thoughts and feelings were at war within me, though I didn't realize the battle was a holy war yet. It began on a Sunday evening while studying for midterms at Cain's apartment. Cain was a member of Jason and Derek's fraternity. He was close friends with them and had been like a big brother to me over the past few months. Everything about him was non-threatening. He was average in height and looks, with short blonde hair that was cut for the business world. Plus, he had a girlfriend who was fun and that I adored. I felt very safe and secure. We had economics together, and when he offered to study with me, I jumped at the opportunity, because I was awful at anything besides talking and writing.

My car was in the shop, so Cain picked me up from the dorm and we went to his apartment to study at his kitchen table. Two hours into studying, he got up and stretched. "I think I've had it with economics," he said. "I'm going to watch a movie." Then he walked to his door and locked it.

I had my head down and was reading a paragraph in the book when I heard the click of the lock. I looked up, not registering what he had done, and went back to reading.

"Shannon, take a break and come watch this with me!"

"You might be done with economics, but I need to finish reading this," I said. "I can't fail this test!" I looked up to see him sitting on the loveseat holding a remote.

"Take a break! Come on! We've been studying for two hours!"

He made a face that made me laugh. "OK, let me finish this chapter, and I'll take a break."

When I was done, I got up and stretched. I did need a break, because all the information was beginning to run together. I went and sat down on the couch next to him. "OK, what are you watching?" I asked.

"*Twin Peaks* the movie," he answered. "Have you ever seen it?"

That was when it happened. A feeling I hadn't felt in many years snuck back up my spine and burned the back of my neck. I had heard very little about *Twin Peaks*. It was a movie that had first been a TV series. I wasn't really certain of its plot, but I did know that it had to do with the murder of a girl and was supposedly quite mystical. For some reason, I had no desire to watch the movie.

"Not for me," I said, getting up to head back to the kitchen table.

Cain leaned over and grabbed my arm, pulling me back down onto the couch. "Watch the movie with me."

I want to say it was Cain that I saw—that it was his blue eyes and gentle smile that spat out the words like venom. But it was not. His eyes were a black abyss, and his face literally dripped evil. His hand was still on me, and it was ice cold.

"Cain?" I whispered.

"You will watch the movie," he said with a voice that wasn't his and in such a way that I knew that my only option was to sit there.

I sat there with my forearm in his death grip, but I refused to watch. Instead, I kept my face on Cain's, cursing myself for being the most naïve girl in the world and getting caught in another predicament. But this wasn't like the other ones. This was evil in its rarest form. There was even a familiar stench of burning in the room that hadn't been there moments before. It awakened memories of that day when I was eight years old, standing on the sidewalk in an El Paso evening, looking into the same face of evil.

I had been brought back to a battle I hadn't encountered in nearly ten years. Out of instinct, I began to pray the Our Father and Hail Mary over and over again in my mind, and pleading for the evil to go away in the name of Jesus.

About halfway into the movie, the stench went away, and the oppression in the room lifted. I recognized Cain again.

"Cain," I said, my voice shaking, "would you mind taking me home? I need to get some sleep."

Without looking at me, he let go of my arm, hopped off the couch, and switched off the TV. "I know!" he said in a shrill voice. Cain was back but not himself. "Let's do the Ouija board!"

Standing, I screamed, "No!"

He disappeared down the hall, and I heard him say, "Oh, come on, Shannon. It's fun!" Then he came back with the board in his hand.

"Cain, please take me home now!" I yelled. "You are scaring me, and I don't want to do the Ouija board!" I was shaking.

In a split second, Cain snapped to. "OK," he said in his normal gentle tone. "Are you done studying?"

"Yes," I said, afraid to say anything more for fear he'd switch again. I went to the table and gathered my books. He unlocked the door, and we got in his car for a tense and silent ride home.

At the dorm, he turned to me and said, "I'll see you in class!" as if nothing was out of the ordinary. I hopped out of the car and stumbled, trying to get to the door as quickly as I could.

That must have been my imagination. What was wrong with me? Why was I attracting these evil people? Dear God, was I really crazy? My mind spun with uncertainty.

When I walked in, the room was dark, so I knew Lauren was asleep. Afraid to be alone in the dark, I turned on the bathroom light and cracked the door so there was enough light to get ready for bed. When I was done, I was afraid to turn off the light and get in bed. The eerie feeling of an evil presence was still toying with my nerves.

I shook it off, quickly turned off the light, and hopped into bed. I tried to take deep breaths and relax, but the feeling held on. The air was thick, and, as I lay in bed, I felt out of place.

When I turned to rest on my side, I saw him—or rather, it.

It was a demon crouching in the corner.

Bursting through its hideous, shadow-covered face were its green eyes. For a split second, I truly believed I had come undone.

"I've gone mad," I thought, panicked. "Take me away and lock me up."

I didn't want to believe it was there, but I felt the fear it was trying to instill. I flipped over onto my back and prayed as I had as a child. I prayed that a legion of angels would come and knock it out of the room. My heart thumped, bruising my chest as I began to battle for my soul.

"In the name of Jesus Christ, go away. Our Father, who art in heaven…"

It was still there. I didn't have to look. I could feel it.

It wanted me back.

"In the name of Jesus Christ, go away. Hail Mary, full of grace, the Lord is with thee…"

My eyes squeezed tight. I crossed my arms over my chest and settled in for the prayerful fight. "I am saved by the blood of Christ. Our Father, who art in heaven, hallowed be thy name. Hail Mary, full of grace, the Lord is with thee. Pray for me, Mary. St. Michael, the archangel, defend me in battle. Be my protection against the wickedness and snares of the Devil. Our Father, who art in heaven…"

Over and over and over again, I repeated the Our Father, Hail Mary, and the prayer to St. Michael. I asked any and every saint in heaven to pray for me. I had no choice. For my life, I knew I needed to pray.

Sunlight peeked through the blinds of our room. My eyes were wide open, and, although the feeling of fear, evil, and despair had passed, I remained on my back with my arms folded across my chest. I was lost in a world of peace, unable to blink, speak, or move. Lauren began to toss and turn in her bed, and finally I could hear her talking to me. It was as if she were in a vacuum. Her words were there, but they were not coherent.

She stood over me, looking down at my face, waving a hand in front of my eyes. She reached down, picked up my arm, and I felt it flop back down on my chest.

A look in her eyes pulled me from the peace in which I had been floating.

"Shannon!" she yelled. "What is wrong?"

"It's OK," I managed to whisper, my voice sounding muffled, as though it were miles away. I knew there was no plausible excuse to give. "I'm—just—exhausted." I tried to swallow, but my throat felt like sandpaper.

She stood up straight and then bent back over to feel my forehead. "Well, you don't have a fever."

"I'm fine," I managed again, finally convincing her to get ready and go to class.

It took all morning for me to gain strength enough to sit up in bed. I was mentally and physically exhausted.

It took a while to come around and get dressed. I didn't want to speak to anyone for fear of losing what little strength remained. Plus, I was afraid my emotions would betray me, and I would wind up sobbing and spurting out the entire strange ordeal landing me in a mental institution. I *knew* I wasn't crazy because the peace given to me as a child had returned.

"The Devil wants you." These were the words spoken by the first face of evil I had ever met, and it was the same face I saw in Cain. That night, the rush of understanding had taken my breath away. I was no longer under the Devil's influence. My choice had changed, and I was listening to God again. I had pissed the Devil off, and he was trying to show me what he could do.

Walking to economics to take the test, I shuddered to think the Enemy could be so real that he could reach me through someone like Cain. I avoided Cain as best I could, not looking in his direction for fear of catching a glimpse of his eyes. I did my best to focus on the exam. Afterwards, I skipped out of class and went down the hall, hoping to avoid any chance of him following me. But I wasn't fast enough.

"Shannon! Wait!" Cain called, his hurried footsteps close behind. As I opened the door of the building to the courtyard, the following sentence came from behind me like an impact from a baseball bat:

"I know you had a visitor last night."

It knocked the breath out of me.

A crowd of students wanting to exit pushed me into the sunlight.

Bewildered, I looked around, but Cain was nowhere in sight.

"He didn't say it," I reasoned with my sanity. My heart pounded in my chest. I was just stressed. I had lost Daniel, and no one knew about

Nick. A lot had happened. I was not losing my mind. No one would understand, but I was not crazy. But why? Why me?

The following week was spring break. I made no plans other than to take a trip home and get away from the insanity. I left two days after the economics exam, and for the first time all year I was anxious to get back home.

It was nice reestablishing a relationship with Morgan. When I got home, the last thing I wanted was to be alone. The past few weeks had left me vulnerable, and constant companionship was what I needed. I wasn't ready to tell anyone about Nick, and it would have made no sense to divulge Cain's behavior. Besides, Morgan seemed excited to have me home, especially since I had taken an interest in going places with her. We went to the movies, out to eat, and shopping. We did all the things we should have always done as sisters.

Unfortunately, by association with me, Morgan became an innocent bystander caught in the battlefield of my malevolent reality.

A few days into the break, while I was upstairs with my mother talking about a bent towel hanger, Morgan let out a scream of terror downstairs. Mom and I dropped the items in our hands and ran downstairs.

Sitting in the living room in a rocking chair with a pair of headphones on her ears, Morgan's skin was practically translucent, and her already big blue eyes were in obvious shock.

"It moved by itself!" she yelled, her voice piercing through the room as she pointed at something on the floor.

Mom and I walked around the couch to see what she was pointing at and saw the lid of a china dish on the floor. As if on command, Mom and I swiveled our heads to the right to find its base. It was as it should have been—five feet off the floor, resting in place on the mahogany china cabinet.

Full of life again, Morgan tore the headphones from her head and scrambled off of the chair. She circled the lid as if it held lethal volts of energy. At the china cabinet, she pointed to the base and said in the same hysterical voice, "That lid lifted up and then out and floated over here." She gingerly retraced the path of the lid to where it rested. "And then it just fell and landed!"

Following every word and every move that she made, Mom and I both looked at her with mouths agape.

"I'm not lying!" she screamed.

The phone rang.

I hesitated before answering the phone because I wanted to tell Morgan I believed her. I knew more than anything that she was speaking the truth. Mom picked up the lid and put it back on the base, and on the third ring I answered the phone.

"How did you like that?"

"Hello," I said, not sure I heard the caller clearly.

"Wasn't that fun?" said a voice, laughing.

My hand gripped the receiver. "Who is this?"

"You know who this is, Shannon. You couldn't hide from me. The spirits were anxious to be called to your house."

A smell like burnt rubber filled my nostrils. "Cain, this isn't funny. I don't know what's gotten into you, but these tricks you are playing aren't cool."

"Tricks? Oh, they aren't tricks. These spirits have been with you for a long time. It's fun getting to see what they see. I know that you're wearing black shorts and a striped shirt, and your sister," he said, pausing to laugh, "is cute as can be, listening to her music and then screaming her head off like a baby. It was a harmless act, really."

"You are sick," I hissed into the phone. "You are evil and you need help. Do not ever contact me again and don't even look my way on campus." I hung up the phone and raced into the living room.

Morgan was sitting in the rocking chair crying. I went over to her and knelt down. "I'm sorry," I said. "I do believe you."

"It really happened, Shannon. I don't know why, but it did. I'm not crazy!"

"I know you're not." I knew better than anyone that she wasn't crazy.

# Same Life...
# New Chapter

Take no part in the fruitless works of darkness; rather expose them, for it is shameful even to mention the things done by them in secret; but everything exposed by the light, becomes visible, for everything that becomes visible is light.

—Ephesians 5:11–13

CAIN AND HIS world were far beyond anything I could comprehend. I knew that what had transpired was real, but the logical side of me wanted to push it to the recesses of my mind and continue on with what little life I had left at school. I was in survival mode. I continued to ignore Cain in class, and, since the "visitations" stopped, I think the message was clear.

Despite the fact that my experience of literally seeing evil should have turned me into an overzealous, religious fanatic and made me fight for whatever good was left in my soul, I continued to feel unworthy of having God in my life every day. I wasn't being disrespectful to him; I simply felt I was doing God a favor by staying away. What could he do with me? Besides, who would listen to a young girl who had been raped twice and now said she had seen demons? The thought was a stretch, even for me, and I had lived it. It was easier to try to morph into what was normal and sane.

At the end of the school year, close to finals week, despite myself (and probably as a way to prove that I was still normal), I developed a friendship with a guy who reminded me of Matt. He was six foot seven inches tall, and his vivacious attitude and smile melted the iron I had built up around my heart. Desperate to feel normal and find the love that had proven itself unattainable, I fell for him hard.

His name was John, and we started as friends. We studied together, talked about life, sat outside, and looked at the stars. But soon, the day came when he leaned down and kissed me.

Wow!

I'm not sure whether he made his move because I was desperate or because it really is true that some people have a chemical connection, but that kiss left me weak in the knees. We were inseparable those last three weeks of our freshman year. He never did anything but kiss me, and he didn't expect any more from me, either.

There was something about John that I wanted to hold on to. I became clingy, and my desperation showed through my words and actions.

When the time came to move back home for the summer, we promised to take turns traveling between hometowns. We did this a few times, met each other's families, and talked on the phone every day when we were apart.

Then, just like that, it ended. We were on the phone at the time, and he had just asked how my day had been.

"Oh, you know, it sucked," I whimpered. "Work is lame, I don't have a car to drive, my parents are nagging me to do more around here, and I miss you. I can't wait to come see you this weekend." I ached to see him. He was the only thing that made me happy.

Apparently, that was too much pressure.

"Uh, about that," he said, "I don't think you should come visit me anymore."

My heart stopped, and my body tingled from lack of oxygen. "What? Why? It's all planned."

"Shannon, I think...I don't think we should see each other anymore."

My heart crumbled and spread throughout my chest. The pain was excruciating. "Why?" I whispered through a clenched, dry throat.

"I don't get you anymore," John said. "You are always negative. You complain about something every time we talk. Nothing seems to make you happy but me, and that's not normal. I don't get it. I've never heard someone so cynical before."

"I'm happy!" I pleaded, sitting up and tightening my grip on the phone. "I'm sorry, John. A lot has gone on with me and..."

I tried to continue, but the words were choked by the tears that wouldn't stop flowing.

"I can tell a lot is going on with you, but you don't ever talk about it and you seem pissed. Mad at the world. It's not fun. I'm sorry," he said, and he hung up the phone.

My wails were so loud, they brought my mom into the room. "What's going on?" she asked.

I was curled up on my bed in a fetal position, clenching the bedspread in my fists. "John just broke up with me!"

"Oh, Shannon," she said, patting my back. "Why?"

I turned my head towards her. "He says I'm too negative."

Her face dropped, and I could see the worry in her eyes. "What do you think?"

I think I'm going crazy, I thought. "I don't know. I don't mean to be."

"Would you want to go talk to someone about it?"

I lay there in silence, allowing the idea to register, and finally, I asked, "Like who?"

"A counselor," she said. "I can make you an appointment."

The air was coming back into my lungs, and as I struggled to catch my breath, I hiccupped and then relaxed with a long sigh. "OK," I said, anxious to find out if I was really insane.

On Wednesday afternoon, as I walked into Alice Birmingham's tranquil office for my first counseling visit, I felt an impending doom. To have to dredge up all of the pain that had been inflicted upon me was like sticking my hand into a vat of hissing snakes that were ready to strike.

After being called out of the waiting area into an adjoining room, I was relieved to see a pleasant looking woman in her late forties or early fifties. She was my height, with a firm handshake and gentle voice. She directed me to a seat in front of her desk, and we both sat down.

"It is so good to meet you. I know your mom and dad, and they are both so wonderful," she said with a smile, adjusting her legs to make it easier to write on the legal pad that was on her lap.

Inside, I frowned. Everyone knew my parents. "Do you talk to my parents a lot?" I asked.

Sensing my discomfort, she sat up, and a more serious look came across her face. "Oh, I would not tell them what we speak about in here," she said. "This is our session. You have client confidentiality."

My shoulders relaxed a little, and she looked at me, waiting for me to say something. I wished I could hit some sort of button inside that would spew forth everything that had been poisoning me. I wanted to get it all out, but saying even the first word of the first sentence proved to be more difficult than I had anticipated.

After a very long minute or two, Ms. Birmingham spoke up. "When your mom called, she said you seemed very sad or upset about something. She said it wasn't like you to be so withdrawn. Maybe if we talked about this feeling your mom is sensing, we can work from there?"

My mom had noticed? Without warning, I released a flood of bottled emotion, and, leaning forward from the pressure of it all, I wept into my hands.

Pain. Pain. Pain.

Pain coursed through my veins and ran through my body, tightening my heart and searing the tips of the memories of my stupid actions. "It's all my fault," I managed to say.

Immediately, she was at my side with a box of tissues and a supportive hand on my back. "What is your fault?" she asked.

"Everything," I said, crying louder. I sat up, took one of the tissues, and wiped my face. Oh, boy, it hurt.

"Why don't you tell me," she said, "and maybe we can work on who's at fault."

I had bubbled over. Through puffy eyes and blurred vision, I looked at Ms. Birmingham and realized that I was desperate to talk. "I'm not the person my parents think I am," I began.

For the next hour, I tried my best to give her an overview of everything that had fought to consume my joy. I spoke of Matt's death, the violent loss of my virginity, of Nick raping me, not once but twice, due to my insecurity and stupidity, and of my absolute loss of trust in any friend or man.

Until the buzzer ended our session, I spoke so much that she had been unable to interject through my laundry list of shame and sorrow. "We have a lot to cover, don't we?" she said.

"Yeah," I laughed. "I guess we do."

"I don't normally see clients twice a week, but because of all that you are working through, I'd like to begin next week seeing you on Mondays and Wednesdays. How do you feel about that?"

"I'd like that," I said, surprised at the relief it had brought.

"Good, then over the weekend, think about what you want to work on the most, and we'll go from there."

It felt good to tell. I had thought that because I had made my decisions alone I would have to live with the consequences alone. Talking to Ms. Birmingham, however, shed light to a clearer path.

At home, oblivious to what I was working through in therapy, my parents refused to allow me the luxuries of sleeping in and lounging by the pool. They encouraged me to get a job.

I was happy to get a job, to meet new people, and have a life.

I got my summer entertainment working as a hostess at a Mexican restaurant. The job was a no-brainer, and the group who worked there instantly became my new party buddies. One tall, skinny, refreshingly cute guy named Steve latched onto me and saved me from myself.

Steve didn't come on strong. In fact, he didn't come on to me at all. We were like two lost puppies, pathetically trying to find their way back home, where it was nice, warm, and comfortable, but who, along the way, had been shoved into a garbage bag and thrown out of a truck onto a deserted road. When Steve and I found each other, we found the courage to walk a new path.

One night, after a long day of work, we sat with each other and allowed the stories of our lives to unravel. After marrying very young, he had recently been divorced, and he had a beautiful one-year-old daughter. His marriage hadn't been able to withstand the lack of maturity and infidelity brought into it. After hearing his sorrow, I found it easy to share my own, feeling camaraderie in pain.

As the night progressed, the moon illuminated the parking lot, where we sat on the hood of my car. I let out a long sigh, and felt the foreign feeling of release. In a matter of days, I had been able to tell my story to two strangers, and neither of them had mocked me.

"Do you pray?" Steve said, breaking the silence and stopping his fiddling with the cuff of his long-sleeved Oxford.

"Pray?" I said, sitting up and crossing my legs. My heart started racing, and the events with Cain came to mind.

"Yeah, I mean I know you're Catholic. I heard you tell Fred you couldn't work till noon on Sundays because of Mass or something?"

I shrugged my shoulders. "I go to Mass because my parents go to Mass."

"Why don't you like to go?" he asked.

"I never said I didn't like to go," I said as my chest tightened.

He sat up, hopped off of the car, and stood in front of me. "Hey, I wasn't trying to make you mad. I was just asking a question."

"I'm not mad," I said, trying to sound indifferent. "To be honest, I hadn't really thought about it." In fact I had, though. I felt guilty for my lack of prayer, especially after the unexplainable night of prayer in my dorm room. But I couldn't get past my feeling of unworthiness.

"But do you pray?"

"What is with this guy," I thought. "Yeah, I guess," I lied.

"You guess? Huh…"

"What?" I said. Now I was irritated. "What's that supposed to mean?"

"I didn't figure you to be the type."

"Type?"

"Yeah, you know. Mad at God. Might as well do what I want because he doesn't care."

"I'm not mad at God!"

"OK, OK!" he said, throwing his hands up in the air. "I was, and I thought I saw that in you, too. Sorry, forgive me."

Hopping down from the car, I searched in my purse for my keys. "Whatever," I said, as I found them and unlocked the door. "I mean, where did all that come from, anyway?"

He came over, and, with concern, he looked into my eyes. "Because I used to be angry, too, and I don't want you to end up like me." He extended his arm and turned his hand over to reveal two ragged, ugly scars along his wrist.

The blood left my face.

"If I wasn't such a coward, I would've cut deeper, and it would've worked. It's the one time I thank God for being a coward."

Like a flash of light, the awkward moment turned into red hot anger. "Well, I'm not like that. I don't ever intend on killing myself."

He dropped his hand, smirked, and shook his head. "Yeah, maybe you won't literally kill yourself, but when I listen to you talk, you are going through the motions. You are negative about life, and your eyes have no life in them."

"Whatever," I spat out petulantly. But I knew he was right. Inside, I was dying. I was going crazy, and I knew that a huge part of me had been lost. Here I was with a mere stranger who was saying the same things John had said. If there was truth to their words, that meant that I had to face reality and realize that my brave persona wasn't fooling anyone.

"Let me go to Mass with you tomorrow," he said. "It's been a long time since I've been to a Catholic church."

"Why? It'll be confusing." Now he was stepping on a foreign boundary. I felt uncomfortable, but I wasn't sure why. It wasn't like I attended Mass faithfully. I kept my faith, or lack of it, private, mainly because I didn't understand where I stood with God.

He shrugged. "You can explain it to me."

"I barely know you," I said. "You haven't even met my parents."

His smile widened. "This bothers you, doesn't it?"

"Yeah!" I nodded, grateful to be honest.

"Well, don't let it." he said, jumping back and laughing. He appeared to be filled with a new burst of energy. "OK! You need to get home and go to bed, and I'll see you in the morning!"

"Do you know where the church is?"

"It's the only Catholic church in town. Yeah, I know where it is. Which Mass do you go to?"

"The one at 9:30," I said, opening my car door and getting in.

He leaned over the door before I could shut it. "Thanks for listening tonight."

"Yeah," I said, pausing to appreciate the peace I felt inside. "I need to thank you for believing me."

He winked and shut the door, waving as he jogged to the other side of the parking lot to his car.

"Strange," I thought. "He didn't even try to kiss me. He listened, and he believed me. Plus, he wants to go to Mass?"

The next morning, on the way to Mass, I nonchalantly told my parents I had a friend joining us. Mom turned in her seat and raised her eyebrows, and Dad moved forward with the expected interrogation.

It was a relief to pull into the parking lot and find refuge in the church. Steve was waiting inside, dressed in a nice pair of slacks and dress shirt. "You clean up well," I whispered with a smile. He looked good, and different, away from the restaurant.

He grinned and reached past me to shake Dad's hand and introduce himself. Dad gave his usual gruff greeting and ushered us into a pew.

Mom, Dad, Morgan, and I knelt down to say a prayer. I never knew what to pray so I only pretended as I scanned the rest of the pews for friends and familiar faces.

Steve knelt down beside me and whispered into my ear. "Are you praying?" he asked.

I turned and creased my brow as if to say, "Yeah, of course I am," but when I turned away and closed my eyes I felt a familiar longing I hadn't felt in a while. I used to be close to God. He was there for me that night in the dorm room. Maybe he would accept me again if he knew that I wanted to be a better person.

"Father, I don't know what to say," I prayed. "And I'm probably the dumbest person you know, but I need your help." It was too much. I didn't want to cry in Mass, I didn't want my parents to ask what was wrong, and I didn't want Steve to know how hard that was. I took a deep breath, made the sign of the cross, and sat back in the pew.

When Mass began, Steve asked questions. "Why do you say that prayer?" "Why do you kneel here?" "What is the priest doing with that and why did he kiss the table?"

Again, I felt stupid. I wasn't sure of the answers to his questions. To play off my stupidity, I either made up an answer or shrugged my shoulders, holding a finger to my lips to be quiet. In reality, I was screaming inside. I didn't know! I knew nothing about being a Catholic, and I had been one all of my life.

In all my years of Catholic schooling, CCE, and Confirmation classes, what I had mostly gotten was the opportunity to meet cute boys. It was not the fault of my teachers, or my parents; I had simply chosen not to pay attention or care, and that led me to emptiness.

After Mass, I rode with Steve to meet my family at Denny's for breakfast. "The Catholic Mass seems to be so rich in tradition," Steve noted.

I nodded.

"Don't you want to know more about it?" he asked. "You know, why you do all that stuff?"

I stared straight ahead and contemplated the question. "You want me to be honest?"

"Yeah." he said, turning to look at me with raised eyebrows.

"I never felt that knowing all of that stuff was important. When you're younger, they teach you about Jesus and his love, and about his sacrifice, which I get. When I was in middle school, we were supposed to be learning about why we kneel, what all of the prayers mean, and really everything that probably makes us Catholic. But I was also going to another church that didn't have any of those rules. It was easier to accept that God was God and all we needed to do was believe in him than learn all these things about my Catholic faith. Even though I stopped going to that other church, I guess all along I was becoming more a part of who they were than becoming a Catholic."

"What do your parents think about that?" Steve asked.

I turned and looked at him. "They don't know," I answered. "I am good at deceiving. Actually, in high school, I was very involved in church. I was a lector, you know, like that guy that stood up today and read the first two readings?"

His eyes got big. "Really?"

"Yeah," I said, my stomach beginning to sour. Hearing me say that out loud was embarrassing. "I went to CCE all the way through high school. I enjoyed classes because my friends and I would get a chance to talk. It was never about my faith."

"That's sad, Shannon." he said as he pulled into a parking spot at Denny's.

"Yeah, I know."

# Tell The Truth, The Whole Truth, and Nothing But The Truth... So Help You God

For God did not give us a spirit of cowardice but rather of power and love and self-control.

—2 Timothy 1:7

ON MONDAY MORNING, when I went back in to see Ms. Birmingham, I decided it was time to lay it all out on the table. I would talk about everything but the evil. That was still too much to admit, and I wasn't ready to hear what it would sound like if I brought it out in the open.

I started with the most recent things and conquered my feelings of stupidity in going back to Nick twice. In the moment my self-judgment was clouded by guilt, but in reality it didn't matter if I went to him a dozen times, I said NO.

She had me describe, in great detail, the first and second incidents. As I told my story, I expected to receive looks of disapproval, but instead I was met with nods of understanding.

"Shannon, have you told anyone else about this rape?" she asked.

"No, not really." My memory went back to the night I sat on the toilet and confessed to Daniel, but his rejection was something I did not want to relive.

"You haven't told your parents?"

"No!" I said, sitting up straight in the chair.

"You said last week that you had been raped by a close friend when you were still in high school. And that was your first time having sex?"

I nodded as my hands fiddled with the hem on my shorts.

"Do your parents know about that?"

I laughed at the absurdity of her question.

"What's funny?"

"Ms. Birmingham, you know my dad. He'd kill me if he knew I'd had sex."

"Really? You think finding out that his daughter was taken advantage of would make him want to harm you?"

I stopped fiddling. I knew Dad wouldn't want to hurt me; it was his look of disappointment that I didn't want to see. I wasn't supposed to be the one causing him pain.

"Shannon, don't you think your parents would want to know that you've been hurt? Don't you think they would want to be there for you?"

The nerves in my legs rattled, and my chest tightened. "Yeah," I said, "but I can't tell them that."

"Why not?"

"Because," I said, struggling to gather up the courage to say the words, "they'd be disappointed in me. My dad wouldn't understand why I had allowed this to happen, not just once but with two guys!"

Ms. Birmingham leaned forward in her chair and took off her reading glasses. "I know your father well enough, Shannon, to know that he loves you very much."

"But Dad always thinks of me as being strong. He wouldn't understand how I could have let this happen!"

"You think that because these guys raped you, you are weak? Do you think you should've been able to fight them off?"

I nodded and bent over, putting my fists up to my face, and fighting back the anger towards myself.

"Shannon, the first thing you are going to do is tell your parents the truth."

My head shot up. "I can't!"

"Yes you can," she said. "You need to know that you have family around you that supports you and believes you. You will not be able to forgive yourself if you can't fall back on some kind of support system. We can bring them in here, if you want, and I can be here with you, or you can tell them on your own."

I continued to stare at her, but I wasn't seeing her. In my mind, I envisioned telling Dad that I wasn't his good girl.

"Shannon, do you understand why this is important?"

I blinked back the vision and looked at her. Suddenly, as if a wave of understanding had swept over me, I wanted to embrace the task. I felt like that little girl that had been rescued from the bad guy and I needed comfort and consolation. At that moment, I needed my parents' love more than anything. I sat up and nodded.

"Do you want to have them come in with you on Wednesday?" Ms. Birmingham asked.

"No," I answered. "I think I'll tell them before then, maybe even today."

"Well, if you need to talk before Wednesday, call the office, and I'll fit you in."

"So, you don't think it was my fault?" I asked, shocked at myself for speaking out loud what had been on my mind the whole time.

"What? The rapes?"

"Yeah, you know, I should never have put myself in that position."

Ms. Birmingham leaned over, grabbed my wrist, and squeezed it lightly. "Did you tell them 'no'?"

I nodded.

"Then it was not your fault. I don't care how many times you went back to them or what you might have said before the dates. None of that matters. When a woman says 'no' to a man, he needs to respect her wishes. You were not respected."

The buzzer sounded, ending the session. I walked out of her office, and, for the first time in two years, I wanted to come clean.

At home, I sat in the game room, watching Oprah with Mom, waiting for Dad to come home. My nerves were on fire with anxiety. I was anxious to tell them, but not out of fear. I was anxious to finally have someone on my side. My only source of dread was the anticipation of Dad's disappointment.

His car pulled up an hour earlier than expected, and I could feel my heart beating in my throat. I let him walk through the door, put his briefcase down on the bar, and kiss my mom as she stood at the ironing board. Mom hung up the shirt she had just finished and made a comment about the pool equipment.

Together, they walked outside, and I followed behind them. The day was unusually overcast for July, and in the air was the slight bitter stench of an impending electrical storm. I stood on the sidewalk that led from the back door to the pool and waited for them to come back towards me. As they did, Dad stopped and leaned down to give me a kiss hello.

"How was your day?" he said.

"I need to talk to you and Mom," I blurted out, unable to stop the tears from rolling down my cheeks.

Mom stopped next to Dad, and they stood there looking at me, confused and worried.

"What's wrong?" Mom asked, reaching for Dad's arm.

There was no way to begin, so I just put it right out there. "I have been raped."

The look on their faces will forever be branded in my memory. It was a mixture of horror, helplessness, and anger. Dad reached out to hold me, but I backed away. I needed to tell it all before I could feel his comfort.

"I was raped when I was in high school," I said. "I was a virgin, Daddy. I really was, and I didn't want it to happen. And I know that I was weak and I should've fought him off, but I didn't. I never said anything because I didn't want you to be disappointed in me."

"Shannon," Mom said, reaching out. I backed further away on the sidewalk and sat down on the steps of the back porch.

I was bawling like a toddler who had confessed to breaking a precious heirloom. "But I'm stupid," I cried, "and it happened again. In April, this guy, Nick, raped me, and I was stupid because I let it happen again. I'm sorry." I leaned over and buried my head in my lap.

Mom sat down at my side and cradled me in her arms. "Ssshh, stop it, you are not stupid. I'm so sorry."

Dad paced the sidewalk. I could hear his footsteps come close and then retreat. "Who are these guys?"

"Tom, calm down," Mom said.

I sat up and saw the pain in Dad's face. He was pacing, gathering his thoughts like he did when he was angry. Abruptly, he turned back to me. "You said one of these guys was here? Does he still live here?" His eyes bulged, and his face was a deep crimson.

Oddly afraid for Paul's life, I defended him. "Dad, there's nothing you can do."

"Oh yeah? What about that guy at school? Did you go to the police? Did you turn him in?"

"No," I mumbled, ashamed.

"What's that guy's name?"

"Nick."

"Well, how do you think Nick would feel if I went and snatched him out of his home, violated him with a broomstick, tarred and feathered the son of a gun, and dragged him through the streets?" He proceeded to continue with a line of shocking language.

Never in my life had I heard the "f" word come out of my dad's mouth, and never had I heard such violence. And by the look on his

191

face, I knew that if I had given him Nick's number, in seconds he would have been in his car, driving to school to do exactly what he said.

"Tom!" Mom yelled, tightening her arms around me.

He stopped pacing and finally looked down at me. Nothing hurt more than what I saw next.

Tears.

He leaned down and took me from Mom. "Honey, it hurts me that they have hurt you. What can I do? What can I do to make this better?"

I shook my head.

"Don't let them get away with this. We'll do whatever it takes, you hear me?"

I sagged in Dad's embrace. Acceptance. It was all I needed to hear.

That Wednesday, I went into Ms. Birmingham's office on lighter feet. I explained how it had gone with my parents and told her I was weighing my options on turning Nick in. When my father had accepted me and wanted to stand beside me to fight against the injustice, I had found courage, and it was empowering. I realized that it was too late to do anything about Paul, but Nick was still wading in the murky waters, ready to prey on another naïve and powerless soul, and I couldn't allow that to happen. This could be my chance to fight the evil in a tangible way.

We discussed the various ways in which to expose Nick, and how each of them would affect my reputation at school. When the session ended, I had a lot to think about before Monday's appointment.

There were three weeks left before I was due back at school. My summer had changed, but instead of feeling helpless, lost, and stuck in a void of despair, I had a new understanding of my role in everything that had taken place in the past three years.

My life had purpose. I could be redeemed.

Steve was the first person I told. One night, after work, we hung outside in the parking lot, and I told him my new revelation. He beamed from ear to ear and hugged me tight. "I have never seen you more beautiful than you are right now," he said, stepping back and looking at me in a way that made me blush. "Really, Shannon, there is this hardness that is gone from your face."

I couldn't look at him anymore. I was too embarrassed. I bent my head and shrugged my shoulders. "Well," I said, "I feel different. I mean, it's strange, but I am anxious to go back to school and do something about what Nick did to me. Even if everyone will call me a liar, I don't really care."

"No one's going to call you a liar."

I rolled my eyes. "Oh, you don't know how admired Nick is. I know there will be a huge group that will not believe me."

"Who cares about them, anyway!"

I laughed. "Exactly!"

"Let's go celebrate!" he said, and then we piled into his car and went for a bite to eat.

For the next few weeks, Steve remained my closest friend at home. After every session with Ms. Birmingham, he would wait for me to call and tell him how it went, or we'd meet up at work or the local hangout and talk it over. We spent a lot of time talking about God and faith, and he continued to go to Mass with me on Sundays, even though he wasn't Catholic. His interest led me to seek more from God, but I was still unsure what God felt about me.

In my mind, God was this massive force above, who sat with his arms crossed, face sneering, and eyebrows furrowed, disappointed in the choices I had made. In my mind, I needed to be at his feet on bended knee, begging for forgiveness and pleading for his love to return.

It was a sad vision, and I'm not sure why it ever entered my mind. Even so, I lived with it for the next few years. Steve and I would talk about it, and he would try and convince me that God was love, that he wanted me to succeed and be blessed. But I didn't feel worthy of that God. The God I deserved was the one in my mind.

Steve was not happy with my resistance to his vision of God, and he tried to help me see him differently. A week before I was supposed to leave to go back to school, Steve gave me a journal. I had not written in a journal since the eighth grade. Flipping through its crisp, clean pages brought me back to the days when I shared a relationship with God by writing down my innermost dreams and desires. But one day I became too ashamed of my actions, and at that time my dreams and desires were no longer aligned with anything God would allow. Although I knew that, I chose to continue living in sin.

I sighed and held on to the journal. "Thank you," I said.

"That's not it," Steve said, pulling a small box out of his pocket.

I opened it up and found a silver cross and chain. But it wasn't just a simple cross. It had Jesus at the top, the Virgin Mary below him, a saint in each corner, and the Holy Spirit in the middle. And when I flipped it over, it read, "I am Catholic. Please call a priest." It was beautiful.

"I have never seen a cross like this before," I said.

His smile widened. "I looked everywhere for that. I hope you like it."

"I love it," I said as I ran my thumb over the imprint and flipped it over to read it again. It was just a piece of silver, but by wearing it I was declaring that I was going to be a different person. To wear the cross, I needed to be the person it represented.

The time came when I had to leave the sanctity of my home, counseling, and new-found friendship, and head back to school to see if the spark of courage could ignite into a flame. In the past three weeks at home, I had taken important steps toward finding out who I really wanted to be. I began writing in my journal, and, while I was not yet addressing it directly to God, I felt as if he were the person with whom I was sharing everything. The silver cross around my neck reminded me that I had a faith to tap into whenever I found the strength to do so, and the counseling sessions had opened my eyes to the lies I had been telling myself for years.

Although I hadn't been miraculously cured, I recognized the path out of the dark valley. As I entered my sophomore year of college, I knew that each day would have to be a conscious step on that path.

# Confessing

If we say, " We are without sin," we deceive ourselves, and the truth is not in us. If we acknowledge our sins, he is faithful and just and will forgive our sins and cleanse us from wrongdoing.

—1 John 1:8–9

BACK AT SCHOOL my new roommate and pledge sister, Lindsay, greeted me with open arms. We were there early to prepare for rush week, and many of us gathered together in the dorm to go over the summer details. I remained quiet, not yet ready to divulge the truth of what I had been going through.

When the school opened, I checked into the counseling department and found someone with whom I could continue my treatment. With the counselor's help and encouragement, and, eventually, with the support of a group of other rape survivors, I took the first step in exposing Nick through the Greek system.

I chose this route first because I knew that I had no physical evidence to take to the police. I felt that the Greek system would take care of the situation without creating a public scandal.

Within one week, I was in the sorority advisor's office. Susan's eyes flamed with anger. She immediately called Nick's advisor and planned a meeting.

I, however, was not present for this meeting. That week, I received a phone call from Ms. Birmingham, asking my permission to talk to Susan about our counseling sessions. After giving her permission and hanging up the phone, I realized that my integrity was being tested. That same day, I received a phone call from Nick.

"Shannon, come on," he said. "Why are you telling these people these lies?" His voice was dry and thick with chastisement.

My neck burned, and I could barely speak. "Nick," I said, "I have nothing to say to you!"

"Come on! Why are you doing this? We liked each other!"

"You know what you did to me, Nick. You are the one lying."

"FREAKING whore," he spat as he hung up the phone.

Again, I was not informed of Susan's meeting with Nick and his fraternity advisors. Then, one week after our initial meeting, she called me back into her office. Before I could even take a seat, I recognized the dejected look on her face.

"Nick swears you consented to having sex with him," she said.

"No!" I yelled. At that point, I was beyond tears. In fact, I relished the anger that welled up inside, because it helped me to feel alive when I wanted to die. "I told him 'no' both times. Both times I asked him not to make me. I didn't want to stay."

"But, Shannon," she paused, pursing her lips, "you went back to him, and you did stay. How do you explain that?"

My blood turned to ice. It was the biggest mistake of my life. I knew that, and now I had to defend it. "After the first time, he was apologizing all the time. I wanted to believe him."

"You shouldn't have gone back."

I took a deep breath and swallowed back every word that wanted to spew from my mouth. "So that's it?" I said. "There is nothing we can do?"

"He came in here with his fraternity's advisor and two respected professors who swore on his good character. I don't know of any other way to fight it. It's your word against his."

"But didn't you defend my character? Why wasn't I told about these meetings?"

She looked hurt. "Of course!" she said. "But there is nothing we can do to punish him when he says that what you did together was consensual. Honestly, Shannon, you going back to him doesn't make sense. And I wanted to hear his side before you got involved again."

"Involved? Don't you think I'm involved?" My eyes rolled, and I bit the side of my cheek. "What can I do to keep other girls away from him?" I asked. I was desperate. Nick was sly, and I feared for every girl that had ever come up to me singing his praises.

"Have you told any of the girls?"

"No," I whispered, bending my head in shame.

"Well, would you feel comfortable talking about it to the chapter? I think that maybe if you did you would find the support you need."

I wanted to help, but the thought of telling everyone at once, with eighty pairs of eyes staring back at me, sent a chill down my spine. I could feel the judgment, and it was only a thought. I, however, had been robbed of the opportunity to share my side of the story, and I knew that this could be my only chance.

"OK," I said, surprising myself. It dawned on me that if I told others what he had done, his reputation would be tainted, despite his claims of innocence. He needed to be stopped.

That afternoon, I had a counseling session with Virginia, my counselor at the university. I told her the outcome of the meeting with Susan, and she wasted no time in telling me to go to the police.

"Shannon," she said, "the worst thing that could happen to you is the police will tell you there is not enough evidence. You know this."

"Yeah," I said. "So why keep going? They won't be able to do anything."

"If the detective sees something in your story that is credible, they will have to bring Nick in for questioning. It will go on his record that you filed a report against him. That's better than nothing."

"It will also go public, and the whole school will judge me."

She sat back in her seat and clasped her hands together. "Sure, if it goes public, you will have those that will not believe you because they are friends of Nick's. But," she continued, sitting forward earnestly, "I am willing to bet on the fact that there will also be other young girls who will hear your story and think twice about going out with him and trusting people so blindly."

"Why haven't any of the other girls in the support group gone to the police?"

"Because they are afraid."

My body flickered and began tingling like a Fourth of July sparkler. As much as I dreaded going forward, my spirit was at peace. I needed to do this.

"OK," I said.

Virginia raised her eyebrows. "Really?"

"Yes," I nodded. "I want to do this. When do we go?"

"I'll make an appointment to speak with the detective, and I'll give you a call to let you know, hopefully by the end of this week."

"Will you be there with me?" I wanted to go forward with the case. I wanted the validation that, even though I should not have gone back to him, my "no" still meant "no." But I didn't want to go alone.

"Yes," she said and smiled. "Of course."

On the way home, instead of walking through the campus to the dorm, I walked along the main road on a path that led me to the university's Catholic church. It was a very small, white house that served as the student center, and next to it was a one-story office building that served as the main chapel. Putting a hand up to the silver cross around my neck, I felt compelled to go into the chapel.

The lights were dimmed, a few people were scattered in the pews, and some stood against the back wall next to a closed door.

Confession.

Those who were standing glanced at me when I entered and then went back to their own thoughts, staring at the floor and preparing to receive the Sacrament of Reconciliation. As out of place and uncomfortable as I felt, I couldn't get my feet to turn around.

"*Stand in line,*" demanded a gentle voice from within. I was torn between a desire to walk out and desperation to feel the peace that I knew confession could bring.

The confessional door opened, and a young woman walked out with an angelic smile on her face. She went to kneel in the pew, and the next person in line walked in and shut the door. I walked over and stood behind a young man in line.

"What time is confession over?" I whispered.

He looked at his watch. "We still have half an hour."

I smiled my thanks and leaned against the wall, but I knew I would need more than half an hour. As the minutes passed, the nerves in my body flared and came alive. My vision of God with his arms folded as he stared down at me with an unpleasant look made the wait excruciating. It was obvious that God knew all of my sins, but voicing them out loud to a priest meant I had to acknowledge my actions.

The door opened, and the young man in front of me stepped in. I was next.

I waited in line as my thoughts ping-ponged across the chapel, pulling my will out the door and then throwing it back against the wall.

Finally, the door opened and the young man stepped out. As he passed me, he smiled. The door remained opened, beckoning me to enter, so I took a deep breath, stepped inside, and closed the door behind me.

It was surprising to find the priest sitting right there in a chair and not hidden behind a wall. When I was younger, the confessional was separated by a wall or partition so you couldn't see the priest's face. But there he was, sitting patiently in a seat, next to an empty chair. He turned slightly and motioned for me to sit.

Guided by some unseen force, I moved forward and sat down. The priest was young. He had a head of dark hair, brown-rimmed glasses, and, were it not for his priestly attire, he could have passed for a typical businessman.

"Hello," he said with a smile. He had a purple stole around his neck and a Bible in his hand.

"Hi," I managed to say.

"Do you have any questions before we begin?"

"I've never done this face to face before," I said.

"Well, it's normal to be nervous," he said. "Try to look at it this way. You are not speaking to me but to the Holy Spirit. Jesus Christ is with us, and he knows all that you are about to confess. Don't talk to me, talk to him."

I drew in a breath and let it go slowly. "OK."

He made the sign of the cross, said a little prayer, and kissed the stole around his neck. Then he opened his Bible, flipped through the pages and settled on a page, breaking my resolve as he began to read:

Live by following the Spirit. Then you will not do what your sinful selves want. Our sinful selves want what is against the Spirit... The wrongs the sinful self does are clear: being sexually unfaithful, not being pure, taking part in sexual sins...the Spirit gives love, joy, peace, patience, kindness, goodness, faithfulness, gentleness, self-control..."

—Galatians 5: 16–26 (paraphrased)

As he finished, I felt the ethereal world coinciding with my existence. Suddenly, I had the strength to face my own faults. "Bless me, Father, for I have sinned. It has been six years since my last confession."

After confessing, I wiped my tear-stained cheeks and held my breath. This would be the moment, I thought, when God would unfold his arms, point a finger at me, and say in a loud, booming voice, "You are a fool! You should have been stronger!"

"I'm sorry," the priest said.

I had averted eye contact with him for my entire confession, and, startled, I looked into his face. His eyes did not show pity but sorrow.

"No human should ever have to suffer through such violence. I'm sorry this was done to you," he said.

I don't remember what he said after that, but it didn't matter. He listened to me. He believed me. At the same time, however, we discussed the part I played in it all.

We talked about not only asking for the grace to forgive Nick and Paul, but the mercy to forgive myself.

Through the power of the Holy Spirit, I was absolved of my sins. In an honest, heartfelt Act of Contrition, I told God that I was truly sorry for all that I had done and I promised to do everything in my power to move forward and leave the sin behind me. I walked out of the confessional, knelt before the Blessed Sacrament to offer my penance and began moving in the direction of a new path out of the valley.

On Friday morning, Virginia and I met with a detective at the police station. I pulled into the parking lot and took a deep breath. This would be my last second of anonymity among the citizens. Walking through those doors would open the door to public scrutiny.

Virginia was already inside. When she saw me, she took my hand and squeezed it as we were led into Detective Rinehart's office. He motioned for us to take a seat opposite his desk.

"So, what is it that brings you in to see me?"

I looked at Virginia before answering, and she tilted her chin up reassuringly. I cleared my throat and said, "I would like to press charges against Nick Ferrante for sexual assault."

The detective leaned back in his seat and bounced a ballpoint pen on his knee. "Those are pretty serious charges."

"Yes, I know," I said, a fireball settling in my throat.

"Why don't you tell me what happened and we'll see what we can do from there."

I recounted the story as honestly as I could. By this point, my well of tears had dried up. I had told the story so many times, and all I wanted was justice.

"I have to tell you that every time I hear a story of rape, whether it be acquaintance or not, it pushes my anger to the limit." Detective Rinehart pointed to a picture of two young girls, huddled together, their blonde hair curled, eyes bright, and smiles wide. "If my daughters were taken advantage of, I'd want to deliver justice myself. I have to ask," he said, leaning forward and resting his forearms on the desk, "why did you go back to him? And why didn't you go to the hospital?"

My entire body drooped in the seat. It was a mistake I couldn't undo. "I went back after the first time because he kept calling and begging and crying. I was convinced I'd made too much of the first time, that maybe somehow I had given him the impression it was fine, even though I had told him all along that I wanted to go home and did not want to have sex." I couldn't look the detective in the eyes. "This is probably stupid but he is so good-looking and well known—I don't know, I guess I convinced myself I was making something out of nothing. I know it's stupid. I was stupid."

"Don't say that," Virginia said, leaning over and grabbing my wrist.

"I don't believe you are stupid," Detective Rinehart added. "I just needed an answer. If the district attorney is going to accept this case and take it to the grand jury, he is going to want answers to these questions."

I sighed before continuing. "I didn't go to the hospital after the second time because I blamed myself for going back. I blamed myself for all of it—that is, until this summer, when I realized that I had a right to say 'no,' that none of that mattered because I did say 'no.'" The courage that had ignited over the summer rose up again. This was my chance, and I wasn't going to let it die.

"OK then," he said. "This is what will happen. I need you to write a detailed account of your days with Nick—from the day you first met, to the first rape, what happened afterwards, to the second rape, and even if he's contacted you since you came back to school. Once I receive that from you, we will have it notarized as your statement. It will be turned over to the district attorney's office, at which point they will review your statement and make the decision on whether to investigate or dismiss the case. If they choose to investigate, they will bring Nick in for questioning, take his statement, and both of your statements will be given to a Grand Jury. Once it reaches the Grand Jury, they will decide whether it will move forward to trial. Do you have any questions?"

"So, no matter what, it will be my word against his?"

"Well, that is unless you can find some witnesses to come in and give statements that collaborate your story against Nick's. In fact, that might be a good idea. More often than not, a young man like this hasn't done this just once. Once your story gets out, you never know who might come forward."

"How long does all this take?"

"That's the tough part. Each step may take a few weeks, or it may take months. It depends on how busy the district attorney's office is."

"Will I know if they accept my case? And if they do, will I know when they are going to bring Nick in for questioning?"

He sat up and began playing with his pen again. "I will do my best to inform you of every step that is taken with your case."

"Will this go on Nick's record at all?"

"Once you bring in your statement and your complaint is signed and notarized, it will go on his record."

I looked over at Virginia. "OK," I said. "I will bring in my statement on Monday then." I stood up and offered to shake his hand. He took it and smiled.

Outside the police station, Virginia walked me to my car. "So, how do you feel?"

"You know," I said, pausing to contemplate the question, even though the answer was on the tip of my tongue. "I have been out of control for so long, and now I feel like I'm getting some of it back. So

I feel really good. For the first time in my life, I can honestly say that I don't care what other people will think about me."

"Well, your true friends will believe you."

"That's right. They will," I agreed. I bent down and gave her a hug. "Thank you for being with me today."

"You didn't need me."

"I know," I thought, rejoicing inside. For the first time in a long time, I felt my own strength.

# Justice

"...Do not be afraid, go on speaking and do not be silent, for I am with you..."

—Acts 18:9–10

A S THE NEW school year unfolded, Derek, Jason, and my pledge sisters gave me positive support. No longer did I feel the need to seek the negative in life and experiences. They rallied around me as the story unfolded, and once I turned my statement into the police I felt confident enough to speak in front of the entire sorority chapter.

Standing in front of over eighty of my peers and admitting to ignorance and weakness was the pinnacle of my character change. Afterwards, they came up and hugged me, telling me how strong I had been and that they were going to stand behind me. As bittersweet as it was, the tune on Nick had changed. He wasn't so great anymore.

"You know, I had heard that Nick wasn't all that," someone in the distance said to another member.

"Yeah, I heard he tried to get Nina to do something she didn't want to, so she told him to take her home."

"He seemed too cocky to me."

Liz Rowland waited in the background. After most of the girls had left the room, she walked up to me with tears in her eyes. "Can I talk to you alone for a minute?" she said, walking over to a corner and wiping her eye with the back of her hand.

"I'm sorry I didn't ever say anything before. I feel like it's my fault that you were raped by him."

My eyes widened and my heart sank. I knew the answer to my question, but I asked it anyway. "Why would you say that?"

"Because he almost did it to me. He didn't fully rape me, but he got very close. We were at the fraternity lodge, and he was on top of me and wouldn't get off. I guess they could hear me pleading with him to stop, because two guys came into the room and he did. No one said anything about it, and I never went out with him again."

I reached out and hugged her. "I'm sorry," I said.

She shook her head. "No, I'm sorry. I wanted to say something to you that night at the social, but, I don't know, I guess I thought it was just me."

"You can still help me, you know? You can write a statement to the police station for my case."

She stood up straighter. "I don't know," she said, hesitating.

Her hesitation shocked me. Didn't she want to help me get him convicted? "If you told what happened to you, then it wouldn't just be my word against his!"

"But no one knows what happened to me," she said, bending her head and avoiding my eyes.

"Liz," I pleaded, "you wouldn't have to go in front of a jury unless it was brought to trial. And even then you could choose whether you wanted to or not. But for now, all I'm asking is for you to write a statement to the police."

She heaved a huge sigh. "I'll think about it."

I knew I couldn't force her so I backed off. "Thank you," I said. "And thank you for telling me." We hugged again.

Back at the dorm, my roommate and another one of our pledge sisters, Jordan, were sitting on the beds, talking in hushed whispers. I could see that Jordan had been crying, and Lindsay got up to give me a hug. "How do you feel?"

"Tired," I said, flopping down next to Jordan on my bed.

Jordan sat up straight and cleared her throat. "You weren't the only one Nick got to," she said.

I sat up, stunned, but I didn't dare speak. I knew the amount of courage she would need to tell her story.

"Last summer, I was here for summer school, and I met him while I was living in the athletic dorm. We went out on a few dates, and he was so nice and…" She stopped and shook her head. "He did everything right, you know?"

I nodded. My heart was beating so fast that I thought it would pop out of my chest.

"Well, anyway, one weekend we went with a bunch of people to this lake house to ride jet skis. I hadn't really done anything with him besides kissing, so I was nervous to stay with him for the night. But he had always been nice and had never demanded to go any further so I didn't think much would happen."

"That night we'd been drinking, and everyone kind of ended up wherever they could find a spot. Nick and I were in the living room, where there was a fold-out couch and another one with some guy already passed out on it. We started making out, and I thought I made it very clear that I was keeping my clothes on. But that's not what he wanted. He changed so fast, it was like he was Dr. Jekyll and Mr. Hyde. He was mean and angry, and the more I said 'no' and told him that I wanted to go to sleep, the more angry he got, calling me a tease and whore." Finally, she stopped and allowed the tears to fall.

For the second time in one evening, I had found myself reaching out to comfort another of Nick's victims, both of whom were in my sorority. How many more were out there in the other sororities, and in the student body as a whole?

"So, did he rape you, too?" I whispered.

She shook her head, and my heart sank. "No," she said, "but he was right there. I mean, he had everything exposed, lying on top of me and practically suffocating me." She snorted. "I kept telling him firmly to stop, but he was so strong."

I nodded in agreement.

"He managed to pull my panties down far enough," she continued, "and we'd been fighting for so long that I thought for sure he was going to win. I freaked out and started screaming, trying to wake up that guy on the couch. I kept telling Nick to get off of me. I used everything I had to push him off and keep him from," she shuddered, "from entering me. And he kept telling me to calm down. I guess I put up a pretty good fight, because he finally stopped, called me a name, rolled over, and passed out."

As disappointed as I was that I had been the only one ignorant enough to have fallen victim to Nick completely, I was very glad that Jordan didn't have to deal with the emotional pain that the actual surrender to the act had given me. I hugged her again.

Not wanting to break Liz's trust, I didn't tell them what she had told me. But I did try to get Jordan to agree to come forward. I explained to her about writing a statement and how the whole process would work.

She didn't hesitate. "Yes, I'll do that," she said. "Of course." Tears sprang to her eyes again. "I'm so sorry, Shannon, for not saying anything when I knew you were going out on dates with him. I don't know why I didn't. I guess I didn't know if you would believe me, and I thought maybe he would be different with you."

"Don't worry," I said. "I'm just glad you're willing to help me now."

As the months dragged on, my purpose solidified. I was going to focus on doing well in school. I was elected an officer of my sorority and given the privilege to move into the sorority house for the upcoming spring semester. My grades were excellent, and I became a regular at Sunday morning Mass at the little St. Mary's chapel. Each week, I listened intently to the lectors, feeling compelled to rejoin that ministry so that, for once, I could proclaim the Word of God because *I* wanted to, and not because it looked good for my parents.

I wrote in my journal religiously, and I began to address particularly tough days to God. He was still the "Big Man" upstairs, but after confessing I felt the fatherly connection forming again between us. Once again, I believed that he cared, but I knew that I still had a long way to go before making him proud of me. If only I had realized that God's love had never changed. He had accepted me for me all along.

I wasn't drinking nearly as much as I had in the past. In fact, I was disgusted that I used to drink until I blacked out. I limited my nights out and became comfortable going out and not drinking at all. The alcohol wasn't a vice. I didn't need it. I enjoyed it, but I never wanted to be out of control again.

By second semester, the district attorney had finally taken my case, along with the statement from Jordan, and I began the long process of preparing to present my case before a grand jury. Liz had never come forward with her statement, but Jordan's had helped. The next thing that would happen would be that Nick would receive uniformed visitors at his door.

As expected, he was not happy.

In my new room in the sorority house, the phone rang.

"You freaking whore!" Nick screamed.

I hung up the receiver before he could say more, but he called again.

"What are you doing telling people I raped you? I didn't rape you! You asked for it, twit!"

These calls continued throughout the semester, and Nick began stalking me at parties and clubs, cornering me when I went to the bathroom, or if he couldn't get near me, sending me looks that seared my soul. But it wasn't the sight of Nick that bothered me; it was the constant reminder of my decision to be involved with him in the first place. Could I trust my decisions?

Summer drew near, and there was still no word on a court date. Slowly, the case drifted into a pocket in my life that I only looked into when the detective called me or Nick and I happened to run into each other. I continued to move forward in reaching the goals I had set for myself, and I even became an orientation leader for the university. My sophomore year had been like a rebirth, and I was learning how to set boundaries and be in control of my emotions.

Then everything changed. Toward the end of summer, in July, at an orientation dance for incoming freshmen, I met an intramural soccer coach who was signing freshmen up to play on his team. His name was Neal Deitz.

He was not my type at all—about five foot ten with coal black hair and the most beautiful almond shaped eyes I'd ever seen. A mutual friend introduced us, and before our friend could tell me his name, Neal asked me to guess.

It was an odd thing to do, but I liked the game, especially since I guessed correctly. To be honest, Neal is not a typical name. I don't know why I guessed it, but I did.

After a few more nights of hit-and-miss meeting, Neal and I finally found ourselves on the dance floor of the popular hangout, and at the end of the night he asked me for my number. After a year of healing, I was ready to revisit dating and give my heart a chance.

True to his word, Neal called the next day and we went on our first date. It took him three dates to ask me for a first kiss. He would call after every date to reiterate his good night, and in the morning to start the day off.

For the next two weeks, whenever we were not working with the freshmen, we spent every waking moment together. When I went home for my twentieth birthday, I couldn't stand the fact that my parents did not know who had revived my waning spirit, so I asked him if he'd take a spontaneous four-hour drive with me to our house, which he did. He was amazing with my family, and when we got back to school we sat at the duck pond and committed to being a couple.

Much to my surprise, it was easy to tell Neal everything. I wanted a clean slate, and I knew that in order to get one I would have to tell him about my rapes. His reaction was one of concern and anger—anger toward any man that would aggressively attack a woman. Neal made me feel secure, protected, appreciated, respected, and loved.

For that reason, I was glad to have him with me when I received the call I had been waiting on for ten months.

"Shannon, this is Detective Rinehart. The grand jury met today and your case was no-billed."

I stood looking at Neal with my mouth agape, fighting to find the words and emotions of what I was feeling inside. Anger boiled up inside of me because they had never notified me of the grand jury meeting.

At first, I was devastated, and then I was angry—angry that Nick had gotten away with what he'd done, not only to me but also to other girls.

"That's all?" I finally said, after what felt like a dramatic long pause.

Neal raised his eyebrows, not knowing who had just called or what had made me turn white and start shaking.

"Yes, Ma'am, I'm sorry," the detective said. "They didn't feel there was sufficient evidence to move it to trial."

"So what happens to Nick now?"

There was an uncomfortable silence. "Nothing, Ma'am. The complaint is on his record, but there is nothing more we can do. I really am sorry."

"Thank you," I said, hanging up the phone and sitting down in the closest chair available. "That was the detective and they no-billed my case."

"What does that mean?" Neal asked.

"It means that nothing will happen. Nick gets a slap on the wrist and that's it. Nothing." I started to cry.

Neal came over to the chair, pulled me up, and gathered me into his arms. He let me cry, and when I finally backed away from his soaked shoulder he offered his wisdom. "Look at it this way," he said. "You stood against him, and now everyone at the school knows he's been charged. At least this way you don't have to drag this out another year and suffer through a trial that would've dragged your reputation through the mud. Girls will think twice before they go out with him."

I wiped my eyes and nodded. "I know."

"And don't you do that talk on date rape for all the orientation groups?"

"Yeah," I said as my chest rose in a hiccupped sigh.

"Look at all you've already done," he said with a smile. When he smiled, his eyes danced.

I couldn't help but adore him.

One month later, the fall semester of my junior year began, and I found out that Nick had not made it back to school to finish out his senior year. I couldn't help but feel a sense of relief. It wasn't the victory I had imagined, but I felt confident that I had done all I could.

The rest was up to God.

# For Love

No one has greater love than this, to lay down one's life for one's friends.

—John 15:13

NEAL AND I were inseparable. He was calm, caring, and considerate. He took care of me. He would put gas in my car without telling me because he didn't like me driving on an empty tank. He called me every night to ask how I was doing, what I was feeling, and to tell me how he felt. He also showed me that it was OK to have friends and do girl things. He would do his sports and have his guy nights, but he always checked in, allowing me to revisit trust in a relationship.

I was able to explore my personal interests with the comfort of knowing that he was still a big part of my life. Our relationship allowed me to realize the glaring faults of the other relationships that had tainted my past. Of course, my reasoning was still scarred and bruised by my experiences, and my boundaries were still distorted and irrational. I felt that in order to show Neal that I loved him, I had to have sex with him.

He never made me. He never asked for it. In fact, he would have waited forever if that was my wish. To relive my life beginning with

Neal—*that* was my wish. But I felt that if I didn't have sex with him, I wouldn't be able to hold onto him, and I knew I never wanted to let him go.

Even after we had added sexual intimacy into our relationship, Neal still showed me the gentleness and compassion that all of my other experiences had lacked. Oddly enough, despite our living in sin, Neal and I went to church together. Our relationship was a direct testament to God, who had put us together without waiting for us to get everything right. Neal was a Christian and had attended several denominations, but never a Catholic Mass. It was interesting to watch him become intrigued by the same faith that I had ignored for so long.

After the fall semester ended, we celebrated Christmas with each other's families, first at my home, and then at Neal's. For the spring semester, I moved into an apartment with Sarah, one of my closest pledge sisters. I was no longer an officer, my term was up, and I decided not to run for another office. It was nice to officially "be on my own" and immersed in the final stages of my college career.

For spring break that year, Neal and I decided to visit Carrie in Florida. We had been together nearly nine months, and taking a nice long road trip sounded fun and exciting. Carrie and her husband lived near Orlando, so we would be able to stay with her and go to Disney World for not much more than the cost of gas and tickets.

I had been continuing my relationship with Carrie over the phone, but our conversations had not been very productive. She'd had another little girl, and my family and I had visited her the Christmas before I met Neal. I could see that Carrie was still involved with drugs, but I was also dealing with my own issues at the time and I decided not to interfere.

When Carrie heard we were coming to visit, she was very excited to have the company. I knew that she and her husband had not been doing well, but I didn't venture to ask many details. Carrie and her drug habit was a sore subject. She blamed Mom and Dad for her problems, and I knew that it was only because she didn't want to own up to her own mistakes. My patience with Carrie was thin.

My parents had no problem with us driving twenty hours from east Texas to Florida. In hindsight, I think they knew that God was sending us on a mission, because normally Dad would never have allowed such a thing to happen.

On the way to Florida, Neal did most of the driving. I read a novel to him out loud in the car. We talked about old relationships and how they had made us stronger despite the pain they had caused. We talked about our childhood, and for the first time I told him about all of the mystical happenings in my life. We talked about God, about what we believed, and what we were skeptical to believe.

We managed to drive twelve hours before stopping and resting for the night. Excited to reach our destination, we woke up early the next morning to hit the road again, and we made it to Florida in the afternoon of the second day. As we pulled up to Carrie's duplex, we saw her standing outside with a phone in her hand.

She was emaciated and disheveled, shaking as she stood there. Her face was gaunt and her eyes a glassy red. "Shannon and Neal just got here," she said into the phone. I wanted to hug her and introduce her to Neal, but she handed over the phone instead. "Here," she said. "Mom wants to talk to you."

Neal stood beside me with his hands in his pockets and a look on his face that told me he wanted to run.

"Hello?" I said.

"Shannon, it's Mom. Listen, Dad and I were trying to reach you last night. Carrie is bad off, and you have to help her. She wants to leave Chris, and we need you and Neal to bring her and the girls back to Texas."

As my mom talked, I looked at Neal, and his face mirrored the shock I was experiencing. "Um, OK," I said hesitating, wondering what the heck was going on.

"Shannon, I'm sorry to have to do this to you and Neal, but her situation is not good. We'd come and get her but it really does work out that you and Neal are there. Use the credit card we gave you. Tomorrow,

Carrie will pack up everything she can into trash bags, and you can help her drive."

"OK," I said. I was speechless. What could I say? No? That I had plans? That I was sorry, but this just wouldn't work into my plans?

Two little angels ran out of the duplex, and my heart melted. They were my nieces, ages four-and-a-half and one-and-a-half, beautiful and full of life and energy. Courtney and Zoe both had blonde hair and bright eyes. I knelt down to get a better look at them, and they came up and put their pudgy little arms around my neck.

"Shannon?" Mom continued. "Dad will be getting home soon. We'll call you again to make sure everything is OK. Don't say anything to Chris. We don't want him to know, and we don't want to set him off."

I held onto my nieces and hugged them tight. "OK," I said. "We'll talk later then."

I hung up the phone, looked over at Neal, and introduced him to my nieces. Instantly, he knelt down, and Zoe went right into his arms. He picked her up with ease. "Hello, Zoe. You're a pretty girl."

She smiled with delight.

"What's going on, Shannon?" he asked.

"I'll explain in a minute," I said. "Let me talk to Carrie to get a better idea." I motioned for us to enter the house.

Carrie was sitting on a recliner near the door, and her circumstance was clear. She was going through withdrawal. Her face was placid, her eyes hollowed, and her whole body shook.

Neal walked past us into the house and sat down on the couch with Zoe and Courtney.

I remained standing near Carrie. "What's going on, Carrie?"

"I want to leave Chris," she said. "He's crazy and I gotta get out of here." She reached for a pack of cigarettes on the table next to the chair.

I knelt down by the chair and whispered, "No, what are you on? You look like hell."

"We've been doing crystal meth but I stopped four days ago and I haven't slept since. It's bad, Shannon. We sold our bedroom furniture to get it." Tears welled up in her eyes. "I don't want to do this anymore, Shannon. I don't want to live this way anymore. I can't feed my kids, this place is a hell hole, and Chris is crazy, Shannon. He'll kill me if I stay." Her hands shook as she tried to light the cigarette.

I was frustrated and angry with both of them for being selfish enough to put themselves in this situation when they had two beautiful girls to support and nurture. But it also pained me to see my sister, the one I had looked up to for so long, in such a pitiful state. I stood up, trying my best to hold back my disgust. I wanted to shout out useless words, but I knew they would get us nowhere.

"Why didn't you tell me this was going on when Neal and I were planning this trip?"

She finally succeeded in lighting her cigarette, took a long drag, and held it in for a second before blowing it out. Avoiding me, she looked straight ahead at the cartoons on the small TV set. "I don't know."

Neal looked at me with raised eyebrows. Both girls were content to sit on either side of him, entertained by the TV.

I motioned for him to follow me into the kitchen, and once we were there I couldn't help but gasp. McDonald's bags were scattered all over the table, and other fast food wrappers covered the floor. I walked over to the refrigerator and opened the door.

Neal walked up behind me. "Geeze," he said in horror.

There was nothing in the refrigerator but an old milk jug filled with water. "What is she feeding these kids?" I asked out loud.

I stood up and shut the door. "I am so sorry, Neal." I couldn't contain my tears.

Neal put his arms around me, and I buried my face in his chest. "I don't know why she does this," I cried. "I thought that after she'd had the girls she would stop. Why is she doing this to herself?"

"Shh, she'll hear you," he said.

Lifting my head, I grimaced. "Who cares? She needs to hear it!"

"Hey, yelling is not going to help anyone," he said. "Think about those girls. They need you to be calm."

He had become my voice of reason. I took in a deep breath and shuttered as I let it out. "Well, we can't stay here tonight, and my parents want us to drive them back home tomorrow."

He agreed without hesitation. "That's fine. We can find a hotel."

"Really?" I said, dumbfounded. If I had been him, I would have run out the door, leaving a trail of smoke behind. "You're OK with leaving tomorrow and driving another twenty four hours?"

He held me tighter. "Yes."

"You're not mad at me? I mean, I don't blame you if you are. You can be mad. My family is screwy. You can break up with me. I'd understand." Despite my attempt to seem emotionless, the tears that rolled down my cheeks betrayed me.

"I'm not going to break up with you," he assured me. "Carrie is no different than my brother. Hell, he's in prison because of drugs. At least she's here, and we can try and save her."

Carrie walked into the kitchen. "What are y'all talking about?"

I turned away from her long enough to wipe my face. "Neal and I were talking about getting a hotel room. I don't really want to be here when Chris is here."

Carrie's eyes widened. "But I don't want you to leave me alone with him! He's crazy, Shannon. He'll hit me!" She turned and pointed to a wall in the hallway. "He punched his fist through the wall!"

"Carrie, there is nowhere for us to sleep. We'll leave tomorrow morning, just like Mom and Dad said. But don't say anything to Chris. You can't let him know that you're leaving."

Just then, the front door opened, and Chris called out, "Hey! Shannon, you here?"

I didn't think it was possible, but Carrie's face grew paler.

"We're here!" I called out, trying to hide my disdain.

Chris came in, hyped up, walking on the balls of his feet, and the whites of his eyes were a crusty blood red. His every move and gesture was overly animated as he came over and gave me a giant hug. "Hey. Sis! Glad you made it in OK." He let go and thrust out a hand for Neal to shake. "Hi, I'm Chris!"

Neal took his hand firmly and introduced himself.

"So, you guys are here with us for the week?" Chris said, leaning against the kitchen counter.

Carrie slipped away into the living room.

"Yeah, we want to go to Disney World," I said. "But we probably won't stay here. We'll get a hotel nearby."

"Why?" he asked, unbuttoning his red work shirt with the word "EXTERMINATOR" in white letters on the back. He had on a white undershirt underneath. His hands shook, but he seemed unusually in control in comparison to Carrie's let down from her high.

Neal saved me and spoke up. "I had already made reservations at a hotel by the time we hit the road. We never wanted to bother you guys for a place to stay."

"Well, OK," Chris nodded, "as long as you know you're welcome to crash here." He glanced around the kitchen and laughed. "Shopping's not our thing. Hey, you guys want pizza for dinner?"

I glanced at Neal wondering how they were going to pay for pizza. "Yeah, that's fine," I said, "but let us pay."

"No! You're our guest. You ain't paying!" He walked into the living room, and we followed behind him.

"Where's the phone book? We're getting pizza."

Courtney shrieked in approval. Carrie reached under the side table and handed it to Chris.

Neal and I took a seat on the couch. We sat in silence, watching the cartoons with the girls. The entire scene was surreal. I stared at the animated figures on the screen and wondered what had led Neal and I across the country, through four states, to enter into my sister's nightmare.

After a few minutes, Chris walked back into the room. "Hey, I'm going out back to smoke some weed. Shannon, don't tell your dad. Hey, I'm sure you do it, too, right?"

Bile threatened to well up in my throat. I stared at him, unable to speak.

"Neal?" Chris said, gesturing to the back door. "You want to take a hit?"

Neal sat up straighter on the couch. "Nah, man, I'm good."

"Whatever, guys! You're missing out!"

"He hasn't stopped," Carrie said, her words dry and sad. "The minute he started coming down, he took an upper to get him back up. The pot's just something he does to mellow out."

I couldn't sit there any longer. I leaned over as closely as I could so I didn't have to talk loud enough for the girls to hear—or Chris, if he walked back into the kitchen. "We're going to leave," I said. "I'll call you when we get a hotel, and if anything happens you call me. I'm going to call Mom and Dad when we get there, too. We'll leave in the morning, but you can't say anything to him, Carrie." I looked her dead in the eyes and winced. "I'm not kidding. Don't fight with him. Agree with what he has to say, whatever it takes."

She nodded. "Can't you stay longer?"

"We're tired. Neal's driven all day, and he'll need to sleep in order to drive again tomorrow."

I could feel the relief seep out of Neal as we stood up from the couch. We hugged my nieces goodbye and left before Chris had finished mellowing out.

In the privacy of the car, once we were far enough down the road to be out of Carrie's vision, I broke down into gut-wrenching sobs. Neal reached over and patted my back.

"I am so sorry, Neal. I'm sure you hate me for getting you into this mess."

"Shh, it's OK. Not exactly the vacation I had in mind, but what can you do? You can't leave her there the way she is now." He looked at the directions he had written to the hotel he'd found in the phone book and got us onto the main highway. "What's with Chris anyway? He seemed pretty decent to me."

I rolled my eyes. I had thought that at one time, too, but I had learned over the years to recognize the façade he had perfected. "Yeah, he can fool the best. He even fooled Dad into believing he was a decent and upstanding citizen. But when they skipped town to move to Florida, we heard rumors about a ton of money missing from the restaurant he managed and possibly even a drug deal that had gone bad. I don't know what really happened, but I've seen enough of him to know that he can't be trusted."

"Do you think your sister is serious about quitting?"

I leaned back in the seat and wiped my eyes with the back of my hand. "I don't know." I said. "This is the worst I've ever seen her. I hope she is." The anger began to boil up again. "It makes me mad, you know? I mean, did you see her and that house?" I banged my head against the seat. "This isn't fair."

Neal put his hand on my knee. "Maybe God is using this opportunity to clean her up?"

I turned and looked at him. "Why would God have allowed her to get this bad? Why does God have to ruin my vacation to save my sister? Why does this stuff always happen to me?" Like a petulant little kid, I did not hide my disdain for God in that moment. I wasn't in the position to see it the way Neal had chosen to.

I took the moment at face value—another bad day in my line of many.

As I talked to my parents and listened to their litany of directions, including getting Carrie and the kids and driving as far as we could without stopping unless we absolutely had to, I learned that Chris had a gun. We didn't want him finding out too soon that Carrie and the girls had left, so we decided to get them early.

"We don't know what Chris is capable of," my parents said.

For a twenty-year-old, this talk was suffocating. How could I manage to process this? He had a gun? Drive until we couldn't drive anymore? Would he chase us? Would he hunt us down? We were acting out a Lifetime movie!

All the while, I looked at Neal, dying inside and knowing that my chances with him had been ruined. He was being so kind, sweet, and caring. He held me as I cried, and I knew that he would be strong and sensible when we needed to take care of ourselves and make the next move. We talked more about his brother's drug addiction and how it had torn through his family. I told him more about my relationship with Carrie, the chaos she had caused in our family, and the strained relationship between her and Dad.

Our conversation brought us closer, but I still felt sure that the situation would be the death of our romance. I wouldn't blame him. The fact he was carrying through with the plan was amazing. He could have stayed in Florida and flown home.

That night, we both tossed and turned, unable to sleep. When the phone rang at 3:30 A.M., it wasn't a shock.

"Hello?" Neal answered.

"He won't leave me alone!" Carrie screamed through the receiver.

I sat up and grabbed the phone from Neal. "Carrie, calm down. What's going on?"

"He won't leave me alone. I can't sleep, and he keeps messing with me, and now he won't shut up. He's pushed me up against the wall and…" Her words broke off into a sob.

My heart began to race. "Carrie, listen to me. We can't come and get you until morning. You can't tell him that you're leaving. You'll piss him off, and he won't let you leave. If you want to get out of there, let it go."

"Shannon he's crazy! I don't know if I can do this!"

There was a commotion in the background, and I heard Chris say, "Who are you talking to?"

"None of your business!" Carrie yelled.

"Shannon, I'm not kidding. He's crazy," she said, and then I heard the click of another party on the line.

"Shannon," Chris said, "I don't know what your sister is saying but she's nuts."

"Forget you, Chris!" Carrie yelled through the phone line.

"You are a whore!" Chris retaliated.

I held the receiver away from my ear, looked helplessly at Neal, and mouthed the words, "What do I do?"

He whispered, "Tell them both they are acting like children and to go to bed."

They were still cussing at each other when I interjected. "Hey!" I yelled into the phone. "Carrie, shut up. You too, Chris. Listen to you. You guys sound like you're twelve. I don't know what you guys are fighting about, but this is ridiculous. Just go to bed and sleep it off."

"He won't let me sleep!" my sister said in desperation.

"Oh, come on, Carrie!" Chris yelled back. "I haven't done anything to you."

"Chris?" I tried to get his attention. "Chris, listen. Please go to bed. Let me talk to my sister. It is after 3:00 A.M. Please ignore her, just this once, and go to bed."

I could hear him grumbling something, but I couldn't make it out. I felt the tension seeping through the line. "Fine, talk some sense into her. Everything's always got to be her way," he said, and he hung up his extension.

"Carrie," I said. "Listen and don't say a word. Neal and I did not plan on driving all the way down here just to turn around and drive you and the girls back another twenty-some odd hours."

"I know, but…"

"No!" I said firmly. "Now, Neal is tired, and I am tired. We have a long day ahead of us tomorrow, and we all need to get some sleep. The last thing we want is for Chris to suspect what's happening. If you can't shut up for one night, it's not going to happen. For all I know, we'll all end up dead."

Her end of the line was silent. Finally, she answered. "I can't do this anymore," she whimpered.

Physically, I felt her pain, and the threat of my own tears burned my eyes. "Carrie, please, it won't be much longer. Call us in the morning and let us know when he's gone."

"OK," she relented. "I love you."

"I love you, too." I hung up the phone and cried in Neal's arms.

Less than four hours later, the phone rang again. Neal and I were already up and getting dressed.

"Hello?"

"Shannon, I'm ready," Carrie said, her voice sounding stronger and more in control. A hint of hysteria laced each sentence, but I could tell that she knew exactly what was going on. "Chris left for work twenty minutes ago. I called Ms. Jacobs and she said I could bring the girls to her until we're ready to leave. I don't know if Chris knows anything, and I didn't want him to try and pick them up from day care."

"OK, we're about to leave," I said, "so we'll be there in about half an hour."

"Hurry, OK? Sometimes Chris comes back in the morning before he goes on his first house call."

"We'll be there as soon as we can. Have you talked to Mom?"

"Yes, I called her as soon as Chris left. She told me to pack everything I could in garbage bags and fill the station wagon."

"OK, good. We'll be there soon, OK?"

We hung up, and Neal and I braced ourselves for another long, crazy day.

When Neal and I pulled up, Carrie was dragging a huge, black trash bag to her car. Neal jumped out to help her. She had managed to pack the car tightly with their belongings. "I'm ready," she said. Her shaking had subsided, but her eyes were still bloodshot and her skin was still pasty.

"Do you want me to drive your car?" I asked.

"No, I'm fine to drive. I just want to get the hell out of here."

Less than five minutes after pulling up to her house, we followed her to Ms. Jacobs' to get the girls. They were unusually quiet when they walked out of the house and didn't fuss when they were strapped into their car seats. It was clear from the lack of smiles on their faces and their big round eyes that they sensed the tension in the air.

"Are you sure you don't want me to drive?" I asked again.

"I'm fine," Carrie insisted.

"Ride with her then," Neal said. "I'm fine by myself."

It was settled. I rode with Carrie, and we set out on our race to get out of Florida.

Carrie and I both kept looking in the rearview mirror, expecting Chris to come up on our tail. We tried making small talk, and after a few hours had passed and the girls' silence had worn off, the car ride became torture.

I climbed in the back and tried to keep the girls occupied. We sang, played games, read stories, and did anything we could to distract ourselves. Not until we had driven four hours did we finally stop for gas and something to eat.

All of us were anxious to get back on the road, and this time I could see the sleep settling in Carrie's eyes. "I'm driving," I said. "You need to sleep, OK?"

She didn't argue, and for the next few hours I drove as they all napped in the car. Neal drove ahead of us, like an angel guiding the way. Unlike in our vehicle, where everyone was given the opportunity to rest and switch drivers, Neal drove on his own.

When we stopped for lunch, Carrie insisted that she was fine to drive on her own so that Neal and I could ride together. I was grateful for the time with Neal. Of course, he wouldn't allow me to drive, saying I needed the rest to relieve Carrie. Not once did he complain about the situation we had been forced into.

A few hours into the drive after lunch, when we were well into Alabama, Neal and I were singing along to the radio when I heard him gasp. I jerked my head around to look out the back window and saw Carrie careen across the highway into the grassy median. Then I watched in horror as the station wagon jerked back onto the highway, crossed the double lane, and came to a stop on the shoulder.

"Oh my God," I said, finally letting out a breath. I said the Lord's name in vain, but it was an act of God that no cars had been in the lanes surrounding Carrie. If there had been, it would have been a catastrophe.

Neal pulled to the shoulder with expertise and came to a stop at the time that Carrie's vehicle did. He and I clambered out of the car and ran up the highway to Carrie and the girls.

Inside the station wagon, the girls were screaming as loud as their little lungs would allow. I opened the back door and got them out of the car and onto the grass, far away from the highway. They clung to me, digging their little fingers into my skin, crying so hard that they couldn't catch their breath.

Neal went over to Carrie, who was kneeling and inspecting the culprit—a blown out tire, gone in shreds, the remnants of which were scattered across the highway.

Even from where I was sitting with the girls, I could see Carrie's hands shaking. Neal said something to her, and she walked over to us and sat down. The girls left me to cling to their mother.

Carrie began to cry.

Neal changed the tire and put on the spare. We needed to find a town to get a new tire, but it was late in the afternoon. We knew we would be lucky to find one that wasn't closed.

Once again, in a time of desperation, I found myself praying. "God," I pleaded, "please let us get somewhere safe that is open to get a tire. I don't know how much more we can all take."

We happened upon a family-owned mechanic shop about a half hour down the road. My prayers had been answered. They had the tire we needed, and with the blessing of my parents' credit card, we had the money to pay for it. The whole incident resulted in a two to three hour delay, but we learned a valuable lesson: leaving Carrie alone was not a good idea.

After spending the night in a hotel room and then driving the remaining thirteen hours across Louisiana, we completed our journey. We reached home before dinner and were greeted by my parents at the front door.

Dad walked over to Neal, and instead of offering to shake his hand, he embraced him in a bear hug. "Thanks for taking care of my girls," he said.

At that moment, I knew I could spend the rest of my life with Neal. If he could stick by me in a situation as stressful and mixed up as this, I could understand how couples who had been married for decades upon decades had remained together.

That trip was an answer to a prayer. As a child, I had prayed to God to protect my sister. In the past twenty-four hours, his protection couldn't have been any clearer.

# In Sickness and
# in Health

Husbands, love your wives, even as Christ loved the church and
handed himself over for her to sanctify her, cleansing her by bath of
water with the word, that he might present to himself the church in
splendor, without spot or wrinkle or any such thing; that she might
be holy and without blemish.

—Ephesians 5:25–27

TWO YEARS LATER, Neal and I were married. I had graduated
a year before and lived at home while planning the wedding and
working as a customer service rep for a tailored suit manufacturer that
was based in Dallas. With an eight-state territory, the position kept me
traveling three to four days a week, and then Neal and I would spend
the weekends together.

Despite my nonexistent influence in my Catholic faith, Neal voiced
his intent to go through the process of becoming Catholic before we
got married. My parents were glad to know that we would share the
same faith, and my grandmother was ecstatic to have another soul
come into the church to which she was so devoted. Neal even asked
my grandmother to be his sponsor, which meant that she stood beside

him during his Baptism, First Communion, and Confirmation into the Catholic church, vowing to support him in any faith issue.

Every time I turned around, Neal shocked me. This was a long nine-month process, and Neal had to drive four hours every weekend to meet with the priest for one-on-one instruction. As I look back on this now, fifteen years later, I am able to see this step as a piece of God's puzzle.

Neal was like a sponge as he soaked up everything about our Catholic faith. He would come home asking me questions, and instead of acknowledging that none of my cradle-Catholic upbringing had soaked in, I would get defensive and embarrassed. He got it, and I didn't. It was painful and obvious to me that I had no idea how to get it, too.

The closer he grew to God and understanding his faith, the deeper I fell into a pit of despair. He was happy, and I wasn't—not because of him but because of some unknown reason, and that made everything worse. Although I was pessimistic about life and wallowing in self-pity, at least I wasn't letting anyone else call the shots. There was simply no more room for error. I couldn't understand how Neal could put his trust in God and in a faith that had no real tangibility. I needed something more solid, a list of things to do to assure myself that I was doing everything OK, or at least something that could make me feel in control.

To make matters worse, on the days I stayed at home, I would have unexplainable episodes of feeling that same fear that had haunted me at the ages of seven and nine and then paralyzed me in my dorm room, causing me to see something so outlandish and downright crazy. My phone conversation with Cain after the "flying piece of china" incident still haunted me.

"These spirits have apparently been with you a long time," Cain had said.

At night, I would lie in bed, unable to sleep because I could feel the air become heavy and I could smell the stench of burning rubber. My breathing would speed up, and my nerve endings would come alive, raising the hair on my arms. I would repeat prayers habitually, and the more this happened, the more I withdrew from the comfort and safety I had begun to feel in what little faith I had.

These were not panic attacks. I saw in the blackness of the room a cloud of green light. As it floated around, putting fear into my core, I prayed to God, Jesus, Mary, and to anyone who could possibly help. I pleaded for them to make it go away. I pleaded, but at the same time I fought with the question of how a God who was supposed to exemplify love could allow this to continue.

I *was* going crazy. That was the only sane answer.

I decided to seek help. I found a new therapist on my new medical plan, and she diagnosed me as clinically depressed. She tried to prescribe medication, but out of fear I refused it. I did not want to become addicted. I did not want to lose control.

Armed with a new journal, daily exercise, a cutback on sugar, and two therapy sessions a week, I set out to conquer something tangible—depression.

The diagnosis was a relief. I was depressed. In the past six years, I had suffered the death of my first love, violently lost my virginity, and opened myself up to relationships that were demeaning and abusive to my self-esteem. Then I had been raped again and suffered illusions of pure evil. Not to mention the family secrets that were revealed once I told my parents about the rapes. Because I had the courage to talk about what happened to me, my mom found the strength to tell all of us what my grandfather had done to her. When we brought my sister back from Florida, she too brought her ugly secret into the light. Our family was on the path to healing and there was more for me to work on. Of course, it made sense—depression was the sane answer.

I wanted to be normal. I wanted to give Neal what he gave me.

After nine months of therapy and only two months away from the wedding, I took a step forward in reclaiming the person I felt I could be all along. I prayed to God in my journal, asking him to help me "get right" with him. After Neal and I got engaged, I became a "born again virgin" and stopped all sexual activity until our wedding day. I wanted so badly that dream of having the perfect wedding night. I did everything I could that was in my control.

The world appeared brighter. On July 6, Carrie, who was now divorced and two years clean, stood by my side along with Morgan, as my maid and maiden of honor. It was a beautiful wedding on a beautiful day, and I felt beautiful.

Neal and I moved to Houston, not far from his parents, and my company transferred me there to be closer to my largest account. I was still traveling, but it worked well with our schedule. Once we were married, I felt as though I had been domesticated, and we attended Mass on a regular basis.

I was following God's directions, and life was normal.

Then, one afternoon, I was visiting a new friend at her home. I had been sitting on the floor with my legs crossed, and as I got up my knees groaned in protest. "Oh," I said out loud, caught off guard by the pain.

"What's wrong?" my friend Joanie asked.

"Nothing, I must've strained my knees somehow," I said, brushing the pain away without giving it a second thought.

Later that evening, while changing the sheets on the bed, I went to lift the mattress to tuck in the sheet, and my wrists gave out. I couldn't lift the mattress because the pain was too intense. I stood, stunned, and looked at my wrists. Nothing appeared different. They were a little swollen, but, other than that, there were no bruises and nothing that was shocking to the eye. Again, I wrote it off as a fluke incident, rationalizing that I had carried my luggage on and off the plane and through the airport. I thought that maybe it had caused some wear on my body.

The next morning, my parents drove in from an antiquing excursion in the Austin area. They were going to drive us home so we could drive my new Mazda MX-3 back to Houston. I was very excited because this was the first car I was buying since graduating college. When I woke up, though, every joint in my body felt stiff and achy. I didn't have a fever, feel sick, or have a headache, but there was pain in every step, in every movement, and even in the simple bending of a finger or toe.

My body looked different, too. It wasn't just my wrists and knees that were swollen. My fingers were plump, and my feet couldn't fit into my shoes. But I didn't say anything to Neal or my parents for fear that they would want to postpone the trip.

Since my parents had just driven from Austin, I offered to drive for a few hours to give them some rest. The drive, however, proved to be too much. Every time I extended a leg to brake or press on the gas pedal, a shooting pain tore through my feet and up my shin to my knees, digging deep into my stomach. I could not bear it any longer.

"I can't drive," I whimpered, steering the car to the first exit off the highway.

That woke everyone up in the car. "What's wrong?" Neal asked first.

"I hurt all over." The pain was too much. I stopped the car at a gas station, and we piled out. "I don't know what's wrong with me. I think a spider has bitten me and I'm having a reaction. Every joint in my body aches." I held up my gnarled hands, "I can't even straighten out my fingers, look, even if I want to." I willed my fingers to straighten, but they remained bent and lifeless.

"Why didn't you say something?" Mom said as she held my hands in hers and stood back to look at my legs.

"I don't know. I thought they were just normal aches and pains."

"We'll make an appointment with Dr. Sutherland as soon as we get home."

Neal picked up some BENGAY® in the gas station and helped me rub it on my hands and feet and under my knees. The warmth of the lotion helped for a few minutes, but then it wore off. By the time we reached Dallas and stopped for lunch my walking had been impaired. I could only shuffle along with my knees bent and upper body hunched over.

Mom was able to get me an appointment that same day to have some blood drawn. Once I was in the office, the nurse inspected me and held my hands with great care, but the concerned look on her face worried me even more.

"What?" I asked. "Do you know what it is?"

"We won't know for sure until the results from the blood tests come back," she said. "And unfortunately that's going to take a few days. But let's see what Dr. Sutherland has to say." She smiled and left the office.

A few moments later, Dr. Sutherland entered the examination room. "Well, it's been a long time, hasn't it?" he said, taking a seat on the swivel stool and taking my hands in his the way the nurse had. He asked me a few questions about where and when the pain began, whether I felt it on both sides of my body, and if I had ever experienced it before.

With each question my anxiety deepened. "Do you think you know what it is?"

He pushed back on the stool and flipped through the file to the sheet that my mother had filled out years ago on the family's health history. "Well, Shannon," he said, "I don't believe it's a bug bite. You do show a history of rheumatoid arthritis in your family, but until we get the results of your RA count we won't know for sure. I'm going to put you on a mild steroid to help with the inflammation in your joints and the swelling. Once we know for sure what we're dealing with, then we can go from there on more treatment."

Rheumatoid arthritis? I had never heard of it. I knew what arthritis was, but I was only twenty-three. There was no way it could be arthritis. My grandmother had arthritis, not me. Later, while discussing the examination with my parents, I learned that a great aunt in the family had rheumatoid arthritis at a young age and ended up in a wheelchair by the age of fifty. She passed away early, too, but my parents had never been certain if it had anything to do with the arthritis.

It was easy to assume the worst and picture myself balled up in a wheelchair before my thirties. I thought, "What next, God? Really?" Was this punishment? I was doing what he wanted now. In the safety of my childhood room, I allowed myself to sulk, cursing each shock of pain that coursed through my joints with the slightest movement.

The steroid helped with the pain, and by the following afternoon I was able to move freely with only a hint of aches in my legs, wrists, and fingers. Getting a new car drew me out of self-pity. I was anxious to drive it home that Sunday.

The next Monday, I flew out to Colorado with my manager for a special suit event at the main mall in Denver. Despite moving more slowly than usual and feeling fatigued, I went about my work without complaints. Secretly, I allowed myself to think it was a spider bite as I initially had.

That first afternoon in Colorado, my manager and I took a break in the ladies lounge to check our phone messages. I dialed the number for my answering machine on the payphone and entered the code.

The first message was Dr. Sutherland's nurse, leaving her name and number and asking me to call back. As I hung up to dial the doctor's office, I could feel my knees getting weak with worry.

It didn't take long for the call to go through and for Emily, Dr. Sutherland's nurse, to answer. "Hello Mrs. Deitz," she said. "Give me a second, and I'll pull your chart. OK, the blood tests came back and your RA factor is high, which is an indication of rheumatoid arthritis."

An atomic bomb went off in my chest. I couldn't breathe. My manager looked over from her own conversation with obvious concern in her eyes. "OK," I managed to say.

"Dr. Sutherland suggests that you find a rheumatologist in Houston to get further blood work done and map out a proper course of treatment."

"OK," I said again. My throat was tight, and my face felt like it was going to catch on fire.

After a pause, Emily spoke up. "Do you have any questions?"

I cleared my throat. "No, thank you," I said. I hung up and bent my head, trying hard to remain poised around my manager.

"Is everything OK?" she asked.

"I have rheumatoid arthritis," I said flatly. It was someone else's voice. I couldn't accept that I had to say it out loud.

After returning home from the trip to Colorado, I found a reputable rheumatologist in my health plan network. But before I could go and see her I had to visit a family physician and get a referral. I spent an entire month traveling back and forth, from the doctor's office to the lab, for more blood to be drawn. Usually, they drew between five and six vials of blood. When I finally made it to the rheumatologist, they decided to get it all done in one sitting. They drew twelve vials.

It didn't matter how many vials were taken; the result was always the same. I had rheumatoid arthritis. Until my situation progressed, steroids would be my course of action on a case by case basis. The only problem was that, with the splitting headaches and weight gain, it was as hard to come off of the steroids as it was to suffer the outbreak itself.

To add to misery, my insecurities grew. Why would Neal want to live the rest of his life with a wife who would be an invalid? We were newlyweds, and there were nights when I would scream out in agony because it felt as if someone had been ripping my legs off at the knees. It was far from romantic and it only served to push me back into the depression that had caged me the year before. Neal tried to look on the brighter side, encouraging me to exercise and keep moving to prevent the outbreaks. I recalled something Dad had told me when I was going through the counseling before our wedding: "God will never give you a cross that you cannot bear." More and more I turned to God in prayer, pleading with him to take the disease away.

# New Life

That you should put away the old self of your former way of life, corrupted through deceitful desires, and be renewed in the spirit of your minds, and put on the new self, created in God's way in righteousness and holiness of truth.

—Ephesians 4:22–24

I PUSHED THROUGH the first year of our marriage with the news of my chronic illness and plugged along in my travels, slowly losing interest in what was once a very fascinating and enjoyable job.

Something was missing. Months before, I had begun to feel an ache inside that wasn't physical. I needed to do something. I wanted to change, but I didn't know how.

Alone in hotel rooms for the majority of the week, I began toying with the dream of writing a book. My company laptop was at my disposal, and soon my evening shows were replaced with the new adventure of creating a story for young adult readers that could be entertaining but true to reality. It was my first book, my first dip into the acknowledgment that I could bring a story to life from beginning, to middle, to end.

With each chapter, my passion for writing was born. I loved to write, and I fell in love with my characters. I enjoyed their joy and wept when they made wrong decisions that altered their lives. Writing this book gave me purpose.

Creating the novel led me to lay a new foundation for my future goals and dreams. I wanted to have a family, to stay home with my children, and write while they napped. I could have the best of both worlds when I wrote. I was certain that this was what God wanted me to do.

I knew I had touched upon something that would make God proud. I would write novels that would be real, while helping teens to find direction and stay clear of the mistakes that had led me down my treacherous path.

Without a moment's hesitation, I set out in pursuit of a job in the Houston area that required no travel. It was time for Neal and me to begin our family, and I did not want to be absent for the majority of the week. Through family connections, I managed to land an office management position at an oil company that paid nearly $7,000 more than my current position.

Stepping down from the more glamorous job of traveling to New York a few times a year and from other opportunities of the fashion world wasn't as difficult as I had first imagined. I did not belong in that world.

But I did not belong in the oil industry, either.

The money was great, but I felt like a kitten that had been fed to the wolves. The lack of morals and ethics in the business world was shocking. Despite my own indiscretions as a teen and in college, I discovered lines that I could not fathom crossing. Infidelity raged in our office, parading before my eyes as if it were the norm. Having been brought in to replace a woman who had been "moved over" because of her lack in organizational skills didn't help matters, either. I felt as though I were working alongside the Devil himself. She would hide files that I needed and disregard messages people left while I was out. She blatantly sabotaged my efforts.

I worked hours upon hours of overtime to get ahead so I could counter her attacks. My novel had to be put on the back burner as my type A personality kicked in to help me make ends meet. The office seemed to mirror the universe's black hole.

Neal and I had already begun the process of trying to conceive, and I found myself praying to God to make it happen quickly. Working in that environment challenged me by giving me a purpose that I did not want and pushing me into seeing the type of person I did not want to become.

And finally, in an act of reprieve, the she-devil was fired.

There was a God!

When the new temp came in the following Monday to replace her, I knew that God had a sense of humor to boot.

"In all I do, I do it for the Lord," Monica, a beautiful young Creole woman, said as she sat across from me in my cubicle.

Taken aback by her bluntness and zeal for faith, especially in a work environment, I raised my eyebrows. "OK," I said. We had just been introduced, and I was about to go over her job description when I asked her to tell me a few things about herself.

"God has been so good to me," she said. "I am a single mother with a five-year-old daughter, and although it's been tough to make ends meet, God has always provided. I was released from my job last week because of downsizing and was worried about paying the bills. Before I knew it, I got the call on Friday that they wanted me to come temp in this position. It saved me. Jesus Christ saved me!"

God had replaced the she-devil with Saint Monica!

I smiled, stifling a laugh. Her exuberance was refreshing, but her constant talk of Jesus was a little too much for my conservative box. Anything, however, was better than working with that woman.

"Well, Monica, I'm glad God brought you here because I needed you."

Monica stepped right into place, and I realized that my prayer for balance and harmony in our little work environment had been answered.

Her constant chatter about God and how he was working in her life no longer made me laugh. She intrigued me. How could someone who had gone through so much be so happy? Every day, she came to work with a smile on her face and a bounce in her step.

Sharp-witted and quick with the comebacks, she might have been the greatest Christian I knew. If you crossed her line of ethics, however, she let you know with a sharp but polite tongue.

Monica was contagious. She became the friend I needed to put me in my place, which she often did. She loved to talk about her faith and the faith that I did or did not have. Once Catholic, she had been drawn to the magnetic charisma of Lakewood Church, the largest non-denominational fellowship church in Houston. Her comments and questions often led me to feel ignorant because I had never bothered to raise the same questions.

She made me think, contemplate, and search for a similar kind of happiness.

Five months into my new position at the oil company and three months after meeting Monica, Neal and I finally conceived.

I was thrilled to be pregnant. After taking an over-the-counter pregnancy test, Monica was the first person I told at work. Instantly, she laid her hands on my head and began to pray for the health of my baby. I wasn't used to this outward display of faith, and I was ashamed that I was embarrassed by it. At the same time, I welcomed her prayers because I felt that she had a much closer connection to God than I had in that moment.

About a week after taking the test and one week before my first scheduled doctor's visit, I began to bleed. Afraid that I was experiencing a miscarriage, I called my doctor and went in for an ultrasound.

Because I was so early, only about six weeks pregnant, I was sent to the Woman's Hospital of Texas. With Neal by my side, we looked anxiously at the monitor, not sure how to interpret the wavy gray lines and swirls. Both the ultrasound technician and radiologist were in the room talking in quick, hushed tones. When they turned the monitor away from us, they pushed my panic button.

"What's wrong?" I asked, squeezing Neal's hand so tightly my knuckles were turning white.

Another doctor came into the room to look at the monitor, and finally they turned the monitor back around so we could see what had caused their turmoil. The doctor pointed out two distinct ovals on the screen. The one on the left was not as defined as the one on the right, and she said that both of them were embryonic sacks. Then she used her pen to point to a very tiny speck, the size of a small raisin, in the oval on the right side.

"This is an embryo that looks to be intact at the moment," she said. Then she pointed to the sack on the left. "It appears that this sack has already been terminated." Her pen outlined the hazy, undefined bottom of the sack. "The pregnancy is already being reabsorbed," she continued, "or, as you're experiencing, shedding like a menstrual cycle."

"What is she saying?" a voice in my head kept repeating. I wasn't getting it. Did I have one baby or two? "Am I miscarrying?" I asked with a shaky voice.

"Yes," the doctor said. "At this point you are miscarrying one of the pregnancies. You had two separate sacks. The one on the right is still intact, but it will only be a matter of time before we will know for sure if it will survive."

Neal cleared his throat and asked, "How long?"

"Her doctor will probably have her return in about two more weeks. By then, if this one survives, we'll be able to see a heartbeat."

In sudden panic, I sat up, "So I sit and wait? What about the one I am miscarrying? What happens to it?"

"Your body will shed the pregnancy naturally, and the rest will be absorbed back into your body. It will not be harmful to you or the existing pregnancy. Normally, we would perform a D & C when this occurs, but naturally that's not possible with the existing embryo intact."

The other two women in the room were looking at the strip of pictures that had printed out from the ultrasound machine. "May I have one of those?" I asked.

241

They cut off a picture and put the rest in an envelope. "We're sending these to your ob/gyn. When you go home, call and make an appointment with her to do another check. You might experience some bleeding and cramping, so don't be alarmed. If it becomes excessive, call your doctor immediately."

Laden with the news of the loss of one baby and the impending downfall of the other, Neal and I left the hospital and sat in silence all the way home. I couldn't pray. All I could do was cry.

I returned to work the following morning, not yet suffering any painful cramping or heavy bleeding, but experiencing some spotting. At my desk, Monica came over, and I told her the news.

"Sit down!" she directed in a gentle but authoritative tone.

Tears stained my cheeks. I had cried all night with Neal, and I had neither the strength nor the courage to keep them from coming. I did as she directed and sat down.

She put her hands on my head and began to pray, fervently asking Jesus to be merciful to me and to save the baby I was still carrying. Her words were full of fire and love. They gave me hope.

That afternoon, I felt the pang of a cramp in my lower abdomen, which brought me into the reality of the situation. No longer able to work, I drove home and parked myself on the couch.

The cramping became more intense, and soon I felt my uterus contract, which added panic to my fear. How could my baby survive if everything around him was literally trying to push him out?

I lay there, weeping and clutching my stomach. I cried out, "God, please help me. Please don't take my baby. I'll do whatever you want. Please don't do this to me!" That evening, I stayed on the couch, reasoning that if I didn't move then maybe my pregnancy could stay intact. Trips to the bathroom kept my panic and fear alive, but I held tightly to the simple shred of hope that Monica had given me through prayer. Then the phone rang, and I was surprised to hear my rheumatologist on the line.

"Shannon, your doctor and I discussed what was going on with you this afternoon, and I wanted to call and see how you were doing."

"I'm scared," I said. "I don't want to lose this baby."

"I'm so sorry. I know you don't, and that's why you need to make sure you rest. Stay off your feet until your next appointment."

"I know, but may I ask what you two were discussing?"

"Oh, well, we needed to discuss my diagnosis of rheumatoid arthritis. Because of this miscarriage, we need to monitor all of your symptoms in order to ward off any further complications and make sure we do not miss any other diagnosis, especially lupus."

"Is it because of the disease that I miscarried?" I didn't bother to hide the tears in my voice. It was too much to suffer the pain of the arthritis and know that it was causing me to miscarry.

"Shannon, I don't believe so, but we want to make sure we take good care of you, and we will continue to work closely throughout your pregnancy."

I realized I could not simply give back the disease, and I couldn't reverse the miscarriage, either. All I could do was be grateful that both doctors were monitoring me. "Thank you."

For nearly two weeks, I floated in and out of uncertainty. Neal did his best to make each day as normal as possible. We tried not to get sucked into the despair of discussing the probability of a baby so we played a lot of cards or watched TV. I finally found comfort in prayer, and began talking to God about how I had realized that maybe I *did* deserve the baby and *would* do what I could to change.

Finally, the day came for the doctor's visit. Neal went with me, and we waited in the office, staring at the ultrasound machine.

The doctor came in, cheerful but determined. "OK," she said. "Let's get right down to business and see what we have."

When the familiar waves of gray came across the screen, my heart stopped. Then we saw the ova. And then the raisin. And, finally, a flutter.

She paused it, pressed a button to snap a picture, and then it came back to life again. "Well, there you go," she said. "We have a good, strong heartbeat."

Ryan was born on September 21, 1998.

# Reconciled

Repent, and be baptized, every one of you, in the name of Jesus Christ for the forgiveness of your sins; and you will receive the gift of the Holy Spirit.

—Acts 2:38

LIFE WAS GOOD. During my months of pregnancy, I had acquired a new boss who was impressed with the programs I had implemented to keep the office organized and running smoothly. When I told him that Neal and I had made the decision for me to stay home (although I was making more money than Neal at the time, we felt that it was worth the sacrifice), he began to discuss the possibility of a part-time position, and eventually I was set up at home with a company computer.

I couldn't believe it. Either Monica's fanatic faith had rubbed off or God had changed course and found me favorable again. Whatever the case, things were looking up. Instead of having to suffer the loss of my entire income, I kept half of my salary, worked only two or three hours a day, and visited the office once or twice a week. It was easy money.

Ryan was an excellent baby. He smiled all the time, and he loved to laugh. We were blessed, and I began to feel an even stronger tug toward my faith. How could I deny that God had answered my prayers? I listened more in Mass, embraced the familiarity, and realized that I could relate to the Gospels. They suffered pain then, and we suffer pain now. God saved them then, and he was saving me now.

The occurrences of dealing with evil and its powerful oppression, such as the time when I had been at my aunt's church and the night in my dorm room, never subsided. They continued to happen over the years, especially when I felt particularly blessed by God. Once I began to understand my faith more deeply, however, they took on a new reality. No longer did I view them as strange paranormal attacks that had filled me with fear and scared me into believing that I was losing my mind. Instead, I began to understand the true battle that was taking place.

Monica was the only one with whom I shared any kind of detail about these attacks, and she introduced me to the term "spiritual warfare."

"The Devil will do anything to stop you from doing God's will, girl. You gotta put on the armor of God and fight it!"

I wasn't sure that I was ready to fight anything, but I could feel a heightened sense of awareness of who I was and where I needed to go.

The summer before Ryan's first birthday, while I was in the shower, a thought was literally pushed forward to the forefront of my mind: *Go back to school.*

I laughed out loud. School and I had never gotten along. If I worked hard, I got the grade, but I had never been "book smart." I had graduated with a high grade point average, but I was glad to be finished with school. Until that moment, I had never had any interest in pursuing a master's degree.

That afternoon, the thought continued running through my mind. It was almost like there was a piece of tape inside my head that I couldn't pull off. Finally, because it was only a fifteen minute drive from my house, I began to look into the University of Houston at Clear Lake.

And there it was: a degree in creative writing through the humanities program. It leapt off the page. My heart began to race. I could get a degree in creative writing? I could go to school and do what I love the most? Then, when I looked at the requirements and realized that I had every one needed, my skin began to feel very pasty and hot. The classes were offered Monday and Wednesday nights, and in two years I could receive a Master of Fine Arts degree.

It was like I had been handed a plate of gold.

In one year, I had completed my second novel, and it was one that dealt with a very personal issue—date rape. I had also joined the Houston Writer's Critique Group to get help with my writing. I had even begun sending it off to agents and learning how to deal with rejection. Whenever a possible publishing lead would fall short, I would go to Monica and cry.

"Just have faith," she would say.

Faith? I searched frantically to figure out how to have faith. I thought I had it. I had been getting more involved with the church, listening more, and praying more. What else could I do?

One day, something that had never crossed my mind became a reality. I knew that educating myself more in my craft would allow more opportunities to succeed and fulfill the burning desire in my heart.

Neal was happy to spend time with Ryan two nights a week, and my dad offered to help fund my education. One week later, I enrolled.

Never before had I enjoyed school. I joined a new critique group that was closer to home, and it was refreshing to be surrounded by a group of individuals who shared the same passion in life. Plus, I needed the escape.

As Ryan became more mobile, it became more difficult to juggle motherhood, work, and school. Ryan was a great baby, but there were a few red flags that kept me on my toes. Before he could crawl, he would get up on his hands and knees, rock back and forth, and hum. I knew he was in the beginning stage of crawling, but once he could crawl he continued to do this, especially when he was upset or in his crib.

Sometimes he would rock so hard that his crib would move across the room and hit the wall.

As soon as he could walk, his curiosity took him places no one-year-old should go. And when I put him in a Mother's Day Out program, he began to hit and bite, something many boys would do, but with an anger that alarmed his teachers. If any other child accidentally bumped him, or if you took him away from something he had been concentrating on, he would lash out. His anger was difficult to witness. Most of my girlfriends had little girls, and they certainly didn't find this amusing. It was as if they blamed me as a mother, and I felt inadequate.

I felt ostracized. Going to school and immersing myself in something I enjoyed helped me to feel validated.

Once I had completed the first year of my master's program, Neal and I discussed the possibility of having another child. Although it meant that I would be pregnant in the last months of my final year at UHCL, Neal and I did not want the kids to be too far apart. It took a while, as it had with Ryan, and through the summer we tried our best to get out and have fun. By the end of August, I took a pregnancy test that showed the two pink lines. But when I visited the doctor at six weeks' gestation, the ultrasound showed that I was eleven weeks pregnant! I had sailed through my first trimester, unaware that I was even pregnant. My body had experienced its normal cycle throughout the summer so I had no idea it was even possible.

We were thrilled! Ryan turned two the following month, and it was obvious that he needed a sibling to help calm him down. He was out of control, and, because he had grown stronger and more mobile, his tantrums would leave me with bruises from his constant biting and kicking. Whenever I tried to remove him from an unsafe situation, he would attack me, screaming at the top of his lungs.

These tantrums were not reserved for the privacy of our home, either. I never knew what would set him off but he would scream, kick, and thrash about in public. Mortified, I would snatch him up and leave. The looks that burnt my back as I walked out embarrassed me and fueled my already boiling anger and resentment toward people who judged. I was angry with myself, too, for not sticking up for my own child, but I felt that I had nowhere to go. Except for Neal, no one else could understand.

My closest friends began slipping away, uncomfortable around my son, and around me because I couldn't take the ridicule or criticism.

Paranoia replaced my earlier depression. I felt like nobody liked me, and nobody liked my son. My desire to feel accepted was reignited, but this time I did not want to run to alcohol for a cure.

There was no other direction for me to go but to God. The emotion I had felt at the age of nine, kneeling with my face in the industrial carpet of my aunt's church, returned. At a time when I was overwhelmed with everyone else's burdens, anxieties, and fears, I felt God's peace. Now I was in the midst of my own turmoil, and I wanted that peace.

But I wasn't sure where to begin. Embarrassed that I did not have much knowledge or understanding of God, I made a New Year's resolution to read the Bible from Genesis to Revelation.

By the end of January, I had been invited to participate in a Beth Moore Bible study program called "Breaking Free." Reading God's Word and then examining my life and my past with the guidance of this program opened me up to the possibility that I actually deserved God's love. I was desperate for understanding.

Slowly, the distractions in my life subsided. Some of them came as a relief, but in other areas, specifically with friends, it was hard to let go. My friends were still distant when it came to having Ryan around, and more and more we were left uninvited. It wasn't all about Ryan, either. Their distance left me feeling insecure, and I began to feel overwhelmed with jealousy toward everyone with a "normal" child. This jealousy ended friendships and forced me to look deep within myself. God had cleared the path for his purpose, but I was still too naive to understand.

That spring was my last semester of school before receiving my master's. I was approaching the very end of my thesis novel, Ryan was getting stronger and more difficult to handle, and there was something about the office environment that I could no longer stomach. I quit my job and let go of the easy money because I couldn't handle working on without passion. I was unsettled and desperate for change. The Bible and the study offered a glimpse of new hope and confidence, even though everything in my life remained the same.

In the midst of all of this, just one month before graduation, my second son, Seth, came into the world. As I suffered through every contraction of his labor without medication, I had the distinct vision that Jesus was carrying me.

Without a moment of rest and only a few weeks after Seth's birth, I sat through my dissertation with my completed novel. I graduated in the month of May. Beth Moore's study was complete, but I knew that I had only received a morsel of what God intended. And at the same time, I had never felt more alone.

I believed I was alone because of my son, but in truth I was literally alone. In my paranoid mind, my friends didn't want to be around us. I was alone inside because dealing with Ryan was confusing and exhausting. One second he was a loving, caring child, and the very next he would lash out in a colossal tantrum, often hurting me physically. We tried every form of discipline. Time out. Spanking. 1-2-3. Taking toys away. Nothing worked.

When his behavior began to affect my ability to mother Seth, I began to resent him. I felt as though God had been bringing me closer to him, but at the same time opening my eyes to my reality. I was a monster.

It all came to a head when Ryan decided to smear his feces on the bathroom walls and floor. Seth was one month old and lay squalling in his crib, face covered in spit up, and Neal had left to play a game of softball.

Before finding Ryan in the bathroom, I had been quietly nursing Seth in a chair, and Ryan had been blissfully playing by himself in his room. The sound of the toilet lid slamming against the base of the toilet jolted my nerves. I realized that those ten minutes of silence had not been a good thing after all. Seth finished nursing, I laid him in his crib, and went to investigate the bathroom.

I didn't have to open the door all the way to stop in horror. "What are you doing?" I spat out in disgust and utter disbelief. Ryan stood before me, covered from head to toe in his own poop. Crystal blue eyes the size of quarters looked up at me with fear.

I stood in the tiny bathroom and reached my hands out to Ryan, but then I stopped, unable to touch the filth he had used as finger paint. Ryan had been potty-trained for a few months, but lately it seemed as though he would purposefully wait for me to be busy and slip off to go in his pants or go on his own, always missing his mark in the pot.

I cleaned up mess after mess for nearly a month, and I tried everything in the book to handle the situation. I bribed, begged, pleaded, scolded, and disciplined. Again, nothing worked.

Ryan hesitated as I stood in the bathroom, and then a grin spread across his face. He spread his fingers and reached his hands out in front of him, the incriminating evidence caked all the way up to his wrists. The stench made my eyes water. It was as if he was mocking me, doing this on purpose, and waiting to see what I would do next!

Infuriated, I reached down and picked up his soiled underwear, thinking, "What do I have to do to get you to stop? Do I have to shove this in your face like a puppy?"

The impulsive thought was so vivid, so real, that I could feel every nerve in my arms and chest twitch with a chilling jolt. I dropped the underwear on the floor and stared at my son in shock. What was I doing? I was not this person!

Ryan's smile faded. The confusion in his eyes sucked me back to reality. My hands shook as the displaced adrenaline pumped through my veins. I reached out and held onto him, crying and begging for forgiveness for what I could have done.

High, piercing screams came from Seth's room. "Ryan, you stay right here and do not move," I said firmly.

I ran into Seth's room, careful not to touch anything, and saw him lift up his precious little face, with spit-up in his nostrils, caked in his eyes, and smeared all over the little bit of hair he had on his head.

I panicked.

I didn't want Seth to choke, and I still had a toddler standing in a bathroom covered in poop. Plus, I was covered in poop!

"Oh God," I cried out. "Please help me!" Defeated and sobbing, I kept praying out loud, "Jesus, help me out of this." I prayed over and over until my words rolled off of my tongue like a mantra. I rushed into the kitchen to clean myself off.

The phrase calmed me down and cleared my head. I ran back to Seth, cleaned him up as best as I could, put him in a swing, and ignored his pitiful cries. Finally, I reached a surprisingly patient Ryan, who was still standing in the bathroom, hands away from his body, eyes now the size of half dollars, staring at his babbling mother.

Once I had cleaned the children and cleaned and disinfected the bathroom, I spent a great amount of time hugging them and giving them the love they deserved. I put them to bed and went into my room, exhausted.

I looked over at the dresser and caught a glimpse of the workbook for the "Breaking Free" Bible study. So much had happened in the months that I had been in the program that it had been difficult to give it the attention I knew I should have, especially because it focused on past hurts, pains, breaking the ties of pride, and learning to forgive. It was all about being filled with the Holy Spirit.

I realized I hadn't even scratched the surface of what the Holy Spirit could do.

Suddenly the lesson poured over me again. I had to break free from myself and allow God to lead my life. The mere thought of reacting in such a harmful and out of control manner to my son forced me to realize I had never been in control.

The epiphany was intimidating. I was a control freak. How could I let go of control? I loved God and believed in his son Jesus Christ, but never before had I thought to leave every second of my day in his hands. The scene from that evening consumed me. What would God have done differently?

I grabbed the book and flipped to the beginning. My eyes fell upon an underlined paragraph:

What does it take? Paying attention to God's commands (by obedience) through the power of the Holy Spirit within us. Why should we? Because God is incapable of making mistakes with our lives. Isaiah 48:17 tells us he teaches us only what is best for us. He directs us only in the way we should go. Obedience to God's authority not only brings peace like a river but righteousness like waves of the sea. Not righteous perfection. Righteous consistency.

"Wow," I said out loud. God is incapable of making mistakes with our lives. Why couldn't I have believed that before? Here I was, in my mid-twenties, uncertain if I had ever lived my life as a Christian. I believed in God, but it hadn't saved me. Believing God, believing his promises, and trusting to take my life without pride and need for control—that was faith.

I looked down at the book again, at the scribbles in the margins, and frantic notations of private prayer to take away my worries and make me like him.

God was answering me, and I was finally ready to listen. What kind of mother had I been? My children depended on me to govern their daily patterns, mold their precious minds, and cultivate their faith. They depended on me. And what I wanted most was for them to know that they were worthy. My throat constricted as if smoke had filled my lungs, preventing even the slightest inhale of clean air.

I was done. I crawled off the bed and lay on my bedroom floor with my face down, forehead pressed to the carpet, and eyes squeezed tightly to prevent the sight of the world around me from seeping in. I covered my ears to block out the sound of my defeated sobs. I was done. I could no longer go on living each day thinking I could do it all on my own.

With excruciating effort, I pulled myself into a kneeling position, eyes still clammed shut, too afraid to acknowledge my surroundings.

"God, I don't want to be this person. Save me from me," I prayed. "Either take my life or do something with it."

I had prayed before, and often, but this wasn't a prayer. No, for the first time in my life, I was at God's feet, broken, ashamed, humbled, and ready to be loved and accepted. Suddenly, even in the midst of the darkest valley, my need became clear. No longer would I avoid the person I might become. This was my bottom—my chance to look up.

"Holy Spirit, come alive in my life," I prayed out loud.

I couldn't pray anything else.

Day after day after day, I prayed the same prayer.

A new peace settled into the marrow of my bones. I cannot pinpoint when it happened. It just did. Nothing had changed in the circumstances of my life, but I looked at everything through different eyes. I tasted God that night. He allowed me to know heaven and the reason for living.

All I wanted was to be with God in heaven. And the way to get there was to follow his direction.

I began to maintain a prayer journal in a notebook and would diligently write in it every morning after reading my Bible passage. A fire had been lit inside of me, and I couldn't sit still. In my new skin, things that had never bothered me, such as cussing and gossip, now made me ill. I wasn't going to judge those who were gossiping, but I couldn't participate in it, either. Who was I to judge? My track record was definitely not clean, and my attitude had been even worse.

I had no right to talk about anyone, and if I did, they had every right to turn it around and talk about me. It was clear that the only reason I ever talked about the shortfalls of others was to make myself feel better. I used to feel my shortfalls were worse than theirs, so I figured I might as well focus on theirs instead of trying to change mine.

Oddly enough, seeing my own ugliness and desperation to change felt like being high all the time—high on the Spirit! I felt God smiling down on me.

I understood that I was a child of God. I was his daughter. He loved me even though I had been a horrible person just days, hours, and even breaths before.

Clarity and understanding washed over me in constant, steady, refreshing waves. I woke up in the morning with a smile, and I went to bed with a smile.

Everything was aligning, and all I wanted was to do what God wanted me to do. I had never felt so happy in all my life. In fact, I considered changing churches because I wasn't sure the Catholic church could continue feeding the exuberance the Holy Spirit had given me.

Then one day, in the shower I heard a voice: *Go and teach the teens.*

I laughed out loud at the thought. Why was I always getting these notions while I was in the shower? I knew nothing about my Catholic faith. I went to Mass every Sunday. I received Communion, but in all honesty I knew nothing. And I was thinking of leaving. How could I teach the teens what I did not know?

Not only that, but I continued to struggle raising an infant as my almost three-year-old son wreaked havoc in our home. I knew as I prayed every morning for God to help me find answers for Ryan that he would answer my prayers. Even so, my life was crazy. There were days when I would lose it and revert back to the yelling and frustration, but then I would snap to and regret it. There were so many changes that needed to be made.

Ryan needed help. It wasn't his fault that he was acting out the way he was. He was just a child. I spent an entire month reading up about strong-willed children and typical boyish behavior. Some of the things I read did seem to relate, but there were some glaring issues that I simply could not overlook. He was energetic and extremely curious, but the only time he would ever throw tantrums was when he was trying to communicate something. He could talk as well as any three-year-old could, but it was almost as though he understood more than he could communicate in words. Plus, the rocking, humming, and forcefully

255

hitting his head against the wall or couch did not add up to normal behavior.

I was afraid it was autism so I took him to be observed by some of the top doctors at Texas Children's Hospital. While in their presence, he threw one of his most dramatic tantrums ever, hitting me and eventually hiding under the table to rock himself back and forth. I thought for sure they would be able to diagnose what had been causing his behavior.

Instead, they said that he was too young to give a diagnosis and that I had possibly suffered postpartum depression, making me unable to handle a normal tantrum. I was furious! But instead of turning the accusation inward and feeding off of my anger and frustration, I prayed to God to direct me where to go to get Ryan the help he needed.

I knew that God would answer my prayer.

Neal and I sacrificed our comfortable lifestyle to pay for a school for autistic children in hope that he would be better diagnosed and treated. A few thousand dollars later, though, when he started bringing the other students' behaviors home with him, it became clear that he was not autistic. Possibly Asperger's but it was too early to tell. We quit the school, and not until someone suggested that I begin talking to him as if he were older did we finally begin to get somewhere.

Ryan was smart. His brain had been functioning more quickly than his motor skills would allow. When this realization hit me, I felt an even greater peace in knowing that he would be OK. At least this was something I could work with.

I hadn't left the church. In fact, I began to be intrigued by the meaning and history of our traditions. I wanted to know more. I wanted to know why I should remain Catholic. An unseen arm pulled me to the church to teach CCE. Always in need of volunteers, they put me in the training classes and set me up to co-teach with someone who had experience.

I didn't know what grade I wanted, but the minute they saw me they put me in with the eleventh and twelfth grade class. Armed with the Bible, the Catechism of the Catholic Church, and a great desire to reach these teens before they set out on long, treacherous roads that were similar to my own, I opened myself up to the world of ministry.

I had written about my mistakes before, but I had always disguised them in fiction. Now I felt certain that I needed to be bold and real about the choices that had led me to such anguish, despair, and loneliness.

In class, I saw the students' smiles and overheard their conversations, and I shivered as I recognized the same masks I had worn for so long. There were years between us, but my experiences were theirs. I understood them, and I needed them to know.

All of my insecurities vanished in that classroom. The more I put myself out there, the more they began to respond and look beyond the masks, if only for the hour. Each lesson corresponded with a Scripture passage, and each of the church's teachings fit perfectly with an experience in my life when I had ignored the same message.

As I prayed they got it, I started getting it.

In the center of it all was something I had been receiving since I was six years old.

The Eucharist.

The Body and Blood of our Lord Jesus Christ.

How could I not have known? How could I have gone through life without recognizing that I had been receiving Christ every Sunday, sent out on a mission to do his will?

"On the night he was betrayed, he took the bread, broke it, and gave it to his disciples, saying 'take this all of you and eat it. This is my body, given up for you—do this in remembrance of me" (1 Cor. 11:23–24).

How could I have been so dead?

Like puzzle pieces that had been missing under the couch and found while cleaning the house, the puzzle that had begun when I was nine, when I knelt at the front of my aunt's church and felt the weight of the pain and sorrow of all those people on me, was finally going to be pieced together.

I was inexcusable. There are no excuses for what I went through and thankfully God doesn't even want me to lose breath in giving an excuse. He loves me through it all.

God had given me the gift of free will—the ability to make choices that could either lead me straight to the path of his will or to take detours along the way. I had been tied to God at conception, but he wanted me to love him on my own. God even gave me the special wisdom and understanding at a young age to help me stay on the straight path.

The Devil had misled me by enticing me with sin, oppressing me with guilt, and poisoning me with anger. I had been duped by the Devil. With each choice I had created a new path, formed off the path of God's will.

Abusing my free will had been addictive. One choice had led to others, mixed in with other people's choices that affected me as well, and then others, and then others, and then ultimately it left me on a deep, dark, unstable path.

I had become a free will abuser!

As I had grown further and further away from the tie that bound me to God, I had loosened myself from his will, leaving a void that I longed to replace.

I had wasted thirteen of my twenty-seven years trying to replace an irreplaceable God.

# God With Us

Do not conform yourselves to this age, but be transformed by the renewal of your mind, that you may discern what is the will of God, what is good and pleasing and perfect.

—Romans 12:2

ONE YEAR AFTER I had accepted God's call to teach the teens at church, Neal came home and announced that he was interested in moving. This surprised me, considering the fact that he had grown up in this town and his parents lived only two minutes away. I had just begun to fall in love with our parish, but there was something about this decision that had God written all over it. It was about starting fresh.

As we crossed the bridge over the lake into the livable forest of our new town, a strong feeling of peace came over me. I knew that we belonged here. The feeling was so strong that I couldn't stop from crying tears of joy.

It didn't take long to sell the house, and we were moved within months of Neal's initial announcement. I was excited to get Ryan into the Catholic pre-school and take the time to finally write what I felt that God had wanted me to write all along.

My story.

I, however, was not in control. God had other plans.

Two months after moving in, a woman from the Catholic school stopped me. "Shannon Deitz?" she said.

"Yes?" I answered, walking out of the church with both boys in tow, having just picked them up from Mother's Day Out.

"Didn't you say you worked with teens?"

I was surprised she had remembered so much about me, let alone my name. It had been almost four months since we'd taken the tour. "Yes," I said. "For two years I helped teach a CCE class, and I helped with a few confirmation retreats, too."

She pulled out a piece of paper from the stack in her arm. "I just got through pulling your information for the church. They are hiring an assistant for the youth minister and I thought you would be the perfect person for the job."

I was stunned.

"If you have a second, I can introduce you to everyone right now?"

The boys were already running up and down the hallway, and panic set in when I thought about wrangling them together while meeting all those people.

"Oh, I'll watch your boys for you," she said. "Don't worry, go on in."

After a brief ten minute meeting with the head of Faith Formation, the youth minister, and the CCE director, I was given a description of the job responsibilities and invited to come back and discuss them further with the youth minister.

I couldn't believe it. I loved teaching teens and had entertained the idea of becoming a youth minister after the boys had grown and I had more time. It seemed surreal that the possibility was coming so soon.

I was torn, though, because of my deep desire to write. I knew that God wanted me to write my story. Plus, I had been looking forward to getting involved in mothers' groups and going to dinner clubs, all of which were things that I never had the privilege of enjoying in the previous town.

As obvious as it was that God's hand was in this, the decision was not an easy one. Despite my struggle with wanting to write, and with selfishly having time to get out and meet new friends while enjoying the amenities with my children, I feared the position.

I was not qualified to do what they were asking. They wanted me to start a youth group, to create and implement confirmation retreats, and help with the planning of the entire high school CCE schedule. And the parish was twice the size of the one we had left behind. I had hardly even dabbled in the ministry, and I had gotten into it with the wrong intention of acquiring knowledge for myself.

How could I stand tall and do so much without any experience?

Finally, as the deadline grew closer for me to make my final decision, I sat down with my prayer journal and poured my heart out to God.

"God," I prayed, "I want to write. You've called me to write. I ache inside to write. But now this position to serve the teens has been put before me. But it will take up a lot of time. The time I would've had to write. If this opportunity is of your will then please take away the desire to write."

Two hours later, I received a phone call from a small publishing house.

"Mrs. Deitz? I'm calling in reference to your novel, *Corner of My Mind*. I'm sorry for taking so long to respond. We like the manuscript."

I had sent the novel to them over six months before and forgotten all about it. Hearing her say the words all writers love to hear—"We like your manuscript"—made my hands and feet start to tingle. I remembered my prayer to God and thought, "This is my answer!"

"But," she paused.

That was never a good word to hear.

"We waited so long because of some financial setbacks, and we wanted to work them out in order to offer you a contract. At this time, it doesn't seem plausible for us to do so. We'll have to send back the manuscript, but we would be happy to offer you some referrals."

I thanked her and hung up the phone. Stunned, I sat down on the couch and cried.

He answered me! I cried tears of happiness. God had answered my prayer. He wanted me to write, but not just then.

The desire and ache vanished. I turned in my application the next day, got the job, and a few months later I was offered the full-time youth minister's position. That led me to deeper, more earnest prayer, asking God to give me the courage to follow his will and take a full-time position even though I thought I was supposed to be a stay-at-home mom. A full-time position such as this would not only become a part of my world but a part of our world as a family.

It felt right.

Not only had the puzzle pieces fallen into place, but the puzzle was beginning to grow and form into a three-dimensional masterpiece. With the help of his teachers at school, we got Ryan the help he needed, and after a few months of extensive observation and testing, we found out that he had tested at genius level and had ADHD with impulsivity disorder. He was smart, and the sudden, explosive, and sometimes dangerous tantrums had been brought on by the impulsivity disorder. After a lot of prayer and discussion with Neal, we decided to try medication.

We feared that it would turn him into a zombie and that our very lively little boy would be caged in his own body. But we were blessed, yet again, with a great pediatrician, who helped with the meds. And truly, for Ryan, and for us, it was a life-changing decision. Finally, he was able to focus and be able to communicate in a civil and proper way. His social skills improved dramatically, and now six years later he is a very intelligent, happy little boy and has been taken off the medication.

Through all of these changes, I learned that as long as I persevered through difficult moments, trusting that in the end I would be stronger and wiser with God's mercy and grace, my spiritual gifts would flourish.

The Devil never stopped his tricks, and I never stopped seeing the green or black figures of his army, but I was also given the gift to see God's warriors. A few months before we moved, I had just settled into bed, lain on my side, and closed my eyes, when suddenly I felt someone standing in front of me. Often Ryan would get up in the middle of the night to get a drink of water so immediately I thought it was him. I expected to feel him tap on my forehead. I waited for it, and when I didn't feel anything I opened my eyes. Before me at about the same height as Ryan was a brilliant white light that made my eyes see the beauty of heaven. It was in the outline of a little person, and although I could not make out a face, seeing it made my spirit soar into an unimaginable euphoria. I knew it was the twin I had lost.

It would take a while for these occurrences to stop leaving me in shock, but I no longer allowed the presence of evil to leave me in fear of these rare moments of God's reality to render me speechless. At times, I even witnessed a genuine, ethereal battle of good and evil, caught in a place where the air was infested with oppression, and all it took was the whisper of prayer to exterminate the Enemy. I was not alone in these battles. I had never been alone. What a gift I had been given to be a witness to heaven and hell's true existence.

As each year progressed, my knowledge in my faith grew, and my understanding of God's purpose in my life strengthened. Even in the deepest of valleys, I praised God, because with each moment of suffering I was being changed, and I knew that in the end I would come out with much more knowledge and wisdom.

Finally, the time came when God dropped the desire to write back into my heart. Armed with a better understanding of who I was, why I had made my choices, and the wisdom to know that all I could do was wake up each morning and say "yes" to God, I put no expectations or deadlines on this project.

But God did.

After three months of writing down memories and verifying stories with my parents and aunt, I began to feel a sense of dread. Would anyone believe me? How could I tell my story without including the spiritual part of it as well? Would it make sense? They would think I was crazy.

Then, in a conference for CCE catechists and youth ministers, Archbishop (now Cardinal) DiNardo quoted a statement by Saint Bernadette of Lourdes: "My job is just to give you the message; it is up to you whether you believe it or not."

At that moment, understanding washed over me. "Exactly," I thought as I wrote down the quote. I didn't know much about the saints, so I looked her up and read about her fascinating story, from her vision of the Blessed Mother at the Grotto in France, to the healing waters, and, finally, to the ridicule of the townspeople. I understood her plight, and I began to ask Saint Bernadette to pray for my intercession.

Before long, I began to receive flyers on a Christian writer's contest called "Inspirational Writers Alive!" I ignored them at first, mentally taking note that I might one day like to enter it when my manuscript was finished, but I wasn't ready for it at the time. Then, as weeks passed, more of these flyers showed up. I continued to disregard the information, focusing on my job and family, until, finally, a friend of mine put one of them in my mailbox at work.

The same exact information had ended up in my lap a number of times. I couldn't ignore it any longer, and I prayed to God about what it could possibly mean. I hadn't written anything substantial, only sixty pages of memories that were not even in story format. Despite my reluctance, however, I felt a continuous urge to meet the contest's requirements, which were to submit the first three chapters of a manuscript along with a synopsis.

Of course, there was a catch. The deadline was in three weeks. During the busiest moment of the youth ministry calendar year, I set out to get something into the contest. With all of my education, I knew not to submit anything unless it had been completed, and still I found myself submitting a rough draft!

I knew that if God wanted me to be bold and come out to everyone in such an honest and open way that this would be the perfect push to encourage me to do so.

Two months later, I received a letter from the contest. I had been selected as a finalist.

I couldn't believe it! At that moment, it didn't matter whether I would win. I had received confirmation from God. Two weeks after sending the letter, I attended the Texas Christian Writer's Conference in Houston and walked away with First Place.

On that blistering hot July afternoon I sat in my car and bawled like a baby. God had placed his hand on my head by granting me this gift. I knew that Saint Bernadette had prayed for me, and I was thrilled to know that my desire to write wasn't just a simple whim. I also tingled with the acute awareness that, no matter how difficult it might be, I needed to heed what God was calling me to do.

But did I have the courage? The strength?

Three days after the conference, I left for Europe with sixteen teenagers from the parish to attend the World Youth Day ceremonies in Köln, Germany with Pope Benedict XVI. In Köln, while on the Rhine River waiting for the arrival of the Pope, we were surrounded by fellow Catholics from all over the world and enjoyed exchanging little gifts from each other's countries. I received a special gift from an older gentleman from Poland.

He and I exchanged our little flags and pins and began a conversation about the former and current popes. After about ten minutes, we took pictures, said our goodbyes, and departed. Then, moments later, he returned and tapped me on the shoulder.

"Excuse me," he said. "I need to give this to you." He handed me a small, red velvet, heart-shaped jewelry box.

Stunned, I held the box in my hand, absolutely speechless. "Oh, no!" I finally said. "I don't have anything else to give you! I can't take this!"

"No," he said, gently pushing the box into the palm of my hand. "It is yours. I need to give it to you."

I smiled, wanting him to know that I appreciated his generosity, and I opened the box. Inside was a little cross pendant made out of blue and white rhinestones. It was beautiful. "This is so nice! Thank you," I said. "But I feel bad." I closed the box and held it in my hand.

He patted my arm and smiled. "No, don't feel bad. It is yours." Then he walked away.

Later, when the teens came back from exchanging pins and flags, I pulled the box out of my pocket. "Hey, I got the best exchange ever!" I teased. "Aren't you jealous?"

One of the girls grabbed the box and opened it. "Ah, Shannon, that's awesome!" She took out the cross, and someone behind her took it. As the first girl stood holding the open box, she looked inside. "Oh, wow, this is really cool," she said. "I've never seen a jewelry box that had a saint medal in it."

"What?" I said, taking the box. I hadn't really looked at it when I opened it. My attention had gone straight to the cross. I tilted the box to look inside the lid, and there it was—the Saint Bernadette of Lourdes Medal. How awesome to receive affirmation not only in the mystery of answered prayer but quite literally in the acknowledgment of a saint and her medal!

That same afternoon, while one of the teens was speaking with a young man who was with the Bishop of Dallas along with a group of young adults, my group called me over to meet him, because they knew that the university he had attended was in my hometown. We spoke briefly for a few minutes, and before departing company we exchanged email addresses for youth ministry networking purposes.

Three days later, at the pinnacle of the World Youth Day experience, all of the groups at the World Youth Day ceremonies took on the final pilgrimage and walked twelve to twenty-four miles to a field called Merrian Field. This would be the final venue for an evening vigil with Pope Benedict XVI, and also where we would celebrate Mass the following Sunday morning. When our group arrived at the massive stretch of land, it was like entering into the Woodstock festival—except that the crowd was three times the size and sober.

More than one million Catholics converged on this vast expanse of land, and even though we had been given designated areas for our groups to settle for the evening, there were so many people who had already set up camp by the time we arrived that our group had to move about five sections back, which was about 50,000 people from our assigned spot. There were so many people we couldn't see beyond the crowd to a clear horizon. And they all spoke their native language. In our section, sitting so close to me that our sleeping bags touched, was a group of Croatians. To my right was a group from Belgium, to the left were some Italians, and in front of us was a group of Germans.

The stench of body odor was so high that it singed our nostrils, and eventually we couldn't smell anymore. Christian music blared from loudspeakers that had been set up in every section. The music came from bands playing on the hill where Pope Benedict XVI conducted his evening vigil and morning Mass. There was singing, dancing, and laughter all around, and no one cared about the smell or close quarters. We were there for one single purpose—to praise and worship God and receive him in the Eucharist.

When night rolled around, it covered the land like a cool blanket. When the sun dropped, the temperature dropped with it, and soon our warm summer night was a chilling forty degrees. When the Pope led the vigil, we all lit our candles and prayed in our native tongues. The Holy Spirit's presence was so strong that it whipped around us in the wind, keeping our fires lit. The energy I felt inside validated every insane occurrence in my entire life.

At around 10:00 P.M., the energy of the crowd began to subside, and I got the urge to use the bathroom. I left the others, who had already settled snugly into their sleeping bags, and tiptoed over a field of cocooned bodies onto the path to the outdoor facilities. When I returned to the area in which I thought I had left the group, I looked out over the sea of wrapped-up bodies, who were covered with blue tarps to keep the morning dew from settling on them, and my heart began to race.

I couldn't see my group. I was lost. All of the sleeping bags and tarps looked the same. How would I find my group without stepping over hundreds of people and making them peek out so I could see their faces?

Panic set in, and I felt my throat tighten. I walked up to the next section and looked out over a similar group of covered and protected bodies. Finally, I recognized the Texas flag that one of our teens had brought as it was waving in the wind.

"Oh, thank you, God," I muttered. My heart settled, and I tiptoed back over the bodies to my vacant spot. I settled in and slipped deep into my sleeping bag.

"Shannon Deitz!"

My eyes shot open. I had heard my name. I unfolded the sleeping bag from my head and peeked out.

"Shannon Deitz!"

Whoever it was came closer. "Shannon Deitz!"

My heart pounded, but instead of feeling fear I felt an urge to get up. I *knew* I needed to go. The feeling was so strong that it seemed to take on a form of its own and lift me out of my sleeping bag.

"She's right over there," I heard one of the other adults in our group say to the man who was calling my name.

Before my eyes could adjust, I saw a very tall man maneuver his way over to my sleeping bag. I looked up and realized that it was the young man I had met three days before on the Rhine River. There was no time for my mind to register his name, let alone grasp the idea that he could have remembered mine—or found me among over a million people.

"Shannon, you need to come with me," he said, reaching out his hand to pull me up from the ground.

It was as if I was moving in slow motion. So many senses converged upon my spirit and human intellect. My spirit inside was warm, literally pushing me forward to go with this stranger, yet my human intellect was struggling to take in the situation, hesitating to trust.

I needed to make sense of what was happening. The only question I could mutter was, "How did you find me?"

He didn't answer and waited as I put on my shoes. One of the teens lying near me in her sleeping bag asked, "Where are you taking her?"

"I need to show her something," he said.

"Well, get her back in an hour," she said. This made me smile, and I reached down and squeezed her hand.

He turned and tiptoed across the bodies to the pathway as I followed close behind. Once on the path, I insisted with the question, "How did you find me?"

Finally, he turned and looked at me. "I don't know," he said. "I woke up knowing I had to find you and I was drawn to this section."

I shivered and thrust my hands into my jacket pocket. We continued to walk on the path to the front of the field where the Pope had led the vigil earlier that evening. Candles lit up the side of the hill in rows, running all the way up to the altar. His legs were much longer than mine so I had to work to keep up with him.

We remained silent for the entire walk, which was at least half a mile, if not much farther. My mind raced with questions, but instinct told me to wait. When we came to the edge of the hill, a mighty gust of pressure pushed me in the direction of the candles, and my mind was overwhelmed with a multitude of hurt, sadness, fear, and worry that swarmed around me. The smoke from the candles seemed to draw in a vast array of emotions and took them up into the air. The flames danced before my eyes, converging together as my heart swelled with love and empathy for all the young souls who were fighting disbelief. It was like that moment at Aunt Denise's church when I was nine years old, but this time I understood the united cry from the souls around me. It was a cry for the need to feel worthy.

Just when I felt that my heart couldn't give another beat, the moment vanished and the flames died down to a flicker.

"What did you see?" the stranger asked in a deep and startling voice.

I turned and looked up at him, shocked by the expectancy that had widened his eyes. I knew. Somehow, deep inside, I knew that he had something to say. "Let's sit down," I offered, and we walked over to a row of folding chairs that had been set up for the Cardinals during morning Mass. We sat down among other pilgrims who had journeyed across the world to be a part of their Catholic history.

As the stranger and I sat side by side, his knees bounced up and down, hitting the back of the chair in front of us. I could tell that he was nervous. I prayed silently for the Holy Spirit to speak for me. Whatever this man had to say, or whatever he needed to know, I knew that the Holy Spirit would have to respond. Not me.

"You have something to say, don't you?" I asked. The calm in my voice surprised me.

His knees stopped bouncing, and he wiped the palms of his hands on his jeans. He took in a deep breath and then let it out. "I think, yes, I mean, um…" He stuttered, took another deep breath, and then looked directly at me. "I don't know you, but ever since I met you on the bridge I have had this dream, and I can't make sense of it."

"A dream?" I said, my heart beginning to pound. I feared I had made a terrible mistake. I had allowed myself to blindly follow this stranger, led only by a distinct feeling of the Holy Spirit. What if I had been duped by the Devil? What if he wanted to hurt me?

"Yeah, like a nightmare," he said as he ran a hand through his hair and cleared his throat.

"Holy Spirit, please be with me," I prayed silently, waiting for him to continue. As it had earlier in the evening, a feeling of peace entered my body and settled within my spirit.

Then, all of a sudden, as though a switch had been flipped inside of him, the stranger became animated and full of life. He turned and grabbed my arm. "Shannon, I don't understand what is happening to me, and it's driving me crazy. But one thing is clear. God is using you and wants you to be bold. He wants you to tell your story—all of it. Some people may not believe you, and some will come against you, telling you not to share what you have always kept secret. But he knows they need to hear you and witness what he's done for you."

He was speaking so fast and with such determination that I couldn't look away. This stranger knew nothing about my life. He had no idea about any of my personal sufferings or spiritual battles. How could he be saying these things?

He loosened his grip on my arm. "You need to write and you need to speak," he said. "All of this I know as if he is literally forcing me to tell you. I don't know why and I don't know how."

By the time he was finished, I was stunned into silence. What was he saying to me? I could hear the words, and I felt his urgency, but it was all too surreal. A surge of energy rushed through my body, and I shivered. "I think it's time I get back," I responded, standing up.

The stranger rose from his chair and allowed me to walk past him onto the path. He walked beside me in silence for a few minutes before speaking up again. "I need to find the Bishop," he said quietly. "I need to go to confession."

When he said this, it sent a jolt up my spine. All he had done was deliver me a harmless message from God. Why would he need to go to confession? Alarms sparked my senses. Instinct kicked in, and I realized that the fleeting feelings of fear I had felt coming and going as we sat next to each other were feelings I shouldn't ignore.

Uncertain of what had caused the evil to return, I was afraid to say another word. Apparently, it had to do with his lack of personal strength.

"Holy Spirit, never leave me," I continued to pray silently. "Saint Michael, protect me."

The silence between us was thick. I stared straight ahead, wishing for a shorter walk, and praying that I would be able to find my group among the crowd of cocooned bodies.

"Shannon," the stranger said, breaking the silence and looking down at me. "Do you believe in karma? Do you think that those who do bad things get back what is coming to them?"

I knew what he meant, and as I heard the fear in his voice, I felt my own fear shed like dead skin. I was calm now, and I knew what God needed him to hear. "I don't believe that what goes around comes around," I said, "at least not when we seek forgiveness. I believe God wants everyone to realize we are always given second chances as long as we come to him with a repenting heart. I might be angry at someone for having hurt me, and it might take me time to forgive, but it would not be my place to wish the same hurt upon that person. When you work in circles, it always will come back to you as well."

I thought about my years of counseling and the amount of work it had taken for my spirit to reach a place of forgiveness with Paul and Nick and even my grandfather. I had to forgive in order to move forward with my life. Without forgiveness, I would have been stuck in that circle of anger, sadness, and despair.

We reached my section of the field, and I stopped. He didn't need to take me any further. I would find my group on my own. I turned to the stranger and felt an incredible amount of compassion. He was standing with his hands thrust into the pockets of his jeans and his head hung in defeat. Compelled to offer him a gesture of thanks for sharing what he had with me, I said, "You are a good person, and I forgive you. I know you had it in you to hurt me, and you didn't. Thank you."

He raised his head and his eyes widened, the reflection of a nearby barrel fire blazing in them. "How did you know?" he asked. "How did you know?" His body began to shake as it had earlier and he began to cry.

I looked away, unable to answer, and desperate to get back to my group to feel safe and secure.

"Shannon," he said, touching my arm before I turned to find my group. "It was only a brief moment, and I don't even know what came over me, but I know that's why you have to be careful. Please don't forget what I told you before. You have to be careful, but you can't stop telling everyone what you know. One day I want to know, too, but I'm not strong enough to hear it now."

He let go of my arm, and I turned down the path that led to my group. I searched for the flag that had helped me find them earlier, and instead I saw one of our group's young adults standing and searching the crowds. He was looking for me. When he spotted me, he maneuvered his way toward me. As soon as he reached me, it was as if a dam that had been holding back my emotions busted, spilling everything out. Sobs wracked my body, and as my shaking legs lost all of their strength, he caught me as I fell to the ground.

The evening had been surreal, and the complexity of it all was too much for me to filter. I needed to pray. I needed Christ. My tears subsided, and the strength began to seep back into my limbs. "Where is the adoration chapel?" I asked.

In the adoration chapel, we had the gift of the exposed Eucharist displayed in a monstrance—a gold holder that signified the glory of his presence. In the Catholic Church, the Eucharist *is* the Body of Christ. Catholics believe that, through transubstantiation, the bread, though its physical nature remains the same, becomes in substance the actual living flesh of Christ.

A sense of calm and peace permeated the chapel. I knelt before the exposed Body of Christ, allowing the entire evening to replay within my prayers. With each moment, thought, feeling, emotion, and message, I felt Christ within me, validating it all. His love washed over me, and I bowed before him, thankful for his mercy.

# My Prayer Partner

For where two or three are gathered together in my name, there am
I in the midst of them.

—Matthew 18:20

SOCCER MOM. THIS term bounced around in my head one
morning as I drove my two boys to school. It had been just over a
week since we had arrived home from Germany, and I couldn't grasp
my role. I was the mother of two young boys under the age of seven,
driving a Suburban, and living what appeared to be a normal life. But I
had just come home from a trip that rocked my world. I had been called
by name and given the gift of being told my purpose, but I had no idea
where to begin. Was I strong enough? Was I bold enough?

I found solace in attending Mass, and one morning, upon listening
to the priest's homily, I knew that I needed to talk to him and tell him
everything. I needed to hear from him whether he thought I was crazy.

Like a fire hydrant let loose on a hot summer day, I spilled my
entire life story to the unsuspecting priest. I left nothing out, from the
near-kidnapping by an occult member, to my visions of demons and
spirits, and all the way to the messenger in Germany. After I had finished,

I looked at the priest, who sat across from me, stoic, in a brown leather chair. I could see that he was thinking, but I could not tell by the look on his face what governed his thoughts.

I couldn't take it. I had to ask. "Am I crazy? Do I need to be put in a mental institution?" I held my breath for his response.

A smile spread across face. "Shannon, you are not crazy," he said. "We all have gifts of the Spirit. Yours happens to be a discernment of the Spirit, of what is evil and what is of God. We have all been given this gift, but some are stronger than others. This is your strength."

Whew. What a relief. He gave me what I needed to move forward. I went home that day and continued to write my story.

Three months later, while sitting at my desk, I typed out the words that described one of the scariest moments of my young life. With every word, I felt unworthy, crazy, and ridiculous. A heavy blanket of doubt settled upon my shoulder. "No one will ever believe me," I thought.

I pushed my chair back, stood up, and stretched, trying to get the ominous feeling to go away. "God, I need you," I prayed. Was I the only one? Would anyone understand the things I had seen?

I needed validation. I grabbed my car keys and drove to a Barnes & Noble. If I could find a book that related to mine, then maybe I could talk to the author and find the validation I was seeking.

In the religious section of the store I read title after title, seeking a true story that dealt with spiritual warfare, but I could not find one that satisfied my need. Frustrated, I tapped my fingers on the spines of the books as I read the titles and prayed. "God, I can't do this alone. I need someone to talk to. You have to give me someone to talk to that will understand what I've seen. I need validation. Please give me someone to talk to!"

"Excuse me, do you read much?" asked an older gentleman, who stood next to me pointing at a book. He had peppered hair, wore slacks and an oxford shirt, and stood about an inch shorter than me.

He startled me, and my cheeks burned with embarrassment. I had been praying silently, but I felt as if he had heard every word. "Yes," I

managed to say, holding back a touch of annoyance. I was in Barnes &
Noble, after all. Wouldn't that sort of imply that I spent a fair amount
of time reading?

"Well," he said, tapping the book, "have you read this?"

I looked at the book and smiled. It was *90 Minutes in Heaven* by
Don Piper and Cecil Murphey. Cecil Murphey was the author who had
judged my chapters in the "Inspirational Writers Alive!" contest, and I
had purchased the book at the conference. Ironically, I had just finished
reading it a few weeks before. "Yes, I have," I said. "I just finished it."

The man smiled in return and lowered his arm. "Well, if you believe
that story, I know of a few others you would like that deal with spiritual
warfare."

My senses heightened. What did he just say? "Funny, I am writing
a book that touches on spiritual warfare," I said as my spirit tingled.

"Really? Well, then, I know exactly who you need to talk to. You
need to talk to Dr. Frank Barlow. He's a retired minister who lived in
Mexico for over thirty years, counseling others on spiritual warfare. I'm
sure he would love to speak with you."

Had he really just given me someone to talk to? I stood before
him, stunned, and I felt my spirit swell up inside of me, saturating my
senses. I had to tell him. "You know, I was just asking God to lead me
to someone that would be able to help me."

The man laughed and didn't seem shocked. "Well, then, I suppose I
was your divine appointment." He took a business card out of his wallet
and wrote down a number for Dr. Frank Barlow. "Here you go," he said.
"I'll call him and let him know you will be contacting him shortly. It
was nice meeting you." He turned and walked away.

I stood there silently, holding onto his card, and mentally accepting
this "divine appointment." After running a quick errand, I hopped into
the Suburban and grabbed the man's card off of the dashboard. If I
didn't call him right then, I would never have the nerve. I grabbed my
cell phone and dialed the number. "OK," I thought, "what do I say?
Hi, I see demons?"

Dr. Barlow answered, and without filtering anything I began to explain what I needed. When I finally gave him a chance to speak, I could tell he was smiling across the line. "Shannon," he said, "I think we should meet."

I agreed. It was exactly what I needed. It was what I had asked God for—someone to talk to. He proceeded to give me his address so I could meet with him the following Saturday. There was no need for him to give me directions. God took care of the details.

Dr. Frank Barlow lived five houses away from me, on the corner of my street, in the neighborhood I had been living in for the past three years.

How could I have ever underestimated God? God has a plan for me, and he will make sure it is carried out, especially when I come to him in need. He does this for all of us, because we are his children.

Dr. Barlow validated me. He understood what I had seen and been through, and he had stories of his own as well. We prayed together that day, and we continue to pray together, coming together in Christ's name.

# Epilogue

NINETEEN HOURS ON a plane allow for a lot of time to contemplate life. I was with another group of young adults from our parish heading toward another World Youth Day festival. They only occur every three years and the last one had been my life-changing moment. Many occurrences had taken place in three years' time that had shown God's hand in my life. It was amazing to have desires fulfilled and never have to suffer the longing.

Within a month of completing the first draft of this book, I was asked to give my first public testimony. Terrified and plagued with the feeling of unworthiness, I politely declined. God, however, continued to pursue me, and through Dr. Barlow and my spiritual advisor I worked on acquiring the courage and ability to be bold in my faith. The offer was on the table, so I took it. Before I knew it, one invitation turned into another, and the pieces of my life began to fall into place all along a bright and straight path.

As I leaned my head on the narrow headrest, I closed my eyes. Despite all the evil I had seen in this world, and all the ways the Enemy had tried to stop me from following God's will, I was still alive and strong. I had spent three years speaking to small youth groups and then to larger audiences at conferences across the country, and this moment could not be beaten.

A tear of gratitude rolled down my cheek. As I wiped it away, I sat up, picked up the folded brochure from my lap, and unfolded it once again. I had to see it in writing—for the hundredth time:

World Youth Day 2008
Sydney, Australia
Program Guide
Thursday, 7–9pm: "GOD'S LOVE" – Shannon M. Deitz
Sydney Convention Center

God is good, all the time! All the time, God is good!

*If you or someone you know has survived abuse of any form, please consider confiding in a counselor or to the proper authorities. The only way out of the dark pit that abuse creates is to expose it to the light of truth.*

*For the Rape, Abuse & Incest National Network RAINN, call 1-800-656-HOPE*

*The Maria Goretti Network MGN is a non-profit support group for survivors www.mgoretti.org*

# End Notes

The following resources were used for quotes and spiritual inspiration:

Moore, Beth. "Breaking Free Bible Study – Making Liberty in Christ a Reality in Life." LifeWay. 1999

Piper, Don and Murphey, Cecil. "90 Minutes in Heaven." Revel Publishing 2004

West, Christopher. "Theology of the Body for Beginners. A Basic Introduction to Pope John Paul II's Sexual Revolution." Ascension Press. West Chester, Pennsylvania. 2004

United States Conference of Catholic Bishops. United States Catholic Catechism for Adults. 2008

The Catholic Youth Bible. New American Bible. Saint Mary's Press, Christian Brothers Publications. Winona, Minnesota

**PW**

Breinigsville, PA USA
27 July 2010
242581BV00003B/7/P